COMPOSING EXPERIENCE

COMPOSING EXPERIENCE

Alan Meyers

Truman College

HarperCollins*Publishers*
CollegeDivision

Senior Aquisitions Editor: Jane Kinney
Cover Illustration: Initial Graphic Systems, Inc.
Electronic Production Manager: Eric Jorgensen
Publishing Services: Interactive Production Services
Electronic Page Makeup: Interactive Composition Corporation
Printer and Binder: R.R. Donnelley
Cover Printer: Coral Graphic Services, Inc.

Composing Experience

Library of Congress Cataloging-in-Publication Data

Meyers, Alan
Composing experience / Alan Meyers
p. cm.
Includes index.
ISBN 0-673-46928-X
1. English language—Rhetoric. I. Title.

PE1408.M518 1995
808'.042—dc20

94-28376

CIP

94 95 96 97 9 8 7 6 5 4 3 2 1

In memory of Betty Pomerantz

Contents

Contents

Preface

In recent years, many teachers of freshman composition have aligned themselves into two well-respected but somewhat opposing camps: the defenders of self-expressive writing that emphasizes personal viewpoint and voice, and the proponents of academic or professional writing within a particular social context. Yet many of us have been seeking a middle way, an approach that builds on and shapes the student's writing voice into an effective communicative instrument for a variety of socially defined tasks.

I began my search for this synthesis more than a decade ago, and this text is the outcome of my labors. It establishes protocols for invention, composing, and revision that foster the logical movement from personal narrative to more outwardly focused narrative, exposition, and argument. Thus, the student progresses from storytelling in Unit I to telling the story in Unit II about what she knows or has learned about a particular subject. The context of experience shifts from the personal to the public as viewed throught the eyes of the writer. And the strategy of writing evolves into solving a problem the student has constructed for specific readers within a specific social context in which she has played a role.

I'm using the phrase "played the role" quite literally here. If writing within a social context is to be meaningful (in both senses), then the context must be authentic—that is, as authentic as a classroom experience will permit—and students must be actively engaged in contexts that motivate the writing. To that end, each chapter in Unit II includes one or two simulation games (entitled "Writing Within a Social Context") in which students must assume roles, analyze the issues, and consider how to enlist in an argument both the materials supplied as well as their own—whether personal, researched, or invented. Then students plan and make (optional) oral presentations, rebut opposing arguments, and write for an audience that has not participated in the dicussion: government officials, managers of companies, members of boards, or members of the immediate community. Since several students share the same roles, they may work collaboratively as they discuss the issues and the facts, engage in debate, and then consult with each other while composing and revising their individual papers.

The Assumptions Behind the Text

Since I strongly advocate the practice of explaining what warrants a writer's claims, let me share the assumptions behind this text:

1. **Students develop strong, confident voices as they move from easily achieved to more challenging writing tasks.** The early chapters of the text therefore emphasize writing as a process in which students explore, compose, and revise while developing lucid, fast-paced, fact-driven styles, which they first employ in personal narratives and later in narratives about the experiences of others. The habit of composing from experience—what one truly knows or can find out about, and therefore comfortably discuss—lays the foundation on which the writer may later defend and explain her personal viewpoints in well-supported arguments.

2. **Writing should be taught as a collaborative process that encourages diversity**. Experienced writers approach their tasks in a variety of ways: some writers revise little while some revise a great deal; some plan efficiently while other discover their plans only through experimentation and change. Thus, the teaching of the composing process cannot be lock-step: its recursiveness must be emphasized. And novices should be encouraged to emulate the practices of experienced writers who consult with colleagues, friends, or editors to produce final copy. Indeed, collaboration enables writers to develop an awareness of audience—and therefore shape their messages to the audience—through such devices as predicting (i.e., readers reading a portion of a text and then projecting what follows), oral reading, postdraft analysis (or metacognition, in which writers reflect and comment on their writing), and peer editing.

3. **An "environmental" approach, in which students learn all the requisite skills involved in a writing task, is the most effective method of writing instruction.** This means that students first examine models—typically three—of the writing they will produce; compile a list of traits that characterize the type of writing; plan, compose, and share their drafts with classmates who help them analyze readers' expectations and predict readers' reactions; and then revise extensively. Such an approach engages students in a number of subtasks leading to the completion of the final draft.

4. **All writing—narrative, expository, or persuasive—is argumentation.** Whether the focus is on the topic sentence, thesis, or main idea, effective writing demands that claims be supported. Every claim is argumentation—even if only a "soft" argument such as "I had a good time on my trip to Washington, D. C." Thus, Stephen Toulmin's terminology of *claim, warrant, backing, qualifiers,* and *rebuttal* (discussed in Chapters 8 and 12) aids students in analyzing the content and structure of their writing.

5. **People write best when they know what they are talking about.** Personal experience is a natural beginning point for writing, but even "impersonal" exposition and argument require that students discuss what they know or can find out about. An environmental approach, especially though simulation games, establishes situations in which students gain experience with a problem, attempt to solve it, and then address their arguments to a specific audience. Within this context, the need to support and document one's claims is both natural and essential.

6. **Expository prose, especially criticism, must make the writer's own point and back up its claims.** No matter how objective, all writing ulimately argues a personal viewpoint. And since writing is problem solving, the writer must construct a problem for the reader and then solve or address the problem. Her central thesis must answer the central question: "So what?" which informs the argument with purpose and meaning.

7. **The use of a rhetorical mode should emerge naturally from a context determined by subject, purpose, occasion, and audience.** For example, cause–effect is central to the "Urban Renewal" simulation game (see Chapter 8) in which participants debate the causes of decay of an inner-city building and predict the effects of rehabilitating it. Comparision–contrast is essential to the "Mom and Dad, I Want a Divorce" game (see Chapter 14), all sides must weigh the advantages and disadvantages of the child's severing her ties to parents. Definition and classification are inherent in the "Queen v. Dudley-Stephens trial game (again in Chapter 14), in which laws must be defined and the facts of the case measured against the criteria for determining guilt or innocence. In all cases, the structure must be organic, not superimposed.

Key Features of the Text

Composing Experience includes the following main features:

- **Flexible approaches to composing and revising,** which emphasize both the diversity and recursive nature of the writing process, while allowing students to discover and then refine their own most efficient personal practices

- **Student-written examples,** which provide realistic and attainable models from which students may inductively derive a list of the traits of a particular type of writing

- **Models from unusual sources**—*Consumer Reports,* sports columnists, humorists, popular scientific journals, legal documents, community newsletters—which demonstrate the importance of effective writing within a broad range of contexts

- **Invention activities,** which help students discover subjects for writing, generate support for claims, and explore appropriate structures for their argument
- **Journal keeping activities,** which increase writing fluency, create a repository of materials and ideas for writing, further the process of invention, and encourage metacognition
- **Composing and revising activities,** which guide students through various stages of the composing process
- **Collaborative activities,** which encourage in-class participation, establish writer–audience relationships, refine individual writing voices, and lead to critical examination of topic, point, occasion, organization, and support
- **Predicting activities,** which increase awareness of audience and relate the structure and development of an argument to the audience's expectations and perceptions
- **Stephen Toulmin's terminology,** which provides a vocabulary and methodology for students to examine the soundness, extent, and clarity of their arguments
- **Emphasis on writing as problem solving,** which requires constructing a problem for readers and then attempting to solve (or at least address) that problem in the argument
- **Postdraft analysis questions,** which foster critical examination and revision of early drafts of one's work—either collaboratively or alone
- **Guidelines** for tightening and strengthening prose, creating oppositions, conducting interviews, summarizing, paraphrasing, and quoting
- **Role-playing games,** simulating real-life situations in which students assume roles, examine relevant data, discuss and debate issues, anticipate and hear conterarguments, and write arguments to a specified audience

Acknowledgments

Just as this text advocates collaboration, it also reflects the input and influence of many colleagues, friends, and relatives, to whom I am enormously indebted. First, I'm grateful to the administrators of Truman College and City Colleges of Chicago for granting a sabbatical leave that allowed me to compose this text while maintaining some measure of sanity. I thank my students, especially those whose work appears in this text, for their continuing help in teaching me how best to teach them. I thank my colleagues Carolyn Dennis and Barbara Kessel for classroom testing the manuscript. I'm especially thankful to my colleague Sherry Medwin for reading and commenting on the text in its various stages of development. I continue to owe my love and admiration to my colleague and wife, Ann Meyers, for her perceptive and gentle advice on revising the manuscript. I am greatly indebted to George Hillocks at the University of Chicago, whose seminar on the environmental approach in part inspired the composing of this book. And I am equally indebted to my mentors whose published works have so greatly influenced this endeavor: Ken Macrorie, Peter Elbow, Lynn Troyka, and Charles Weingarten. I again applaud my faithful editors, Jane Kinney and Alison Brill, for placing the full resources of HarperCollins at my disposal. And I thank all my colleagues who have read and commented on the manuscript at various stages of its development:

I wish also to thank my parents Bernie and Birdie Meyers, may they rest in peace, for their sacrifices that allowed me to pursue a higher education and vocation in the teaching of composition. And finally I offer my fondest gratitude to my children Bradley and Sarah, who by their enthusiasm and love continue to remind me of the real values in life.

Alan Meyers

Introduction

Examining the Traits of Effective Writing

So often in school writing assignments, you need to choose a subject to explore. But what? When you consider all the controversies and problems in the world—unemployment, pollution, revolution, starvation, abortion, racism, sexism, ageism, welfare, capital and corporal punishment, cruelty to animals and children—you may justifiably think: "I don't know much about these matters; whatever I say will be naïve, even foolish. How can I write effectively, especially when I'm not quite sure what effective writing is?"

While such uneasiness may be justifiable, it's unnecessary. You do know—or can learn—more than just clichés about many issues. But don't begin hunting for material in an alien world. Start with the world you know best: the world of your own experiences. There's nothing trivial about them. You've lived, worked, acquired skills, learned information, and formulated viewpoints that others have not. Start by composing from your experience and gaining experience with composing. Then you can broaden that experience to include what you read or see or encounter. And finally you can seek out further experiences that enable you to write with authority about important contemporary issues.

If I had to give a young writer some advice I would say to write about something that has happened to [him or her]. . . . It always amuses me that the biggest praise for my work comes for the imagination, while the truth is there's not a single line in all my work that does not have a basis in reality.

—*Gabriel Garcia Marquez*

Addressing an Audience for a Purpose

Let's begin by defining our terms. *Effective writing* is a *social, purposeful* activity in which a writer addresses a specific reader or group of readers on a specific occasion to achieve a specific purpose—getting a job, making a complaint, helping a client, selling a product, solving a problem, touching someone's emotions, earning a grade. The writer also speaks in an authentic voice and is truthful to his or her experiences, whether real or imagined. Here, for example, is a journal entry a student revised to share with an audience of classmates in hopes of amusing them:

> Any time I have to wait, my nerves are shorter than the lines I'm waiting in. The lines feel like a traffic jam. I'm in my lane, bumper to bumper, inching slowly forward only to stop and wait again while someone breathes in my ear or kicks at my heel.
>
> Once at the grocery store, I shopped for half an hour but waited in the check-out line almost twice as long. The couple ahead of me was smart. One got the groceries as the other kept their place. Meanwhile, I started to melt and drip like the fudge ice cream in my bag.
>
> Just recently I had to renew my driver's license. First I waited in line for information, then waited in another line for an application form, and afterwards waited in line to pay. By the time I finished the eye examination and the written test, my legs and temper were sore.
>
> Finally I staggered to the picture line where I displayed an exhausted, angry face. The lady suggested a big smile, so I smirked. Then I waited again for the picture to develop. When I finished, I was late for work so I rushed to the el station and waited for the train.
>
> —Mary C. Fahey

Fahey doesn't moralize on the great issues of our time, but describes her first-hand experiences instead: the lines at the grocery store and driver's license facility. She knows what she's talking about and conveys the message through examples we can recognize and smile at. Despite her exaggeration for humorous effect, we recognize in the events some truths about the frustration of having to wait.

Moreover, Fahey doesn't write pompously (and awkwardly) in language intended to impress. Instead, she renders her experiences through

- tight yet graceful phrasing [" my legs and temper were sore"].
- metaphors ["feels like a traffic jam. I'm in my lane, bumper to bumper"];
- oppositions ["The lady suggested a big smile, so I smirked"];
- and emphatic repetition ["First I waited in line for information, then waited in another line for an application form, and afterwards waited in line to pay"].

Making Readers Believe and React

While Fahey's experiences are familiar and somewhat universal, effective writing needn't be limited to events readers have already encountered. Writing is *art*, a word derived from the same root word as *artificial*, and the kinship between these words is not coincidental. The Greek philosopher Aristotle said that art does indeed imitate nature, which he defined as *what is or was, what is thought to be, or what ought to be.* This next piece of writing, by Nancy Jean Farrell, describes a less common—yet nonetheless recognizable—event because of its specific detail:

Leaving the freeway, I follow a road east into a canyon. To both sides, the road reaches up to houses and farms. The only ways out are back or on foot through the woods and over the hill into the next canyon. As I walk, I think how my life has been like the road. I moved from the city to the double-wide trailer where I spent my last five years with my parents. Then, I wander through the woods until I begin to go back the way I have come.

A mile later, I turn left and climb the gravel driveway to the trailer. Through the carport and up from stone steps, cobwebs cling to the walls of a workshop. Behind it, the upward slope is alive with the fleshy green leaves and bright yellow flowers of ice plant. A path meanders through it up into the foliage.

At the top of the path, but not of the hill, sits a stone bench, a place for the wanderer to rest. I gaze across the canyon at the fields and houses, and along the ridge at the eucalyptus trees that sway in a breeze and fall in a gale. Turning, I step carefully across the path. An underground spring bubbles up, breaking through the seemingly solid ground. Before me is an inhospitable area filled with poison ivy and blackberry bushes. For a moment, these vines step back and it is peaceful and serene, mysterious and beckoning, hidden but accessible. Here I buried my animal friends. The grave markers are now covered by rain-washed soil and fallen leaves.

To the west, past the triangle of vegetation, a periwinkle vine spreads an inviting carpet of deep grown leaves and dusky blue-violet flowers beneath the strong limbs of a huge evergreen. From one of these caring arms, two ropes dangle earthward joined by a simple length of plastic. A swing, a joy. Pulling myself up, I begin to glide. Back, forth, soaring ever higher. Leaning back, I gaze into the branches. The breeze lifts my hair, caressing my skin. The tree is strong, its limbs are strong, and I am safe.

It seems a fairy world here. Glittering gold sunbeams filter through the nettles. The light is subdued, the air gentle and warm. Moths of a hue almost equal to the flowers flicker between the shadows. A gentle mist begins to fall. The tree catches the drops. Playfully, the breeze shakes some loose; they drift down and spatter on the leaves. Scents of trees and flowers, rain, and sea blend into the aroma of life.

Here, life is nothing more than this place, this time. Here, I can feel alone as I watch the world pass by around me. Here, the place one yearns for inside herself, where she can remove to and find peace, is manifested in a physical reality. Here I can reach out with all my senses and touch a feeling.

—Nancy Joanne Farrell

While Fahey's piece makes us nod in recognition ("Yes, that's the way it is"), Farrell's elicits a different response: "Yes, that's the way it must be." She puts us in the scene so we can see, hear, and feel it as she did. She employs strong—but not pompous—verbs that move the action forward: *wander, cling, meanders, sway* and *fall, dangle, glide, caressing, flicker*. A less accomplished writer leans heavily on weak verbs that collapse under the weight of ideas: *is, get, go, make, do, run, have, put,* and *take*. And Farrell doesn't belabor her point—her return visit brings her comfort and pleasure—but lets the facts speak for themselves.

The abstract is seldom as effective as the concrete. "She was distressed" is not as good as, even, "She looked away."

—*John Gardner*

Writing Knowingly—And Thus Confidently

These essays from students sound authentic because they reflect the writers' own first-hand experiences and reactions. However, professional reporters and columnists usually discuss more public and impersonal issues, so they must read and research and interview until they feel comfortable and familiar with the subject matter. Part of that familiarity arises from specializing in a particular field: politics, education, crime, medicine, race relations, or sports. Here, for example, is the beginning of a column by Chicago *Tribune* sportswriter Bernie Lincicome from November 1992, the day after the Colorado Rockies and Florida Marlins baseball teams completed their drafting of players from the rosters of the National and American leagues. Note his confident, convincing tone.

A TALENT-THIN SPORT GETS THINNER

The American dream is that anybody can play major-league baseball, and now they all are, for Colorado and Florida.

What did those new National League franchises pay to be part of Tuesday's piñata party, $95 million each? Ross Perot only paid $60 million to finish third [in the 1992 presidential election].

If either team wins more than 50 games next season, it will mean they were allowed to play each other every week.

The general thinning of major-league talent has reached near transparency. These new teams ought to come with curtains.

The good news for the locally curious is that no matter how hard [General Manager] Larry Himes and [Field Manager] Jim Lefevbre work at it, they cannot make the Cubs the worst team in the league for at least another 10 years.

If these guys were baseball cards, and I suppose they are, you swap 20 Jesus Tavarezes for one Kirby Puckett.

All of baseball just got worse. Two more teams sharing the scarcity means that baseball is spending more and more money for less and less ability.

Lincicome knows and cares about his subject, states his opinions without apology, and conveys his message in tight, forceful sentences. He also knows his audience—Chicago sports fans—and thus refers to teams and people they will recognize. He writes in a genuine human voice communicating genuine human responses. And like Fahey and Farrell, Lincicome doesn't show off his vocabulary; he just makes every word count.

Establishing a Clear Structure

Effective writing needn't explore profound subjects; it need only accomplish its purpose. The following article from *Consumer Reports*, for example, delivers honest, straightforward advice about buying juice extractors. Thus, each paragraph begins with a topic sentence that clearly states its point. But despite the article's emphasis on giving practical advice to consumers, the writing is neither stodgy nor stiff. Note the rhythm and directness of the sentences, the strong verbs and adjectives, the metaphors and oppositions:

If you want juice because you like the taste, our tests can help you find the best juice-maker. But if you think juice can cure whatever ails you, think again.

The 1990s already has its very own food fad—fresh-made juice. Ads for juice extractors command entire newspaper pages and turn up on late-night cable TV. In department stores, juice extractors garnished with plastic produce sit beneath colorful displays. Macy's flagship store in New York City has even created a special department called "Juiced Up."

Credit the boom in juice-makers to feature-length TV commercials starring people like Jack LaLanne, or "The Juice King," or the champion of them all, Jay "The Juiceman" Kordich. Combining the persistence of used-car salesmen with the fervor of televangelists, Kordich and Company have convinced hundreds of thousands of people that healthful eating requires a juice-maker priced close to $300. But in their zeal to sell juicers, they make claims for the power of juicing that range from fanciful to misleading.

In fact, juice cannot be any better than the produce from which it's made—and can sometimes be less nutritious because it lacks all the fiber in fresh produce. Fruits and vegetables are good for you, whether juiced or whole, cooked or raw. They provide essential vitamins, minerals, and trace elements.

—"The Juice Craze"

Writing Honestly and Entertainingly

This final example, a report of scholarly research, could have easily sounded dull and mechanical. But its author, Clifford Adelman, is not afraid to let his voice be heard, to write metaphorically, and to acknowledge the concerns of readers who might only reluctantly accept his conclusions.

> Because the . . . [study] was designed more than 20 years ago, without reference to contemporary cultural wars, it has no ax to grind. It is what social scientists call an "unobtrusive" source. Its validity stands on a stronger toe than does that of contemporary surveys with loaded questions. Some readers will not like the data in this [study], but the numbers are resilient, and they tell a clear story.
>
> —*Tourists in Our Own Land: Cultural Literacies and the College Curriculum*

One more point about effective writing. It evolves from a process of composing and revising, then further composing and revising. As someone once said, "Writing never gets published; only *rewriting* does." Each piece you've read in this chapter is a revision, the end product of two, three, or more drafts. So don't be intimidated; don't try for perfection in your first drafts. Just get your ideas out so you can return to them later. Relax and draw upon your personality and powers of language so that a human voice emerges—clear, direct, and honest—that speaks of real ideas or events to other humans.

In writing, you can make a silk purse out of a sow's ear, but first you have to create the sow's ear.
Your first draft is the sow's ear.

—*Charles Parnell*

A Short Summary of What Makes Writing Effective

Despite their differing purposes, topics, and audiences the examples in this chapter share a great many traits. Here's a list of the most important, not all of which need occur in every piece of effective writing, but that nonetheless appear with great frequency. We'll continue to examine these traits throughout this book:

1. Effective writing accomplishes its purpose for the audience, occasion, and medium of communication (a book, a memo, a magazine ad, or a scholarly paper).
2. It therefore makes and sticks to a point. ["If you want juice because you like the taste, our tests can help you find the best juice-maker."]
3. It's persuasive; the writer knows what she's talking about. ["Some readers will not like the data in this [study], but the numbers are resilient, and they tell a clear story."]

4. It backs its claims with specifics. ["It seems a fairy world here. Glittering gold sunbeams filter through the nettles. The light is subdued, the air gentle and warm. Moths of a hue almost equal to the flowers flicker between the shadows. A gentle mist begins to fall."]

5. It's truthful to an experience, whether actual or imagined.

6. It's clear and direct. ["By the time I finished the eye examination and the written test, my legs and temper were sore."]

7. It employs strong verbs and adjectives. ["Finally I staggered to the picture line where I displayed an exhausted, angry face."]

8. It fashions oppositions in fact or style or idea. ["the scarcity means that baseball is spending more and more money for less and less ability."]

9. It's often humorous. ["The American dream is that anybody can play major-league baseball, and now they all are, for Colorado and Florida."] Or metaphorical. ["Its validity stands on a stronger toe than does that of contemporary surveys with loaded questions."]

10. And it often employs strong repetition. ["First I waited in line for information, then waited in another line for an application form, and afterwards waited in line to pay. . . When I finished, I was late for work so I rushed to the el station and waited for the train."]

UNIT I

Writing from Experience

Chapter 1

Generating Ideas

You're staring at a blank page or computer screen and encountering those familiar questions: How do I start? What do I have to say? Everyone shares the problem, so don't let it disturb you. First drafts are only preliminary acts in a *composing process;* they rarely follow a formula or formal outline, but record the thoughts and language that enter your mind. Since the average person can think ahead only four to ten words, you probably cannot begin a sentence knowing exactly how it will end—or what the next sentence will say. You therefore cannot anticipate the exact content and wording of an entire paper; you can only explore your thoughts as they arise. And while some (usually experienced) writers approach their first drafts with clear notions of what they'll be saying and where they'll be going, you may not—and need not—be one of them. Don't worry, therefore, if your thinking is disorganized, your phrasing unclear, or your language repetitious. Putting words on the page or screen is as much a process of discovering ideas as it is of communicating them. From these discoveries come further discoveries and refinements until you approach the form that conveys your message to your audience and achieves your purpose.

How can I know what I think until I see what I say?

—*Graham Wallas*

The beginning of the composing process is thus a time to write quickly, without censorship or concern about perfection. There's an ocean of ideas in your unconscious mind, awaiting entry into your consciousness. Your task is to open the flood gates and channel the flow onto the page or screen. The Nobel Prize winning author Isaac Bashevis Singer was once asked how he went about composing his stories. "There's no plan, no formula," Singer replied. "I may write something once or a thousand times." Like most professional writers, Singer was mystified about how his ideas took shape until they reached their final, publishable form.

I just say OK, I'm going to make the biggest fool of myself as possible and just go right ahead and don't stop. I just get it out. . . . Often my first draft is a very complete draft. It may not be the one I use or anywhere near what finally takes place. But it's in my own handwriting and very few people can read it but me.

—Horton Foote

Once you've captured your ideas on paper or in computer memory, you can look them over, see what point is (or could be) emerging, and decide what to discard, replace, expand on, or refine. You may change your mind and wording five or ten or thirty times until the language feels right, sounds right, and says what you've finally determined it should say.

First drafts are for learning what your novel or story is about. Revision is working with that knowledge to enlarge and enhance the idea, to reform it. . . . The first draft of a book is the most uncertain—where you need guts, the ability to accept the imperfect until it gets better.

—Bernard Malamud

BEGINNING TO WRITE FREELY

One of your choices for getting started (you'll examine other options in Chapter 2) is through what Peter Elbow, Ken Macrorie, and others call free writing—quickly recording whatever comes to mind on a topic, without concern for exact wording. The process allows you to take chances, play with words and ideas, fool around. Don't censor yourself or hold back. If you go too far, say something silly, or offend, you can always remove those parts during revisions—but at least you can work with something that's lively and fresh. Free writing requires little or no planning. Don't be concerned about an introduction, a body, and a conclusion—or even about always sticking to the point. Digressions often lead to new discoveries and insights. If the words or ideas stop coming, then simply jot down ideas grocery-list style until you can write freely again. Much (or even all) of what you say will be unusable, but the experience of saying it may allow you to compose a focused first draft.

Many people's first experiences with free writing may result in little worth keeping, mainly because the process takes getting used to. But the experiences often foster inventiveness and insights. Note that when the following writer struggles to settle into a topic, he finds some powerful imagery emerging, imagery that he could revisit later in an extended composition:

This is harder than I thought it could be. Where am I to start? Where am I to begin? Confusion is crippling. I had a girl over. . . . There was no light except for what filtered in from the streets. I was looking at her face, or at the place I thought her face would be, and for an instant I sat there, frozen. The visage then flattened and shattered, into a mosaic, into a million, uncountable pieces that I could not work together into one with either my hands or mind. All I could do was close my eyes and try to make sense of what was happening, but it was out of my grasp. That night she looked so fine. In an instant, though, she was just a photograph, and it was with my eyes that I realized this.

Form is virtually irrelevant to free writing. The author of this next piece chose to mark his place by repeating words until he decided what to say next.

Can't think. Wait a minute. . . . Music is an awkward friend for our most awkward moments. Piece by piece, note for note, it gives you a sensation which you can't quite clarify. It's just a growing mass of of of pleasure and it keeps on growing. Rock, jazz, classical and so on, and these are genres of music which not all of us are accustomed to but which some of us find particularly interesting. . . . So I leave with these words said by someone else music is the art and the capacity to re-experience one's innocence.

—Otto Castillo

The primary audience for free writing is yourself as you discover and explore ideas; later, you can return to those ideas to decide which to explore further in a first draft. Notice the private nature of the following passage; only the writer knows the specifics behind her generalizations:

I'm supposed to call Jim later. . . . He is a headache. Extremely negative. . . . I'm glad I am out of that relationship.

The writer may never wish to reveal the details of the relationship she alludes to (nor should she have to). But the ending of the passage carries a delightfully candid admission:

Goes to show money cannot buy happiness. A nice vacation though.

The punch line is worth using, but only if the writer decides to write more publicly about her experiences with Jim. Otherwise, she should discard this piece and move on.

This next free writing also leads to honest and surprising statements:

I can't seem to lose this weight I put on over the last two years. I remember when I was in high school I couldn't put on weight if it was a pair of shoes. Somehow I've bulked from a slim hundred sixty pounds to a plus two hundred over that period of time. I don't feel I eat any more or less. It just keeps adding on. There was a time when I didn't have to lift a finger to be in shape. Now I find myself working out with the rest of the fat people.

My stomach was flat as an iron board; now it's swollen like a pregnant woman's. I'm working out three or four times a day just to lose a pound or two a week. I guess it's just a sign of getting older.

—Terrance Mhoon

Much of this free writing holds potential. Notice its oppositions, for example: "I've bulked from a slim hundred sixty pounds to a plus two hundred." "My stomach was flat as an iron board; now it's swollen like a pregnant woman's." And its surprises: "Now I find myself working out with the rest of the fat people." The writing is not perfect, of course; parts could be cut or rearranged. (The first two sentences of the second paragraph might be shifted to the first, for example.) Nonetheless, this free writing could easily be expanded on, revised, and then shared with an audience.

Composing Activity: Getting Started with Free Writings

Do at least three ten-minute free writings (preferably at different times or even days), writing as fast as your hand or keyboard skills allow, without concern for spelling, punctuation, or exact wording. Don't worry about straying off the subject; just keep going. If you run out of things to say, describe an object in the room or your sensations at the moment. If you land on a subject you'd like to explore beyond the ten-minute time limit, continue to write. And if you produce nothing of particular interest, don't despair. Just let your voice emerge and your hand keep pace with your mind.

Collaborative Activity: Sharing Your Writings with Classmates (25 minutes of class time)

Bring one of your free writings to class and read it aloud to a group of several (perhaps three or four) peers, who will also share their free writings with the group. Read your paper twice: the first time so your classmates can listen without analyzing, the second so they can comment on only what they like best—be it a small piece of description, a surprising phrase, or a particularly apt word choice. When you're just starting out (and indeed at just about any time), praise works far more effectively than condemnation. Once writers hear what readers enjoy—as well as learn what works for other writers—they subsequently attempt to replicate these successful practices while abandoning unsuccessful ones.

FOCUSING ON A SUBJECT

Now that you've become accustomed to free writing, you can begin to employ the technique to discover and explore your ideas about a particular subject. Don't plan too much. Write about a matter that interests you, describe an object or person, or reflect on an issue of importance to you. Perhaps you can then make your topic interesting to your readers.

Here's an example of a focused free writing whose playfulness may arise in part from a sense of liberation from "the rules." Note the lack of concern for correct punctuation throughout.

> If I didn't know any better I'd swear the city's sanitation workers had found a new dumping ground in my apartment.
>
> Pizza boxes, pop cans, clothes everywhere and garbage piled to the clouds in the sky would make you think I'm a bachelor, which I am. I go through this every weekend, where do I start? I promise myself I will clean up after each meal, wash clothes at least twice a week and vacuum daily but that's like finding and ending the national deficit.
>
> Yet I am color coordinated. I have matching pizza stains on my wall and couch. Thinking to myself this is the life. Like one wise man once said, or at least that is what I'm told all good things must come to an end.

Composing Activity: Bringing Focus to Free Writing

Compose two more ten-minute free writings in which you stick to a single topic. If you cannot think of anything to say or how to express a thought, stop for a moment and list your ideas until you can resume writing again.

Collaborative Activity: Sharing and Revising a Focused Free Writing (25 minutes of class time)

Read one focused free writing aloud twice to a group of several peers, who should then offer responses to the following matters:

1. What seems to be the point, and—if the point is unstated—how and where should you state it?
2. Where could you add more details and clarify matters?
3. What irrelevant or unimportant parts could you delete?

After everyone has read aloud and heard the group's comments (this should take about twenty minutes), spend three minutes making notes about what to incorporate or change in a first draft of the paper. Don't write the first draft now.

KEEPING A JOURNAL

There is nothing too trifling to write down so it be in the least degree characteristic. You will be surprised to find on re-perusing your journal what an importance and graphic power these little particulars assume.

—*Nathaniel Hawthorne*

A journal is not a diary; it is not a private log or a summary of your daily activities. Instead, the journal serves as a repository of materials you gather for potential use in your writing and studies, whether in or out of school. Here, for example, is a student's journal entry from the beginning of the term. In it, she reflects upon her fears about returning to school after a long absence:

> Last night I woke myself with definitions of words from my psychology book. I'm even in school in my sleep.
>
> I am still very nervous about this college scenario. Wondering if my retention and comprehension will keep up with the quizzes. I feel my mush mind is in competition with these younger, sharper minds.
>
> Only by the grace of God and a lot of persistence will my dream of a career in nursing become a reality.
>
> The math placement test I took on registration day boggled my mind when it came to algebra. I knew it twenty years ago but today it looks like Japanese. I've decided to take a tutoring class in order to boost my score next time I take the test. I was glad the math class was filled. A young Nigerian woman, Marilyn, will be my tutor. I had to push away in my mind she is only twenty-one.
>
> How ironic, the young teaching the old.
>
> —Linda Novak

Like a diary entry, this journal entry examines personal matters. However, the journal directs its topics more outwardly, toward an audience. While the writing is not polished and the insights are not profound, the entry includes specific detail and oppositions that hold potential for a fuller and more compelling exploration of its subject matter later.

Journal writing is essentially focused free writing. In ten or more minutes a day, you can explore whatever concerns, interests, puzzles, or angers you. You can register your doubts, questions, impressions, and plans. You can record, respond to, and interpret events, ideas, or actions. Many professional writers keep journals in which they capture surprising happenings, observations and insights, patches of dialogue, humorous or troubling moments, and unusual looking things or people. These journals are both private and public—private because the writers may choose not to use many of the entries, public because the writers always compose the entries with an audience in mind. When writers reread and reassemble the entries later, the result may uncover truths and insights the writers hadn't considered before.

That familiar lament, "I don't know what to write about," becomes less insistent when you examine your journal entries for ideas and information to adapt or expand. Furthermore, a series of journal entries over several days may lead you to view an experience or idea from several angles—an opportunity college students rarely encounter during a short semester or quarter. The following entry from the journal of a recently arrived foreign student supports the contention that whoever discovered water certainly wasn't a fish. The student's mastery of the idiom of his second language may be limited, but not his ability to observe and analyze:

A few days after coming to the U.S. I made a great decision: buying an American newspaper. I define the decision "great" because it was and still is (but less) hard to understand all the words of the articles correctly, and figure out the meaning of some sentences.

The first time I purchased a newspaper I thought "Be careful. You are taking two of them!" But I wasn't; it was only one big newspaper! In Italy, and probably all Europe, the journals are not divided into sections, but all the articles are contained in only one part, which is much thinner and much more expensive than the giant American papers are.

When opening it, I was surprised with the quantity of issues it treated. I thought: "Who can read this mountain of paper? Only a retired or ill person has the time to do that!" But on the other hand, there is specialized news like business, sports, real estate, and so on. Thus, a person who is interested in that kind of information need not buy other journals and can save money; another advantage is that all the family can read it because it contains news and columns that could interest the kids as well as the grandparents. Finally, it can be read by more than one person at the same time. At home when two of us wanted to do so, the paper had to be torn apart into several pieces, because sports pages were linked with business, local news with world news, and so on. When we finished reading, the pages were scattered all around the room, and we needed ten minutes to reassemble the paper! A disadvantage of living outside America.

Despite the writer's stilted phrasing in spots, he succeeds in constructing a lighthearted contrast between a particular instance of American culture and his familiar one in Italy. But his journal also provides a vehicle for examining a far more serious matter:

One of the worst faces of the United States is its subways. . . . The subways of New York are notorious for their robberies and various crimes, but the subways in other cities don't have a good reputation, either. I heard that the Chicago subway is also dangerous at night, but not at the NY levels.

I think everybody who comes to America and immediately takes a subway will not have a good or accurate image of the nation. When you enter some stations, they smell so bad that it is like putting your head into a garbage can, and certainly no one would think the floors are clean.

When I take the train, I feel like I'm entering a tunnel and going back to the past; everything seems old, abandoned, as if trains and structures don't need repairs or modernization.

The first time I came to Chicago with my parents, I was a child; when we took the train, I was scared that it could fall down, because the supporting structures were covered by rust. Now I'm not afraid of that, but, anyway, I watch the structures with suspicion, because they are more deteriorated than they were ten years ago.

The train and subway system here in Chicago is very strange, but I guess these conditions are similar all around the states, although the nation is one of the richest and technically advanced in the world.

Anyway, taking the train helped me to figure out why Americans use so many cars.

—Aldo Ronchetti

Continuing in this vein, the writer could record further observations in subsequent entries. These observations might provide material for an extended composition on the complexities of American society.

Journal keeping can fulfill academic functions in a variety of courses. For example, you can employ journals to assess your progress in learning as you record and react to new concepts and material. In the following excerpt, a student examines his own writing practices:

The only times I can find myself writing well are times when my attentions should be focused on other things. It is difficult for me to write whenever I actually make myself sit down, pick up a pen and take out a fresh piece of paper. It is impossible; often times I'll discover that an hour has passed, though an instant ago I had situated myself, and the paper, spread out before me boundless and infinite, has remained blank. There is a numbness affecting me, probably originating from an aspect of my self. . . that restricts my thought and sentiment. It . . . hinders my capacity to relate what I feel.

—Carlos Orellana

You can also respond to reading assignments in your journal. Simply copy down memorable passages, and then explore your reactions and questions. Or you can summarize important ideas and reflect on them. This separation of notes and responses is often called a "double entry" journal. Here's an example from an American history course:

Notes: The War of 1812 was both a battle between the British and Americans and a battle between the Indians and the Americans. The British, I suspect, were conducting an aggressive war—attempting to hold onto their practice of capturing (kidnapping?) American sailors from private ships and impressing them into service on British ships.	*Reactions:* I've often wondered why an Indian leader like Tecumseh seemed so attractive to Americans. The Civil War general was named William Tecumseh Sherman. Odd that he would be named after an enemy of America. But I'm beginning to understand the admiration for Tecumseh. He was really a visionary, a man who wanted to

When they grabbed four Americans off the *Chesapeake,* a public not a private vessel, it was an overt act of war. The Indians (or, more properly, Native Americans) fought a more defensive battle. They wanted to preserve their lands against the trespasses of the Americans, who, according to the Indian leader Tecumseh, had negotiated a series of illegal treaties with small tribes who gave land they did not own to Americans.

unite all Native Americans in a federation to oppose the white settlements on their land and prevent further attacks on their villages. (It seems that attack on the Indians at the Battle of Tippecanoe was naked aggression by the Americans.) What really blows my mind is that the British made Tecumseh a Brigadeer General in their army. Some savage! I want to find out more about this guy.

Questions: How did Tecumseh feel about torture, gauntlet running, and scalping? Was he more "civilized" than many of his comrades? Did their British allies permit such brutality?

You'll employ the journal often for gathering notes and planning strategies for later assignments in this text as well.

Composing Activity: Keeping a Journal

Maintain a journal for several weeks. Make your entries on 8 1/2 x 6 loose-leaf paper kept in a binder. That way, you can periodically remove and hand in entries to your instructor. Or keep a journal on your computer, handing in a diskette or a printout of several entries from time to time. Try to write about matters you usually don't examine (Reactions to other people? Musings about your future?) and in ways you usually don't attempt (Specific descriptions? Dialogues? Narratives in the present tense?). Use subsequent journal entries to evaluate your successes and difficulties with these attempts—that is, to write about writing and think about thinking.

Composing Activity: Keeping an Academic Journal

In another section of your journal (set off by a colored divider page) or in a separate computer file, maintain a record of your responses to class lectures and assignments. If you write in a notebook, keep class notes on the left-hand pages, and use the right-hand pages for recording your reactions to, questions about, and insights concerning lectures and the comments and questions of your classmates. If you use a computer, set up a two-column format, or record your response entries in italics. On the right-hand pages, discuss your feelings, both favorable and unfavorable, about the ways classes are conducted. Note your responses to and questions about reading assignments. Such inventory taking often helps you identify and articulate issues to investigate, to ask questions about in class, or to review. Reexamine these journal entries from time to time and then record any further ideas, questions, and responses they provoke.

Collaborative Activity: Revising a Journal Entry (15 minutes of class time)

Bring one or more journal entries to class to read aloud to a group of peers (as you may have done with free writings earlier in this chapter). Then, based on the listeners' responses, revise and sharpen the focus of the material so it more closely resembles a composition you could hand in to your instructor. Look for a leading idea and shape the paper so that each of its parts addresses and clarifies that idea.

Chapter 2

Discovering and Shaping Ideas

No two writers compose in exactly the same way. While their ultimate goal is to produce a clear, convincing, and engaging piece of prose, the process of arriving at that goal varies from person to person—and often from task to task. On one extreme are the *Planners*, who can frame their ideas before beginning to write and who tend to revise only once or twice. On the other extreme are the *Discoverers*, who find shape for their ideas only through multiple revisions. Neither approach is better than the other; they are simply different.

I plan quite a bit. But I'm not too aware of it. That is, I've not got it all down, but I've got a good deal of it thought through or felt through, before I begin writing. So that the whole world of it is very much alive and urgent for me. . . . The world that I'm going to write has already been created, somehow, in the physical sensation before I go about writing it, shaping it, organizing it.

—*William Goyen*

I don't know what I'm thinking about a particular thing until I have some kind of draft. It's the actual execution that tells me what I want to say, what I always wanted to say when I started.

—*Elizabeth Hardwick*

Like most writers, you probably stand somewhere between these extremes but lean toward one or the other. However, inside every veteran writer's mind is a filing cabinet full of resources that make the composing process more efficient. The previous chapter supplied you with a few of these resources, and this chapter will suggest even more. As you sample each one, try to be both a participant in and an observer of your composing behaviors. Determine which practices most comfortably suit your thinking patterns and therefore should occupy a place in your own mental filing cabinet for further use.

You're who you are, not Fitzgerald or Thomas Wolfe. You write by sitting down and writing. There's no particular time or place—you suit yourself, your nature. How one works, assuming he's disciplined, doesn't matter. If he or she is not disciplined, no sympathetic magic will help. . . . Eventually everyone learns his or her own best way. The real mystery to crack is you.

—*Bernard Malamud*

EXAMINING WAYS TO DISCOVER, EXPLORE, AND SHAPE IDEAS

Two thousand years ago, the Roman orator Cicero advised that writers (or, in his case, speakers) begin the composing process with what he called the *invention* stage. In this stage, writers investigate and study the subject matter, select the materials to include, and analyze occasion, audience, and purpose. Cicero obviously was a Planner, so this structured procedure made sense for him. Now, however, after several decades of research into the actual practices of both professional and novice writers, we view invention differently. Rarely do writers consider and resolve every important issue prior to composing a first draft. Instead, they engage in a more dynamic and often unpredictable interplay among discovering and drafting ideas, analysis, and revision that continues throughout the composing process. We say that the process is *recursive*—that is, the steps in it recur, or loop back on themselves. For instance, you may plan and compose a first draft, begin revising (often in consultation with others), realize you've omitted an important idea, and stop to compose a new section. You may change your mind during the planning or drafting stages and therefore stop to revise— or start all over again. You may shift passages from place to place at any point in the process, cutting and pasting the passages by hand or in your word processor. You may even compose new sentences while proofreading your final draft.

Your perceptions of audience and purpose may shift throughout the process, too. You write primarily for yourself while exploring and discovering ideas, but you revise with an eye toward the interests and needs of your readers. And, whether you begin with a clear idea or only the vaguest notion of what you hope to accomplish, your goal may change or emerge later in the process—and may lead to further revisions.

Today, therefore, we generally regard invention as a time to discover and shape ideas, but not necessarily as a time to resolve every issue relating to audience, purpose, occasion, and point. These matters are important— indeed, they're critical—but they tend to switch from background to foreground throughout the drafting, revising, and editing stages of your work. We'll examine audience, purpose, and occasion later in the chapter, but first let's take a look at additional discovery techniques.

Brainstorming

Brainstorming is simply the process of listing ideas as they occur to you. You jot down whatever comes to mind about the subject, narrow the list to develop a point, add additional items to the list, and then consider how these items should be organized. Suppose, for example, that when a student we'll call Melissa Barnes decided to inform (and entertain) her classmates about what it's like to be the daughter of a professional baseball player, she generated a list of her ideas about the subject:

> father a pitcher for Pittsburgh Pirates
> pitched only a few years in the majors
> traveled a lot
> the players wore their different colored uniforms
> Mom raised us
> I was five through seven years old
> didn't understand the significance of his job at first
> hard making friends with kids at school—did they like me for what I was or for who my father was
> I wanted to be a professional ball player, too
> loved going onto the field and looking at the players up close
> learned that the men in blue suits were umpires
> we had to be well behaved
> got autographed baseballs
> the seats in the stands were hard
> the weather was often too cold or hot
> always wanted to eat peanuts and hot dogs, but Mom restricted our diets
> would get candy treats after the game
> when dad left the game, mom took us to the rest room
> if Dad lost, he was sometimes in a bad mood
> the umps gave my father trouble from time to time
> brother wore Pirates' jersey and we both wore Pirates' caps

After finishing this list, Barnes realized that her ideas needed some focus, some central point around which she could develop and organize her materials. She decided that the most important ideas concerned her experiences at the games: what she saw, heard, and felt there, along with how she had to behave. Thus, she crossed out the details about her school experiences, her father's travels, and her mother's responsibilities for raising the children. She then compiled a second brainstorming list in which she rearranged the items into categories and added new items:

> father a pitcher for Pittsburgh Pirates
> I was five through seven years old
> didn't understand the significance of his job at first

loved going onto the field and looking at the players up close
the players wore their different colored uniforms
got autographed baseballs

learned that the men in blue suits were umpires
the umps gave my father trouble from time to time
we could tell by what the men behind us yelled at the umpires
when dad left the game, mom took us to the rest room

I wanted to be a professional ball player, too
the seats in the stands were hard
the weather was often too cold or hot
brother wore Pirates' jersey and we both wore Pirates' caps
we had to be well behaved
always wanted to eat peanuts and hot dogs, but Mom restricted our
diets

got good treats after the game, especially if the Pirates won
if Dad lost, he sometimes was in a bad mood

going to games like going to church
sat in hard chairs in both places
men in the aisles collected money

The final draft that follows emerged from such beginning efforts:

There's a basket full of autographed baseballs in my living room. Each one has a different story to tell. Some are shiny and white, and have never been used in a real game. Others are soiled with grass stains, and some are smudged with blue ink by the sweaty palms of the players who signed them.

My love for baseball goes back a long way to the days when my father was a pitcher for the Pittsburgh Pirates. I loved going onto the field with my dad while other, less fortunate kids had to sit in the stands. At the same time, I didn't understand the magnitude of being on the same turf as America's greatest heroes. I only knew that they all dressed in the same suit on our team and a different suit on the other team. The guys in blue suits were the umpires. Sometimes the umpires were the enemy, like when my dad threw a strike and they called it a ball. My cues came from the men sitting behind us who would boo and yell nasty words at the ump. Then the manager, the man who got to wear a suit but never played, would come out to the mound and take the ball away from dad. This is the time when my mother would take us to the rest rooms.

What I really remember about growing up in a baseball stadium was how hard the seats were. Sometimes it was too cold. Often it was too hot. I remember my fashionable mother in hats that matched her shoes that matched her handbags. My brother always dressed in a black and gold jersey, and we both wore wool baseball caps that made our heads itch. People would always come up to talk to us. They often told my mother how well behaved we were. They would laugh when they asked my brother what he wanted to be when he grew up and he said a farmer. I once said I wanted to be a Playboy bunny and my mother told me I would rather be a nurse. Once I said I wanted to be a ballplayer like my dad and everyone just looked nervous.

We also went to church a lot back then. We would spend Sunday morning at church and Sunday afternoon at the ballpark. Sometimes it seemed hard to tell the difference. We sat in our chairs. Mom read us the program, and we watched the proceedings faithfully. Men would come through the aisles and collect money. At the ballpark, you received Cracker Jack in exchange for your quarter, at the church only salvation.

After the game, there would be a treat if we were good. We always had a better treat if my dad's team won. He would meet us at the car, sometimes with beer on his breath, and pick us up and hug us. Sometimes people would be standing around, waiting to have their baseball cards signed, and always in pursuit of those prized game balls.

Things have changed since then. The last baseball I had autographed was given to me by a man I dated. My girlfriend and I were at Wrigley, jumping up and down, drinking beer, and swearing. He was a left-handed pitcher from Pittsburgh. Maybe things haven't changed as much as I think. Next week I'll be back in church.

Melissa Barnes found sufficient information and direction to compose a story after just two attempts at brainstorming, but there's no limit to the number of brainstorming lists you could compile. In fact, you may return to brainstorming any time you need to generate and organize new material within the composing and revising process.

Collaborative Activity: Brainstorming (25–30 minutes of class time)

Prior to coming to class, brainstorm for ten minutes in your journal about a frustrating experience: dealing with a bureaucracy, registering for classes, arguing with parents or someone in authority, encountering numerous delays on a trip, struggling to learn a new concept or skill, or putting up with a dogmatic boss or supervisor.

Then, in five-minute sessions in class, take turns reading your lists aloud to a group of several classmates, who will share their responses to the following questions:

- What is the leading idea or theme of the experience?

- What details in the list best support that idea—and what details do not?
- How might the details be reorganized?

Don't respond to their comments or try to defend yourself; just listen to your classmates' suggestions and perhaps take notes. Immediately following the discussion, spend five minutes composing a sentence that expresses that leading idea. Cross out the entries on the brainstorming list that do not support it, and number the remaining entries to reflect your reorganization. Reorganize, rewrite, or expand the brainstorming list in your journal later.

Clustering

Another way to generate and organize ideas is through clustering. You start the process by jotting down and circling the central idea in the middle of the page. In Melissa Barnes's case, the first circle might look like this:

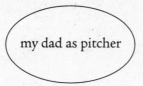

Then you branch off the circle in whatever general directions occur to you, as illustrated from Melissa Barnes's emerging diagram:

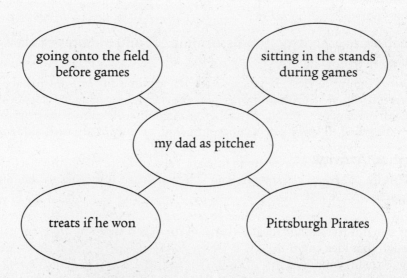

Continue generating ideas by adding branches off branches, as in this partial view of the completed clustering diagram for Barnes's paper:

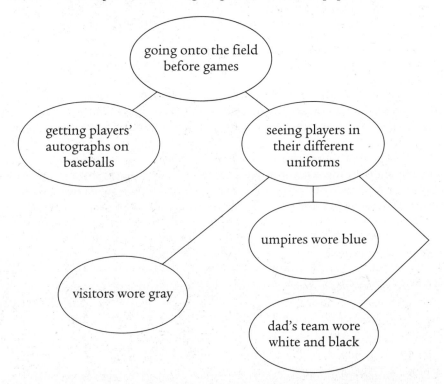

Then scrutinize the diagram, add further circles, erase and then reattach lines to different circles, and decide which parts of the diagram to include in the first draft of your paper. (A number of the circled details from Barnes's final diagram would not be included.) Of course, as you change your mind or narrow the focus of the topic, you can also draw new diagrams.

Because it not only generates but also connects ideas, clustering often lightens the burdensome task of arranging a complex body of thoughts and data. Clustering therefore appeals to business people, lawyers, academics, and many other professionals who must compose letters, memos, lectures, or presentations under the demands of a deadline.

Invention Activity: Clustering

Choose a journal entry you'd like to expand and shape into a story for your classmates to read or hear. Draw one or more clustering diagrams in which you produce and organize the material. Before, during, or after drawing the diagram, consider the leading idea or theme your story should emphasize (although that idea could change as you compose and revise); then begin structuring (or redo) your diagram to include only materials that support that idea.

If formulating and expressing the central idea prove too difficult, try the following invention activity, called looping.

Looping

Looping, a variation of free writing, allows you to write quickly but then return to your topic in ever-narrowing focus. Moreover, since looping requires that you write in sentences, it strengthens your ability to examine your ideas and the relationships between them. Sentences are complete statements, so they tend to express ideas fully. They also establish a natural and logical progression of thought.

Begin by writing quickly on a topic for five or ten minutes. Try to discover and explore your ideas without pausing to revise or ponder word choice. Allow yourself to digress, but always try to return to your topic. When you finish, scrutinize your work for the most important idea, what author Peter Elbow calls "the center of gravity." What you find may be a powerful insight, a connection between ideas, or a potential theme. Compose a sentence that states this idea, and use it as the opening sentence of another loop.

Look for the center of gravity again, summarize it in a sentence, and repeat the process as often as necessary—two, three, or even four times—until the summarizing sentence clearly expresses an idea or theme that you can comfortably develop in a paper. Of course, the looping process may also produce a number of valuable supporting ideas to include as well. After arriving at the summarizing sentence, you may brainstorm, cluster, or compose a first draft of the paper.

Composing Activity: Looping

Return to either your brainstorming list or clustering diagram and do several writing loops until you clearly state the leading idea or theme of a paper. (If the leading ideas have clearly emerged already, you might practice looping with an entirely new subject.)

Collaborative Activity: Writing and Revising a First Draft (25 minutes of class time)

Outside class, compose a first draft of a paper based on one of the products of your earlier invention activities. Then read the draft aloud twice to a group of several peers: the first time so they may listen without judging, the second so they may listen critically and comment on (1) what they like, (2) what they'd like to hear more (or less) about, and (3) what questions the paper raises but doesn't answer. Again, don't respond to their comments or try to defend yourself. Instead, take notes on the advice you think might help you most in revising the draft. Later on outside class, look over both the draft and your notes. If other ideas occur to you, record them in the margins or at the end of the paper. Then revise your first draft.

The invention practices you've explored here and in the previous chapter should broaden your choices on how to generate and organize ideas before beginning a first draft. You may find them useful or totally unnecessary, but keep them in your mental files nevertheless. Later chapters of this book will discuss further invention practices that are appropriate to specific writing tasks.

CONSIDERING AUDIENCE, OCCASION, AND PURPOSE

You can't ignore the remaining items on Cicero's invention agenda—considerations of audience, occasion, and purpose—for they help determine the effectiveness of your writing. Therefore, we'll introduce those items here but return to them more specifically in later chapters.

Remember, invention is a dynamic practice that precedes—but usually continues throughout—the composing process. At some point, therefore, you should examine and shape your writing with the following five questions in mind. Planners will probably wish to do so early, Discoverers after composing one or more drafts. How you respond to the questions doesn't matter: ponder them, discuss them, make notes or formal responses, or write nothing at all.

1. *What Is the Occasion for Writing?* Are you writing a term paper or an essay examination in school? A lab report in a science course? A letter to apply for a job? A memo to a supervisor or colleague at work? A sales presentation to a customer? A letter to a client? An article in a professional journal? A desktop-published newsletter for a business or community group? A letter of complaint to a store manager? An informal note to a friend? An article for a newspaper or magazine? Each of these occasions governs your choices about what (and how much) to say, and how to say it.

2. *What Is Your Reason for Writing?* What is your goal: to earn a grade, get a job, make a sale, demand a refund, correct or apologize for a mistake, suggest a change, explain a task, record the minutes of a meeting, outline a procedure, amuse a friend, or announce a public event? Each of these reasons helps you determine how to address your audience (formally or informally, politely or angrily, seriously or lightheartedly), how to structure and phrase your ideas, and how to use the material you've gathered.

3. *Who Is Your Audience?* Although you write for yourself when exploring and discovering ideas, what you ultimately say about a topic depends greatly on whom you expect to read your final draft. How familiar is your audience with the subject matter, and, therefore, what do they need (or not need) to know? What are their attitudes and prejudices toward your subject (and toward you)? What are their concerns and interests? What is your relationship to them: employee to boss, expert to novice, friend to friend?

4. *What Is Your Subject and What Do You Know (or Need to Know) About It?* No writer can intelligently discuss subjects he or she doesn't understand. Write about what you know—or can find out about. Then you can say a great deal, and can say it clearly and authoritatively.

In business or everyday experience, the subject of the writing connects naturally with the occasion and reason for writing. (An advertisement, for instance, tries to sell some product to a target audience: a stock mutual fund to wealthy investors, a minivan to suburban families, a large-screen television set to middle-class families, a line of basketball shoes to athletes or their coaches, or even a denture cream to elderly people.)

In school assignments, where the occasion for writing is most often to earn a grade, you may be assigned a topic or be required to select one from a list. Then you must narrow the focus of the topic so you can discuss it effectively within the limitations of space, time, and format allowed. You can say something meaningful and interesting only if you take ownership of the topic (that is, convince yourself that you want to write about it), decide what point you wish to make, and then shape the writing to develop that point.

5. *What Is Your Point?* Since you always communicate for a purpose, you don't simply write "about" a subject; you must make a *point* about the subject. Your writing must always answer one question: *So what?* A letter in which you apply for a job should not only discuss your educational and vocational background; it should also demonstrate *how that background qualifies you for the job.* A letter in which you complain to the management of a restaurant should not only describe the inferior service you received; *it should also demand a refund, a free meal, or at least an apology.* Making a point is such an important issue that we'll devote a full chapter to it later in this book.

Once you've answered these questions, no matter how tentatively, you can experiment with what to say first, second, or even eighth. You can consider what ideas to explain and when to explain them. You can consider what to include and what to leave out. In the limited space of a letter, an essay examination answer, or a 500-word composition, you can't say everything, so you must decide what's most important, most relevant, and most interesting. With practice, answering the questions will become second nature to you, and will heighten your awareness of what to look for when you revise.

LOOKING AT PUBLISHED WORKS

To practice analysis according to Cicero's criteria, read the opening paragraphs of the following three published works (that is, works made public for readers). Each addresses a specific audience, on a specific subject, on a specific occasion, for a specific reason, and makes a specific point. Then answer the questions that follow.

I: Life insurance is one of the most difficult purchases people ever make. Policies are confusing, their terms opaque, their true costs often obscured. That's especially unfortunate because life insurance is not a luxury but, for many people, an essential purchase. If you have young children, for example, you need life insurance—probably more of it than you have now.

If you ask people how they picked a policy, they're likely to answer that they had confidence in the company or in their insurance agent. The insurance industry likes people to buy on trust rather than on facts about the policies themselves. "There's really no best policy," the president of one major insurer told us. There are certainly very good and very bad policies, however. Our nine-month investigation reveals that major differences do exist in the cost and quality of life-insurance products. Over the next three issues, *Consumer Reports* will rate more than 400 policies and demonstrate that some are clearly better—and some are clearly worse—than others. We will show you how to save hundreds of dollars a year on life insurance and get the best possible coverage.

II: When in the course of human events, it becomes necessary for one people to dissolve the political bonds which have connected them with another, and to assume among the powers of the earth, the separate and equal station to which the Laws of Nature and of Nature's God entitle them, a decent respect to the opinions of mankind requires that they should declare the causes which impel them to separation.

We hold these truths to be self-evident, that all men are created equal; that they are endowed by their Creator with certain unalienable Rights; that among these are life, liberty, and the pursuit of happiness. That, to secure these rights, governments are instituted among men, deriving their just powers from the consent of the governed; that whenever any form of government becomes destructive to these ends, it is the right of the people to alter or to abolish it, and to institute a new government, laying its foundation on such principles and organizing its powers in such form, as to them shall seem most likely to effect their safety and happiness. Prudence, indeed, will dictate that governments long established should not be changed for light and transient causes; and accordingly all experience hath shown, that mankind are more disposed to suffer, while evils are sufferable, than to right themselves by abolishing the forms to which they are accustomed. But, when a long train of abuses and usurpations, pursuing invariably the same object, evinces a design to reduce them under absolute despotism, it is the right, it is the duty, to throw off such government, and to provide new guards for their future security. Such has been the suffering of these colonies, and such is now the necessity which constrains them to alter their former systems of government.

III: This is the story of an extraordinary voyage in time, and of a young woman who devoted three years to a singular experiment. In 1979, Patty Moore—then aged twenty-six—transformed herself for the first of many times into an eighty-five-year-old woman. Her object was to discover firsthand the problems, joys and frustrations of the elderly. She wanted to know for herself what it's like to live in a culture of youth and beauty when your hair is gray, your skin is wrinkled and no men turn their heads as you pass.

Her time machine was a makeup kit. Barbara Kelly, a friend and professional makeup artist, helped Patty pick out a wardrobe and showed her how to use latex to create wrinkles, and wrap Ace bandages to give the impression of stiff joints. "It was peculiar," Patty recalls, as she relaxes in her New York City apartment. "Even the first few times I went out, I realized that I wouldn't have to act that much. The more I was perceived as elderly by others, the more 'elderly' I actually became . . . I imagine that's just what happens to people who really are old."

What motivated Patty to make her strange journey? Partly her career—as an industrial designer, Patty often focuses on the needs of the elderly. But the roots of her interest are also deeply personal. Extremely close to her own grandparents—particularly her maternal grandfather, now ninety—and raised in a part of Buffalo, New York, where there was a large elderly population, Patty always drew comfort and support from the older people around her. When her own marriage ended in 1979 and her life seemed to be falling apart, she donned her costume more than two hundred times in fourteen different states.

Here is the remarkable story of what she found.

—Katherine Barrett, "Old Before Her Time"

Issues for Investigation and Discussion

1. Who is the intended audience for each of the published works? How do you know? Describe each audience in detail: What is their age? What are their concerns? What is their educational level? What is their social standing? Why would they be interested in reading the work?

2. What is the occasion for each of the works—in other words, why did the writer (or writers) choose to publish the work?

3. What is the main purpose (or goal) of each of the works? What does the writer or writers expect the audience *to do* after reading the work? What evidence supports your answer?

4. What point does each work make about the subject matter? Summarize the main ideas of each, and, based on what you've read, predict what the remainder of each work will discuss.

Composing Activity: Writing About Writing

Return to the first draft you wrote earlier in the collaborative activity on page 20, and consider how you might reshape the paper for a student publication at your school. Who reads the magazine and what do they expect to find in it? What purpose would you hope to accomplish by publishing the work (aside from achieving fame and glory)—that is, what would you expect your readers to do and feel after reading your work? How could you further clarify, strengthen, and support your point? What haven't you yet explained that readers would need to know? What aspects of your subject don't they need to know?

Write a journal entry that explores your responses to these questions. Think about specific changes you might make concerning the details to include or exclude, the phrasing of ideas, and the organization of the whole work. Don't worry about the form and shape of your responses; just get your ideas down on the page. Alternatively, you may simply make notes for changes in the margins of your first draft.

After considering these issues and planning changes, compose a revision of your first draft.

Chapter 3

Telling Stories

Find a subject you care about and which you in your heart feel others should care about. It is this genuine caring, and not your games with language, which will be the most compelling and seductive element in your style.

—*Kurt Vonnegut, Jr.*

Storytelling is the oldest of the writing skills, and also among the most important. The philosopher Immanuel Kant said that our fundamental way of thinking and communicating is through narration. Because we are human, the stories of other humans engage our intellects and emotions far more powerfully than any set of abstractions or statistics. Moreover, good stories (also called *narratives*) entertain, providing an essential ingredient of strong writing. Whether we intend to inform or persuade our readers, stories animate, enliven, illustrate, and prove our point. An audience may soon forget abstractions, but they won't likely forget good stories—and, as a result, the message behind each. The meat of any writing is its ideas, but narratives often make them more palatable.

LOOKING AT NARRATIVES

Writing from personal experiences should come naturally. Just choose any one of the thousands of funny or embarrassing or powerful moments from your past. Virtually any one of them can be developed into a lively and entertaining story. Put yourself back in the event, visualize it, listen to it, feel it, and record what you find. Here, for example, is a humorous account of a childhood experience written by a college freshman.

When I was eleven, my brother and I became famous in one day. It all started because we felt persecuted by our mother's mad obsession with wholesome food. Even my little sisters stared blankly at her lima beans. We wanted ice cream and my father hadn't uttered the code word—ice—for what seemed like years. We sat in the summer heat and swallowed our vegetables with disgust. Something had to be done, so after dinner we began plotting.

The next day my brother kept mom busy while I slid into her bedroom. After finding her purse, I gently pulled a bill from her wallet, put the purse back, and retreated into the hallway. I took a deep breath, stuffed the bill in my pocket, and tried to walk casually past mom without looking at her face.

As I went out the front door I gave my brother the sign. He ran out to the curb where I was waiting and panted, "Whaddya get?"

Glancing at the kitchen window nervously I said, "She didn't have any change; all I got was a buck." I held out a crumpled bill.

"That ain't a buck, that's ten bucks!" my brother said in amazement. Then he looked and me and said, "You're gonna get in trouble for this." I looked at the kitchen window again for signs of my mother. My brother stood on the curb waiting until he asked, "Well, whad're we gonna do now?" I felt like strangling him. My hand fidgeted with the bill in my pocket as I imagined the business end of my mother's ruler on my butt. "Are ya gonna get ice?" my brother said, interrupting my reverie. Then the taste of ice cream mixed with Bosco came to mind. Every time my mother caught me in a lie she washed my mouth out with Lava soap. I imagined looking innocent and saying, "I found the money, Ma; I didn't take it." The Lava soured the Bosco in my brain.

But my mom's face never appeared in the window and the sun kept telling me how good and cold ice cream would be.

We took off for town, arguing all the way. We decided to change the bill at the Ben Franklin, but we had to buy something to look legitimate. A Duncan see-through yo-yo caught my brother's eye. We argued, agreed on co-owner-ship, sealed it with spit-on-the-palm, and left. Eight dollars and some change remained. We were rich.

The saleslady in the Ben Franklin stared at us like goldfish in her five-and-ten fish bowl as we stood on the sidewalk tearing the plastic wrapper off the yo-yo. I pointed to a sign on Jansma's Bakery window across the street: "Chocolate Eclairs—Four for a Dollar." We weren't allowed these cream-filled dreams at home—my mother was too mean—so we had to make up for lost time. After buying four eclairs we stood on the boulevard imitating pus-filled sores at each other.

But ice cream was still on my mind, so like two millionaires we strolled down to Rexall's. My mother's words, "Thou shalt not . . ." were lost in the noise of the swarm of kids inside the drugstore. My brother and I debated over the cooler filled with ice cream. We couldn't agree on what kind to buy. A small crowd gathered. We decided on a whole carton of Fudgsicles. Suddenly everyone liked us.

Even Gustuli, the kid that used to beat me up every day, was my pal. The power of money made my head swell and I couldn't see myself sitting down to lima beans ever again. We were now philanthropists, revered and respected for our wealth. In the alley behind the drugstore we stood like Mafia bosses, Fudgsicles jutting from our mouths.

Someone had fireworks for sale, but the deal had to be made in a secret place. We decided to meet in Hank's barn. My brother and I got there before anyone else, so we sat in the sun-lit straw and waited. Hank never seemed to be around and it looked like he never used the barn. As big to me as a cathedral and filled with dark corners and a nice musty smell, Hank's barn was one of my favorite places.

We were forbidden to play in the barn because it was dangerous and Hank didn't like trespassers. I sucked on a Fudgsicle and thought about the time Hank had caught my brother and me in his pear tree. He looked old and angry while pointing his gun at us. I thought he would shoot, but he let us down and told us to get.

Finally, the kid with the firecrackers showed up, accompanied by a bunch of other guys. I bought some Chasers and Black Cats while my brother and the other kids ran around the barn hollering. Someone with a deck of cards suggested a poker game. We played cards in the tiny loft room, filled with streaming sun and straw dust, while the little kids played their games on the barn floor. My brother kept taunting me to walk the beam. Bored with cards, I finally agreed, but dared my brother to walk it with me. We went out, one at a time, tippy-toeing over the narrow joist above the barn floor to stand in the middle, where we had to raise one leg and then get back to the wall without falling off.

Walking the beam was exciting, but the fireworks in my pocket promised new thrills. My brother and I talked about throwing some in a huge barrel, but someone suggested putting one in a rat-hole. Toward the back of the barn, in one of the stalls, we found a huge rat-hole. We rigged a string of firecrackers together, lit the wick, jammed them into the hole, and backed away as the fireworks fizzled. Smoke trailed from the rat's front door. I looked for water in the barn, but the only buckets around were filled with dust. We tried to smother the fire by stuffing the hole shut. Our friends vanished. A disoriented rat appeared from nowhere and ran for the door where Hank stood holding a shovel.

I can't recall much of what happened after that, except the look of sadness on my mom's face when the police officer opened the back door to let us out of the squad car.

—Mark Schlitt

Here's another story from the adolescent years of a college freshman, this time with a far more serious point. Note that, unlike Mark Schlitt's story, which develops a single incident, it discusses the typical and habitual activities of two friends.

THE BUTTERFLY IS FREE

The butterfly is free to fly
She spread her wings and . . .

This was part of the eulogy I wrote and read at my best friend's funeral when we were eighteen. She had attempted suicide twice and failed. Her doctor had given her three bottles of anti-depressants which she took her last day.

Her name was Sonya Rodriguez but we all called her "Stone." Stone was a modern-day Cinderella, a ward of the state at the age of four. She lived with her wicked stepmother and two wicked step-sisters. She was expected to clean, cook, shop, and do the laundry for the entire family. Her free time was to go to studying, to maintain a straight "A" average. At fifteen, she did all this but looked for more. She created a life-like dummy to lay in her bed, and we'd crawl out the bedroom window to hang out and party all night. When we were together they called us Orange and Yellow Sunshine for the colors of our hair.

The week her stepmother took a vacation, Stone and I, another girl named Sonny, and some guys we hung around with went wild. We took Stone horseback riding, partying, to shows, concerts, and everywhere we could get to.

Shortly after turning eighteen she stopped by my house with a suitcase and asked if she could stay. My mother left the decision up to me. Sure, why not?

I introduced her to B. S. Phil and they laughed, danced, and romanced. But he broke her heart one weekend and she was still very fragile. Unfortunately, the same weekend I went off camping. The following Tuesday I came home from work to find Stone had O.D.'d on pills her doctor had prescribed for depression.

Phil and I were pretty blown away. After the funeral we were sitting in my mother's backyard. We saw one hundred butterflies or more only in the yard, none to the right, none to the left. We both knew then that the dead can communicate. We knew she came to say, "Until we meet again."

Once when we were fifteen, I asked Stone, "If you believed in reincarnation, what would you want to be?"

She answered quickly, "A butterfly, because butterflies are free."

—Christine Mueller

We needn't dwell in the distant past for stories to capture and hold the minds of readers. This next example from an older student tells a compelling story from his adult life:

After twelve hours of patrol in the cold and rain, we were tired and hungry. The area had been heavily mined and the Viet Cong were setting up rocket positions to shell Da Nang Air Base. Our job was to search out and destroy these sites.

Having accomplished our mission, we decided to dig in for the remainder of the darkness. The squad formed an L-shaped ambush zone, a tactical defense position, while I stationed myself about twenty meters out to act as a listening post. All was quiet for some time, when suddenly the V. C. were ahead of and flanking my position. Communication with the squad was impossible because Charlie was jamming our pre-determined radio frequencies. I picked up my rifle and began crawling toward the squad. The V. C. spotted me and opened fire, and after a few seconds, my boys opened up with everything they had. I was trapped between friendly and enemy fire without cover, except for a pagoda altar on my left. My machine gunner was shouting, directing me out of the line of fire toward the altar, but movement was impossible. I kept firing at the origin of the green tracer bullets as they burned past my head. A concussion grenade exploded somewhere in front of me, causing my ears and nose to bleed and helmet to disappear. Someone launched an illumination flare, and I knew it was time to move or die. Running as low as possible, I made it to within a few meters of the altar and was suddenly blown senseless by an anti-personnel device. It felt as if I had stepped on a trampoline, bounced into the air, but come down on a cement slab. I think I recall saying out loud, "What the f–ck did I do?" There wasn't any pain at first, but then I realized all my clothes had been blown off. I turned my head and saw my left boot lying next to me with part of my leg still inside. The rush of pain was unbearable. The fire fight continued, but the fear of being killed by an enemy bullet no longer held a place in my mind. My brain could only tell me to scream. Luckily, the force of the booby trap had propelled me forward, far enough to land behind the altar, safe from enemy gunfire. At that point, nothing else really mattered except pain. I tried to lift myself up on my elbows, when I felt a hand on my shoulder and a soothing voice, telling me to relax. The squad leader gently placed my head in his lap while a corpsman began applying tourniquets to my legs and I suddenly realized the fire fight was over. The V.C. disappeared as quickly as they had appeared. He stroked my head and assured me the med-corps chopper was on its way. The chopper finally arrived and was forced skyward again because someone had popped a red flare, meaning enemy in the area. I was so weak from loss of blood that the morphine injection had no effect on the pain. My screaming turned to laughter, then crying, then screaming again. I knew I was going to die. Finally, someone popped a green flare, meaning friendliness in the area, and the chopper returned, hovering a few feet off the ground. The squad leader and the corpsman placed me on a poncho, laid their field jackets over me, and the rest of the squad picked up the corners of the poncho and heaved me through the hatch. By this time, I was delirious and when the corpsman on the chopper tried to keep me from looking out the hatch while in flight, I punched him in the face. I may have realized that the instinct to survive was still in me.

I was later awarded the Bronze Star with Combat Valor, my second Purple Heart for wounds incurred in battle, and the entire squad received the Presidential Unit Citation for bravery in the field on that November 6, 1968. And, after several operations and months of physical and mental therapy, I was able to return to civilian life.

—Al Schulze

Issues for Investigation and Discussion

1. What did you enjoy most about each story? What parts are most memorable?

2. The "voices" of the three authors of each story differ radically in their level of formality, use of slang, and attitude toward the subject matter. How would you characterize each voice? Cite some examples to back up your claims. Why do the voices differ? Is slang ever appropriate, and, if so, when?

3. Are the first two stories told from a child's viewpoint, an adult's viewpoint, or both? How does this viewpoint affect your perceptions of events? Support your claims with examples from the stories.

4. What passages in each story develop suspense or lead to a climax? In each case, what makes you anticipate a less than happy ending to the story?

5. The first story—and to a lesser extent the second—employs more dialogue

than the third. Why? What effects does that dialogue create?

6. The opening paragraph often establishes a story's tone (humorous, tragic, nostalgic, etc.) and theme. In each of the three stories, what issues and feelings does the opening paragraph introduce? After reading each opening paragraph, what predictions can you make about the events to follow?

7. The opening paragraph also establishes a story's setting, telling *who, what, where,* and *when.* Examine the first paragraph of each story. How does each introduce the four w's of its setting?

8. Is each story told chronologically (that is, with events unfolding consecutively in time) or do some stories employ flashbacks or flash forwards? How do these techniques influence your reactions? Back up your claims with examples.

9. What is the point of each story? Is it stated explicitly? In the first sentence of the first story, what does the word "famous" mean? What kinds of "fame" have the brothers experienced by the end of the story?

10. As a way of summarizing your ideas in response to these questions, or to any other matters you observe in the stories, turn to your journal or a computer file and list a dozen or so common traits of effective stories (or create a list with several classmates). Let this list guide you as you compose and revise your own story later.

COMPOSING YOUR OWN STORY

The three stories you've just read illustrate an important advantage of talking about the past: you can recapture the immediacy of the event through the distance of time and maturity. This double perspective creates rich possibilities for discovery and understanding—both for you and your readers. Try it, but don't reject a potentially entertaining or significant story because you can't remember the precise details. No one can recall every fact or piece of dialogue exactly, so include specifics that remain faithful to the general outlines and feelings of the experience. You needn't travel back to the distant past, either. Last week's experience will suffice, provided you can detach yourself from your emotions at the time—if, for instance, your genuine anger or humiliation isn't too painful to share.

Collaborative Activity: Getting Started on a Story (50 minutes of class time)

Spend five minutes brainstorming in your journal about four or five incidents that taught you a lesson or affected your life significantly.

- First choose the topics, and then jot down whatever comes to mind about each.

- Then meet with a group of several classmates, spending ten minutes in which each will read his or her notes aloud and hear the group's opinions about the most interesting topics.

- Immediately afterwards select one incident to explore fully, and write or brainstorm on the experience for ten minutes in your journal. Close your eyes from time to time to help yourself concentrate. Focus on details, both physical and psychological. Let your dimples show—and your warts, too—for readers appreciate honest and specific experiences.

- When you've finished free writing, read your work aloud to the group twice: the first time so the members can listen without judging; the second time so they can comment on the parts they like best, identify the places where they'd like to know more, and indicate where they think the story is going or should go. Listen to and weigh their reactions without responding or trying to defend yourself.

- After everyone has read and heard the responses to his or her materials (this should take about twenty minutes), spend a few more minutes with your journal, jotting down ideas for completing and revising your narrative.

- Then compose a full first draft of the narrative at home. If you run into a dead end, return to brainstorming, free writing, and/or clustering (and perhaps take some time off to let your ideas incubate). But if all these activities prove fruitless, consider choosing another topic from your initial list.

If meeting with the group isn't possible, try this activity with a friend or relative, or choose one topic from the list by yourself and then follow the remaining procedures.

Composing Activity: Shaping Ideas Around a Point

Take a few minutes to reread—but not revise—your narrative, either alone or aloud to your group. Then ask yourself (or your group members): What leading idea emerges or should emerge? What lesson does the story convey? Consider what might be added to strengthen that point (without hammering readers over the head), and consider what parts might be eliminated because they're unnecessary or irrelevant. Compose a statement of the main idea (it's often called a *thesis*), and consider including the statement either at the beginning or the end of the paper (or consider omitting the statement entirely if the point of the story is clear). In any case, let the thesis guide you in revising. Then write a second draft of your narrative.

DEVELOPING THE NARRATIVE THROUGH FACTS AND DIALOGUE

Although some stories will never burn with excitement, even the most inflammatory event can be doused by a soggy presentation. Igniting a reader's interest is crucial to all effective writing, and specific details—facts and dialogue—usually provide the spark. Don't despair, however, if your early drafts aren't generating much heat. Successful storytellers are made as well as born. You can master the skills of employing facts and dialogue.

Facts are statements that can be proven, generally through simple observation. Unlike airy abstractions or esoteric theories, facts ground your ideas in reality. They allow readers to perceive—to see, hear, feel, smell, and perhaps even taste—a place, a thing, or an event. Abstractions rarely touch and move us emotionally, but facts can clarify and enliven almost any claim. Accomplished writers establish the dimensions and action of a visible, palpable world. Note the specific details in one last story from the childhood of an older college freshman.

It was me and Ronald Oliver and his brother Donald on our way as usual toward the railroad tracks over on Blue Island. Just about every day we would go there. Most days we would have fun running and playing on the railroad ties. Some days we would look for produce, fallen or thrown from passing trains. On a few days we would force open a box car that was sometimes left parked on the siding.

The sun was high in the heavens on this late summer afternoon. Our eyes squinted against its searing radiance. Heat waves launched from the concrete, gumming the thin soles of our Woolworth black hi-tops. The rotting sweet smell of produce from the nearby South Water Market bounced in our nostrils. We darted in and out among the parking meters as we skipped toward the tracks.

When we got to the railroad yard there was a very high embankment of black, slippery gravel to climb to get up to the tracks themselves. Past experience had taught us that the easiest way to go was to get a running start and "haul ass" up the gravel, trying not to slip back to the sidewalk. My first attempt at running up the tracks netted me four slips, two scraped knees, one lacerated elbow and a pair of re-ruined jeans. The physical agony of many such attempts had guided me to a technique in which I attacked the embankment not straight but on an angle. I had to run farther but with hardly ever a slip.

We were seven- or eight-year-old boys who felt like world-conquerors after we made the top. In addition to the embankment climb, there was one last chore of physical fitness to accomplish. We had to stop our bodies' upward motion before getting across the first railroad track which lay about two feet from the summit. From the sidewalk below, we could not see or hear if there was a train coming. Only young boys could enjoy the thrill of a near miss. Ronald, cruel child that he was, thought it funny sometimes to charge up right behind Donald or me and fake like he was going to push us onto the tracks.

All the warnings of being dismembered by a mile-long freight train, all the stories of railroad hoboes kidnapping little boys and putting them into a campfire pot, all the theoretical problems of being lost in a Kansas railroad yard had been forgotten long ago. We did this just about every day. No sweat!

Successfully, we all reached the top. We simultaneously slid to a halt and yanked our necks left and right to view the tracks up and down. There were no trains or boxcars anywhere. Up the tracks the bright sun bombarded the gray strips of steel so they looked like long pairs of nervous rubber bands. Down the tracks—the same view.

I thought for a moment we would just play a couple of games of "100 ties" and then head for Fosco Playground when Ronald shouted, "Look!"

Off the side of the tracks about three hundred yards east sat an old well-kept railroad shack. This was no discovery except that this time the door was swung wide open. We had spent a lot of time inspecting the shack for a way into its secrets. The shack's good construction and two-foot-wide, always-shining brass railroad lock had withstood our efforts.

Using a whole microsecond to think, we broke into a run toward the open door. Our feet pummeling the railroad ballast sounded like a mini wheat-thrashing party.

Long-legged Ronald was soon about fifty yards ahead of me and Donald. He was sure to reach the shack before us. The code of seven- and eight-year-old boys states that Ronald could then lay first claim to whatever treasures were lying behind that door. I had no formal track training and knew nothing of going into a "kick" to overtake the front-runner. So Donald and I settled into an easy jog, our eyes remaining steadfast on the door.

About five yards or one second before Ronald reached the door, a huge man stepped out. His arms were spread out like he was trying to hug the Goodyear Blimp. A faded brown slouch hat covered his eyes and shadowed a clean-shaven face. A dark blue suit jacket hung over a pair of coveralls. His feet were slabbed over by heavy black work boots. The next sight I saw was Ronald flailing in the man's arms like a Daddy Long Legs' belly stuck in a Roach Motel.

By now Donald and I had reversed direction but could hear Ronald wailing to our backs, "Put me down. Donald! Jerry! Don't leave me, Mama!" Then a voice like that of every cop in the world sounded, "You boys come back here—NOW!"

Revolving in our spots, Donald and I started toward the man who was still grasping the squirming, crying Ronald. We marched shakily toward the man. When we got about five yards away, I noticed a badge pinned to his overalls.

"I'm a railroad detective. You boys get in that shed!"

Donald and I stumbled into the dark shed and Ronald pushed in behind us. We turned and faced the man. He stood glaring down at us with a very angry look. I could only imagine the life-ending act he would perform next. Instead he began to tell us the same stories about dismemberment, kidnapping, and being stranded a million miles away, etc. We smirked silently until he also informed us that we had broken the law—trespassing on R.R. property. He told us he had to call the police and our parents.

This man then closed the door, locked it from the outside, and left.

At that moment, Ronald, Donald, and I went to prison. We talked about all the horrible things that were going to happen to us. We talked about dining room riots, break-outs, and machine gun fire in "the Yard." We talked about the possible fights with Cagney or Edward G. or maybe even Humphrey. We talked about kickings and beatings from inhuman guards. Our words were punctuated with moans and sobs. And all of this would happen after our parents had finished beating us to death.

Half an hour later, the man returned. He didn't seem angry now. In a slow and ominous voice he re-summarized the stories. He opened the shed door wide and with one outstretched arm invited us out into the sunshine. He faced us squarely and blasted us with a single statement: "Go home!—and never let me catch you on the tracks again!"

We left, ignoring all the acquired skills of negotiating the embankment on the downhill run. We were bruised and battered when we hit the sidewalk.

Many years later, I worked for the Santa Fe Railroad Company. Every day that I went on the tracks, I looked for that man.

—Gerald Anderson

Anderson renders scenes through details that touch all of our senses: the searing radiance of the sun, the heat waves from the concrete that gum the soles of their shoes, the rotting sweet smell of produce from the nearby South Water Market bouncing in their nostrils. We not only see and hear what he did but feel it as well: his slips on the embankment that net him two scraped knees, one lacerated elbow and a pair of re-ruined jeans. Note his inclusion of proper nouns, too. He and his friends don't wear just shoes; they wear Woolworth black high tops. They don't imagine beatings by cons in the prison yard; they visualize thrashings at the hands of their Hollywood heroes James Cagney, Edward G. Robinson, and Humphrey Bogart.

Accomplished writers color a story with precise brush strokes to illustrate and portray rather than merely talk about their subject. Do the same as you write. Don't fall back on adjectives like "beautiful," "large," "enjoyable," "happy," or "interesting." Let facts that exemplify your claims carry your narrative forward and enliven the story for your readers.

In sum, you can achieve two important goals of writing—to be *interesting* and to be *clear*—most comfortably by composing stories from your own experience. But make them detailed, make the details relevant, and make your language lively. Don't just summarize an event from your childhood. Free the child in your personality to play with words and record the facts.

Follow-Up Activity: Adding Facts

Return to your narrative and select at least one incident that could be expanded and enlivened through facts—perhaps the climax of the story. Rewrite the incident by putting yourself back into the scene. What did you see, hear, say, feel—or even smell and taste? If something has a name, use it. Be guided by the main idea or impression you wish to convey. You may wish to read this revised passage to your group for suggestions on what else to include or exclude.

Follow-Up Activity: Adding and Shaping Dialogue

Return to the stories by Mark Schlitt and Gerald Anderson and look at their use of quotations. Consider the following issues:

1. How are quotations punctuated? Do punctuation marks go before or after the quotation marks? Why do some quotations end in periods and others in commas? How are quotations and the phrases identifying speakers capitalized?

2. Are the speakers of every quotation identified? How does paragraphing help us recognize the speakers?

3. Compare direct quotations (those with quotation marks) to reported speech (those without quotation marks). How do they differ in punctuation, word order, and handling of tenses?

Once you understand the technical treatment of quotations, apply these techniques to the dialogue in your story. Perhaps one or more scenes would benefit from dialogue that advances the action. (Odds are, the parts without dialogue summarize rather than fully develop an event.) You may invent dialogue if you wish; no one expects you to remember the exact words of the characters. Revise those scenes by adding dialogue, and then read them aloud. Do the speakers sound authentic?

All dialogue should come out of character. It should never come from the author. If a character speaks in slang, then it is perfectly proper to let him do so. It would obviously be out of place to put slang in the mouth of a character to whom such language would be alien. If you want dialogue to be strong and vivid, make it real.

—Sidney Sheldon

Collaborative Activity: Adding Dialogue (25–30 minutes of class time)

To test whether one or more scenes (or even your whole story) need dialogue, reread your story to a group of several classmates. Have the group discuss the characters involved: What are they like? What would they probably sound like? If time permits, let classmates invent some dialogue. Note their suggestions in your journal, and, after class, revise the story to include the dialogue.

REVISING THE BEGINNING AND ENDING

The latest version of a literary work begins somewhere in the work's middle, and hardens toward the end . . . the work's beginning greets readers with the wrong hand.

—Annie Dillard

Composing is a continual process of revising and perfecting. No serious writer expects to compose a successful story in a single draft. With each revision—literally, as we see our work again—we delete and add material as our ideas change and grow. We see each draft as preliminary to the next until the writing feels graceful and accurate and authentic. Among the most often revised passages of a story are its beginning and end.

Beginnings are especially troublesome. Like someone trying to drive a car over ice, we may spin our wheels for a while before finding traction. We can't sort out our ideas, so we say too much, too little, or too little that is relevant to our point. Consequently, the final draft of a story's beginning is often the last part we should write. We should compose it after the point and mood of the story have taken shape. We can then examine our original draft for empty moralizing and heavy-handed dramatics:

Life is filled with tragedies, and . . . (Doesn't everyone know that?)

The thing that really taught me a lesson was the time when. . . (Why not let the facts of the story reveal that lesson?)

The worst moment in my life was the time when . . . (Again, the facts should make that clear.)

Or for statements of the obvious:

I'll never forget the time when . . . (Of course you won't; you're writing about it.)

The Greek philosopher Aristotle advised that stories should begin *in medias res*—in the middle of things—with a fact or event that carries the action forward. Here are some examples from student papers:

It was me and Ronald Oliver and his brother Donald on our way as usual toward the railroad tracks over on Blue Island.

—Gerald Anderson

Daddy was real mad. I remember him huffing and puffing on the other side of the door.

—Robin Prosser

The priest's voice spoke softly to me through the screen. "Yes, my daughter, I'm listening to you."

—Emese Schweder

Sometimes stories begin with a statement that arouses our curiosity, as in Mark Schlitt's reminiscences from his childhood:

When I was eleven, my brother and I became famous in one day.

Or, as in Christine Mueller's story, by flashing forward to the end and therefore establishing the mood of the piece:

The butterfly is free to fly
She spread her wings and . . .
This was part of the eulogy I wrote and read at my best friend's funeral when we were eighteen.

Beginnings are often clichéd, so in revising you should look for trite sayings to remove. For example, an early draft of Al Schulze's story began sounding like a Peanuts comic strip:

> It was a cold and rainy morning that day back in November of 1968. We had been on patrol for twelve hours and were tired and hungry.

Realizing the problem later, he tightened and rearranged the details so they put us into the action directly, quietly:

> After twelve hours of patrol in the cold and rain, we were tired and hungry.

Don't try for a perfect beginning to a story in your first draft. Expect to revise it several times later to engage your readers' attention through facts, surprise, or suspense. Often a good way to initiate the revision process is to cross out the opening sentences until you arrive at a specific statement or piece of dialogue that puts the action *in medias res.*

Like beginnings, the endings of stories usually require alterations, for in early drafts we're tempted to moralize. After a story about wrecking your dad's automobile on your sixteenth birthday, you needn't conclude, "I'll never forget that day as long as I live." Examine your story's ending closely in the latter stages of the writing process. Can you cross out the last sentence and any that precede it until you arrive at strong statement of fact that needs no elaboration?

You can also consider returning to an idea that was introduced at the beginning of the story, as did Christine Mueller:

> Once when we were fifteen, I asked Stone, "If you believed in reincarnation, what would you want to be?"
> She answered quickly, "A butterfly, because butterflies are free."

There's one other possibility. If a story has been filled with shocks or bumps or surprise, consider ending it quietly, as Gerald Anderson did after his encounter with the railroad detective:

> Many years later, I worked for the Santa Fe Railroad Company. Every day that I went on the tracks, I looked for that man.

Follow-Up Activity: Revising the Beginning and End of Your Story

Examine both ends of your story carefully for signs of sentimentality, moralizing, or heavy-handedness. Revise the beginning so a fact, a surprise, or some suspense emerges. (You may simply cross out your opening sentence and any further generalization until you come to a specific statement.) Consider employing either the *in medias res* technique of Aristotle or a flash-forward technique as in Christine Mueller's story.

Look at the end of the story, too. Does it moralize or drag on? Revise it so it concludes quietly or finishes with a fact or piece of dialogue. (Again, you may cross out generalizations, beginning with the last sentence in the story, until you come to a specific statement.) You may also read the opening and closing statements to your group members to hear their responses or suggestions.

Collaborative Activity: Hearing and Reading Responses to Your Story (25 minutes of class time)

Before revising your paper for the last time, read it aloud to your group twice as you have done in past instances. This time, however, make notes of the group's responses to the questions in the following Postdraft Analysis list. Later, when you are away from the group, look over your notes and then respond to the responses of the group. Do you agree or disagree, or has another idea occurred to you? Consider these reactions when you revise.

Postdraft Analysis
(To be completed by the writer or peer reader)

1. What is the point of the draft? If the point isn't clear, what would clarify it?
2. Look at the details in the story. Do they create a sense of immediacy for readers? If not, what might be added or expanded? Identify these places with bracketed labels.
3. Look at the dialogue in each incident. Should more be included to create a sense of immediacy? If so, indicate where with bracketed notes. Are there any points at which the dialogue seems unrealistic? If so, identify those places with bracketed labels.
4. Can you follow the progression of action throughout the story? If not, how might ideas be rearranged? Look at the logical connections between the ending sentence of each paragraph and the beginning of the next. Identify with bracketed labels where connections between ideas could be clarified.
5. Look for places where the language isn't clear, direct, and natural. Indicate with bracketed labels where it should be reworded.
6. Are all the elements of the setting—who, what, where, and when—established at or near the beginning? Are they introduced gracefully? If not, what should be added or made less mechanical? Indicate in brackets.
7. Examine the ending. Is it heavy-handed? Does it continue on unnecessarily? If so, indicate changes in brackets.
8. What other problems, if any, need to be addressed? If so, how might they be addressed?

Concluding Activity: Revising and Editing Your Story

Based on the responses to the Postdraft Analysis questions, do a final revision of the story, making connections clear, sharpening the details, adding or changing dialogue, and editing the paper carefully for matters of mechanics, grammar, and spelling.

Chapter 4

Looking at Your Language

In writing, short is usually better than long. . . .an article that makes its case succinctly is the highest form of courtesy to the reader. Somehow it never occurs to sloppy writers that they are being fundamentally rude. Most pieces can be cut by 50 percent without losing any substance.

—William Zinsser

You might think that tightening and strengthening sentences have to do with form, not content. But you cannot separate content from form. Once you gain some mastery over the structures of language, you increase your ability to communicate to readers exactly what you mean in phrases that are strong and graceful and direct. Furthermore, when you scrutinize your words, you heighten your ability to think critically. To recognize and eliminate empty language is often to banish empty thoughts. Strong form without strong content is impossible; meaningful sentences generate meaningful ideas.

The most essential gift for a good writer is a built-in, shockproof shit detector. This is the writer's radar and all good writers have it.

—Ernest Hemingway

Make a practice, therefore, of tightening and strengthening your sentences during revisions. The routine of scrutinizing both your language and thoughts will soon carry over into your first drafts. But heed this warning: Don't attempt to compose perfect first drafts, or you will never finish them. Always regard your early work as preliminary; you will revise it later perhaps a dozen times.

LOOKING AT PASSAGES

Readers expect your writing to make a point (otherwise, why should they bother to read it?), and the shortest distance to your point is in a clear, direct style. Compare the two versions of the passages that follow, one version of which has purposely been written to be wordy and awkward:

I. Passage A

The ceremony that is being participated in by us today is being performed not for the commemoration of the triumph of one faction of the political spectrum over another, but instead for the acknowledgment and reaffirmation of the importance of the method by which such triumphs can ultimately occur: through the free exercise of the right to vote. This ceremony can be viewed as symbolizing the termination of one era of government and simultaneously the commencement of another which will replace that era with a different form of government. Consequently, the symbolic meaning of this ceremony is that it expresses a continuation of the practices that have long been established as well as a departure from these practices into different areas. The reason for this observation can be found in the oath to the Creator which I have recited as it was so solemnly attested to by all my predecessors who have occupied this office for the previous 175 years.

Objective observation of the phenomena occurring on our planet would indicate a radical departure from the behavior of any previous time in history. Unmitigated power is our possession, so that the eradication of the factors that are the sources of every type of poverty is possible; additionally, a similar measure of power is in our possession to extinguish each and every person who inhabits this planet. Nevertheless, the beliefs of our forebears that led to a revolution and war continue to be perpetuated in all precincts of the globe: the belief that the universal rights are bequeathed by the Creator and not the various governments.

Passage B

We observe today not a victory of party, but a celebration of freedom—symbolizing an end, as well as a beginning—signifying renewal, as well as change. For I have sworn before you and Almighty God the same solemn oath our forebears prescribed nearly a century and three quarters ago.

The world is very different now. For man holds in his mortal hands the power to abolish all forms of human poverty and all forms of human life. And yet the same revolutionary beliefs for which our forebears fought are still an issue around the globe—the belief that the rights of man come not from the generosity of the state but from the hand of God.

—John F. Kennedy, "Inaugural Address"

II. Passage A

A singular ambition that never changed was shared by me and my contemporaries during the years of my childhood which were spent in a village located on the western side near the edge of the water of the Mississippi River. That ambition was manifested in one desire: to attain the position of the pilot of a steamboat. There were a variety of other types of transient ambitions which were felt by us from time to time, but as time went on, the impermanent nature of these ambitions was soon apparent. Such ambitions included the desires to become entertainers of different sorts, ranging from clowns in circuses to Negro minstrels, and even pirates. However, the passage of time had an effect that led to the loss of interest in these types of professions. Nevertheless, the aspiration to become a steamboat pilot had a permanent place in our minds.

Passage B

When I was a boy, there was but one permanent ambition among my comrades in our village [Hannibal, Missouri] on the west bank of the Mississippi River. That was, to be a steamboatsman. We had transient ambitions of other sorts, but they were only transient. When a circus came and went, it left us all burning to become clowns; the first Negro minstrel show that came to our section left us all suffering to try that kind of life; now and then we had a hope that if we lived and were good, God would permit us to be pirates. These ambitions faded out, each in its turn; but the ambition to be a steamboatsman always remained.

—Mark Twain

Issues for Investigation and Discussion

1. Which passage from each pair did you prefer? Why?

2. Jot down four or five adjectives that characterize each passage. Compare your list to those of several classmates and compile a larger list.

3. Although the paired passages "mean" the same, they communicate radically different messages. Why? Cite examples from individual sentences.

4. Circle any forms of the verb *to be (is, are, was, were)* in all four passages. Which passages contain more *be* verbs, and how do these verbs affect your reactions?

5. Circle any repeated words or ideas in all four passages. Where are the repetitions most numerous, and how do they affect your reactions?

6. Underline the subjects of each clause in the passages. In which passages are the subjects most specific and concrete? In which passages are the subjects not performing the actions of the verbs? How do these matters affect your reactions?

If you characterized both *A* passages as "bad" writing and both *B* passages as "good," you weren't wrong. But let's place the issue in a different context: away from the writing and onto you, the reader. You judge writing to be good when you find it *readable*—that is, when its message and purpose are clear to you, the audience. A writing style is effective when transparent, when nothing in the language inhibits the communication of ideas. Although readability to some degree depends on appropriateness—what works according to occasion, purpose, subject matter, and audience—readability to a greater degree depends on clarity. The two *B* passages differ radically in word choice, use of specifics, and degree of formality, yet both are readable because they are simple and direct. The following tightening and strengthening practices will help you to increase your ability to produce readable prose.

ELIMINATING WEAK REPETITION

What makes me happy is rewriting. . . . it's like cleaning house, getting rid of all the junk, getting things in the right order, tightening things up. I like the process of making the writing neat. When I read a column in the paper and I find I've used the same word twice close together or I've got something dangling, I can't stand it.

—*Ellen Goodman*

In the early stages of composing, you struggle to discover and express ideas, not necessarily to express them elegantly or succinctly. Furthermore, your unconscious mind tends to fix on certain words or ideas and repeat them, sometimes strongly, other times not. You should thus expect to find and remove awkward repetition as you revise. For most writers, expunging the unnecessary is not a chore but a source of great pleasure. Indeed, professionals regard the process of arriving at a finely wrought sentence as a quest for victory, a triumph that the eighteenth-century poet Alexander Pope summed up as "what oft was thought but ne'er so well expressed."

Eliminating Words Repeated Unnecessarily

If it is possible to cut a word out, always cut it out.

—*George Orwell*

A fundamental principle of tightening is simply to eliminate repeated words that neither clarify nor strengthen your message. "Stephen King is a writer who writes exciting books" restates *writer* and *write* for no apparent purpose. "The theme of the novel was unusual, but the plot of the novel was dull" clogs the sentence with a needless *novel*. You could recast both sentences in a more direct, readable form:

> Stephen King writes exciting books.
> The theme of the novel was unusual, but the plot was dull.

Note these further examples:

Flabby: Tuesday was an unlucky day.
Tight: Tuesday was unlucky.

Flabby: My pride fell and my fortunes fell, too.
Tight: My pride fell with my fortunes.

—*Shakespeare*

Begin the revising process by returning to your early drafts. Underline or circle repeated words, and consider each one. If the sentence would be simpler and more direct with some words omitted, then draw a line through or bracket [ ] the words to omit. Often, however, you must recast a sentence to discard the wasted words:

Flabby: After *I* studied for two days straight, *I* felt prepared to take the examination.

Tight: After *studying* for two days straight, I felt prepared to take the examination.

Don't attempt to cut out every repeated word, however. Emphatic repetition lies at the heart of good writing. Language is musical, and it builds, establishes tension, and creates surprise, as in these examples:

And so, my fellow Americans, ask not what your country can do for you: Ask what you can do for your country.

My fellow citizens of the world: Ask not what America will do for you, but what together we can do for the freedom of man.

Finally, whether you are citizens of America or citizens of the world, ask of us the same high standards of strength and sacrifice which we ask of you.

—John F. Kennedy

I've seen too much hate to want to hate, myself, and I've seen hate on the faces of too many sheriffs, too many white citizens' councilors, and too many Klansmen of the South to want to hate, myself; and every time I see it, I say to myself, hate is too great a burden to bear.

—Martin Luther King, Jr.

Revising Activity: Eliminating Words Repeated Unnecessarily

Highlight, circle, or underline repeated words in several of your early free writings or journal entries—or, if you prefer, in the papers you composed in Chapters 1 through 3. Then cross out the words you can eliminate and rewrite the sentence above the line if necessary. Do all your work on the original drafts; don't copy over or rewrite these papers. You might also exchange papers with a classmate and look for further repetitions to remove.

Collaborative Activity: Revising a Passage (15 minutes of class time)

Copy down a sentence or two that you have trouble revising and share your selection with a group of several peers or with the entire class, who should suggest several ways of recasting the sentences.

Change it. How? Easy. Read a stinky sentence over. Figure out what it means. Now . . .
put the sentence's meaning in your own words. . . You may have to expand the sentence
into two or three sentences. That's allowed.

—*Bill Scott*

Eliminating Empty Categories

Academic writing often requires that you examine and classify data, but that
practice can be abused, creating empty categories and wasted words: "Hillary
Rodham Clinton is a *woman* who has greatly influenced public policy" states
the obvious, for her name reveals her gender. Likewise, "Swimming is an *activity*
that many people enjoy" needlessly categorizes, for swimming obviously
requires activity. These sentences could be tightened with no loss of meaning:

> Hillary Rodham Clinton has greatly influenced public policy.
> Many people enjoy swimming.

Look for classifying words such as *factor, idea, type, area,* and *kind,* for they
often signal vacant categories you can cut:

Flabby: Astronomy is an area of natural science that is interesting to many
people.
Tight: Many people find astronomy interesting.

Flabby: Her father was the type of person who expected his dinner to be
on the table when he arrived home.
Tight: Her father expected his dinner on the table when he arrived home.

Flabby: Calculus is a subject that many students avoid.
Tight: Many students avoid calculus.

Another tip: when you state an idea abstractly and then concretely, consider eliminating the abstract term:

Flabby: They disagreed about two important issues: their faith in God and
trust in humanity.
Tight: They disagreed about their faith in God and trust in humanity.

Flabby: I knew what I had to do. I had to stop the wound from bleeding.
Tight: I knew I had to stop the wound from bleeding.

Finally, ideas repeated or implied in other words are also candidates for
cutting:

Flabby: The reason why I couldn't go to summer school was because I had
to work.
Tight: I couldn't go to summer school because I had to work.

Flabby: I must get up at 6:00 A.M. in the morning.

Tight: I must get up at 6:00 A.M.

"Die!" he shouted insanely." The word "die," with its exclamation point, is already too much, "shouted" is implied, and "insanely" overwhelms all three words before it. The effort collapses under its competing components.

—*David Madden*

Revising Activity: Removing Needless Categorizing Words

Look over several more free writings or journal entries (or the papers you wrote in Chapters 1 through 3). Underline or circle any empty categorizing words or ideas implied in other words. Then cross out or bracket the parts you can eliminate, or rewrite the sentences above the line. Once more, you may wish to exchange papers with a classmate or discuss troublesome revisions with your group or the whole class.

Eliminating Relative Clauses

The relative pronoun "which" can cause more trouble than any other word. Foolhardy persons sometimes get lost in which clauses and are never heard of again. My distinguished contemporary, Fowler, cites several tragic cases, of which the following is one: "It was rumored that Beaconfield intended opening the Conference with a speech in French, his pronunciation of which language leaving everything to be desired . . . " That's as much as Mr. Fowler quotes because, at his age, he was afraid to go any farther. The young man who originally got into that sentence was never found.

—*James Thurber*

As James Thurber suggests, *who, which,* and *that* (or *relative*) clauses often convey information in roundabout or awkward ways. Many relative clauses can simply be removed, especially if any form of *to be* follows who, which, or that:

Anyone [who is] concerned about global warming should read this month's *New Republic* magazine.

A subject [that is] often debated on college campuses is required courses.

Thomas Jefferson and John Adams, [who were] the authors of the Declaration of Independence, both died on July 4, 1826, [which was] exactly fifty years after its signing.

Constructions beginning with *there is* or *are* often generate relative clauses and can frequently be recast:

Flabby: There are several issues that we ought to examine.
Tight: We ought to examine several issues.

Flabby: There is only one answer that makes sense: end the program immediately.
Tight: Only one answer makes sense: end the program immediately.

And relative pronouns can sometimes be dropped from sentences:

> I knew [that] the boat was taking on water fast.

Sometimes, however, sentences must be recast to eliminate relative clauses:

Flabby: I held my breath and bought the car that cost $20,000.
Tight: I held my breath and bought the $20,000 car.

Flabby: No one paid any attention to the old man who sat on the park bench.
Tight: No one paid any attention to the old man sitting on the park bench.

Revising Activity: Recasting Relative Clauses

Underline or circle relative pronouns in one or more of your earlier papers, and cross out or bracket those you can eliminate. Consult with classmates again if you need help.

Eliminating Nominalizations and Choosing Strong Verbs

Clear and direct statements place the action where it most logically belongs: on the verb. Less readable statements shift the action to a noun, a process called *nominalization*. Note these examples:

Flabby: I made a decision that I would buy the more expensive CD player.
Tight: I decided to buy the more expensive CD player.

Flabby: We came to the conclusion that the fuse had blown.
Tight: We concluded that the fuse had blown.

Flabby: We reached an agreement to meet again on Thursday.
Tight: We agreed to meet again on Thursday.

Flabby: I had an idea . . .
Tight: I thought . . .

Not only do some sentences shift the action from verb to noun, but they also won't let the subject of the verb perform the action:

Flabby: A *decision was made* for the company to discontinue the manufacture of plastic bottles. (Who made this decision?)

Tight: The *company's board of directors decided* to stop the manufacture of plastic bottles.

Flabby: An *agreement was reached* that no liquor be served at the fraternity party.

Tight: The planning committee agreed to serve no liquor at the fraternity party.

Like nouns that express actions weakly, overused verbs such as *do, get, make, put, take, go, come, run,* and *have* carry so little meaning or force that writers must add words to elaborate on them. For example, the phrase "He came into the room" reveals nothing about the speed, size, posture, grace, state of mind, or emotions of the subject. Providing more information requires additional words and clumsy phrasing:

He came into the room quickly and clumsily and made a lot of noise.

A more imaginative verb choice expresses more precise meanings economically. Note the shades of meaning each of the following verbs conveys:

He barged (roared, barreled, crashed, shot, flew, skittered, pranced, whizzed) into the room.

The verb *have* often wastes a sentence or clause in order to establish simple possession. Compare these sentences:

I have a good friend whose name is Brian. He attends school out of state. My good friend Brian attends school out of state.

Thus, scrutinize your verbs as you revise, challenging yourself to substitute less ordinary (but not overly fancy) verbs that deliver the meaning you intend. As with all tightening and strengthening practices, doing so will help you convey your message to your readers in the most emphatic and graceful way.

I'm very concerned with the rhythm of language. "The sun came up" is an inadequate sentence. Even though it conveys all the necessary information, rhythmically it's lacking.
The sun came up.

But, if you say, as Laurie Anderson said, "The sun came up like a big bald head,"
not only have you, perhaps, entertained the fancy of the reader, but you have made
a more complete sentence.

—Tom Robbins

Composing Activity: Rewriting a Passage

Rewrite the following strong passage to make it far less readable: repeat words
and ideas; add empty categorizing words; express ideas abstractly; transfer the
actions from the verbs to the nouns; and add in relative clauses. You may wish
to compare your version with those of classmates to see who qualifies as the
"worst" writer (and therefore stands the best chance of becoming a governmental bureaucrat).

After a lifetime of writing I still revise every sentence many times and still
worry that I haven't caught every ambiguity; I don't want anyone to have to read
a sentence of mine twice to find out what it means. If you think you can dash
something off and have it come out right, the people you're trying to reach are
surely in trouble. H. L. Mencken said that "0.8 percent of the human race is ca-
pable of writing something understandable." He may have been a little high. Be-
ware of dashing. "Effortless" articles that look as if they were dashed off are the
result of strenuous effort. A piece of writing must be viewed as a constantly evolving organism.

—William Zinsser

Collaborative Activity: Revising a Passage (25 minutes of class time)

In small groups (or by yourself), revise the following poorly written passage to
eliminate weak repetition, empty phrases, and wordy passages. See if you can
shorten the passage significantly without affecting meaning—and see if you
can add specific, enlivening details after making cuts.

Some places are better for studying than other places. When I have to study
after I have finished my classes, the place where I hate to go the most is the
Student Center. There are several different reasons why I despise it so much, but
basically I dislike it because of one important factor. There is so much noise that
comes from a lot of people who are not interested in anything but enjoying
themselves. They talk over the normal voice level by yelling at each other. Some
of them get into disagreements or they have arguments over something stupid,
like which soap opera should be watched on the televisions that are mounted
on the wall that is on the north end of the Student Center. Other students play

music on their portable radios in a loud and annoying manner, which makes it impossible to concentrate. Still other students play in card games and curse in a very angry way when they lose a hand. Any normal student couldn't study in that environment, so the best thing to do is leave and go to a quiet place like the library, which is located on the second floor.

Revising Activity: Composing a Second Draft

Return to a free writing or journal entry that carries an important message. Tighten it thoroughly, but don't eliminate important specific details. If you wish to reshape the entire writing around a central point while adding facts and specific information, do so.

Chapter 5

Creating Oppositions

It's the writer's job to stage confrontations, so the characters will say surprising and revealing things, and educate and entertain us all. If a writer can't or won't do all that, he should withdraw from the trade.

—Kurt Vonnegut, Jr.

Oppositions aren't mere decoration to your writing. Like the contrast control on a television set, they bring ideas into sharper focus—for both your readers and you. In his *Rhetoric,* or the art of persuasion, the Greek philosopher Aristotle said that we employ oppositions to define terms, determine facts, and anticipate and refute unfair counterarguments. He maintained that we uncover truths by challenging them, by testing them against their contradictions. *Darkness* helps define *light, sharp* helps define *dull,* and so on. Aristotle called this exploration of opposites a *dialectic.*

Oppositions also foster intellectual and societal growth. The German philosopher Georg Wilhelm Friedrich Hegel (1770–1831) said that all history is a dialectic in which the clash of opposing ideas and actions leads to progress. One government or philosophy (a *thesis*) provokes a reaction to oppose it (an *antithesis*), which in turn results in some combination of the two (their *synthesis*). Black opposes white and produces some shade of grey. Thus, for example, people might rebel against an absolute dictatorship, establish an absolute democracy, and later replace it with a representative form of government (which they would eventually change in other ways). Thesis provokes antithesis which leads to synthesis—and the synthesis becomes the next thesis for further development.

Finally, oppositions generate tension, an essential to all writing or art. Think of all the stories you've read and movies you've seen that follow "the odd couple" format, in which two people with little in common must get along or compete: Huck and Jim in *The Adventures of Huckleberry Finn;* Pip and Estella in *Great Expectations;* Catherine and Heathcliff in *Wuthering Heights;* and the main characters in such movies as *Rainman; Lethal Weapon; Pretty Woman;* and *Planes, Trains, and Automobiles.* The appeal of these stories lies in how the dissonance between the personalities, attitudes, beliefs, or stations in life will be resolved. We enjoy discovering what synthesis between thesis and antithesis will emerge.

Effective writing thus demands oppositions in ideas, circumstances, and styles. These oppositions not only establish tension, but force you to examine an issue from top to bottom—and even from the sides. The experience should open your mind to insights and truths you might not otherwise discover.

LOOKING AT OPPOSITIONS

Oppositions arise partially through plan and partially through revision. But in either case they enhance your writing. Note how a student's small experience takes on importance and drama in the following story because of her attention to opposing facts and details.

I am walking from school along Racine to the Lawrence Avenue bus stop. Broken glass crunches beneath my feet. The street is strewn with wrinkled papers, cigarette butts and beer cans.

Two dogs trot by nosing in the garbage along their path. Two women and two men sit on the grass in front of the nursing home laughing wildly, taking long gulps from cans of Schlitz. A crumpled figure lies on the sidewalk asleep or maybe dead. A skinny old lady in an oversized shabby wool coat passes, carrying on a heated discussion with herself. Mr. James, of Mr. James's Grocery, stands in the doorway of his shop, watching her. Next door at the laundromat, a fat girl takes a drag from her cigarette while waiting for her clothes to dry. The birds on Pigeon Island, the corner of Racine and Broadway, pick at crumbs left by a little man.

A tall, white-haired bony man in a dirty green overcoat walks toward Lawrence Avenue. He hasn't shaved in weeks and his chin reminds me of my old hair brush. He ambles past the movie house, past the health food store, past Peter Pan's clothing shop, muttering under his breath. When he reaches the street, he turns around and heads back past Peter Pan's, past the health food store, till he reaches the movie theater.

Again, he turns around and retraces his path. I reach the corner with him and start to cross, not paying attention to traffic, not noticing the light is red.

The old man calls out and jumps in front of me, startling me back to the sidewalk. A green Plymouth speeds by with horn blaring and barely misses him.

As the old man stumbles back to the corner, a fat man in dark-rimmed glasses screams at him, "What's the matter with you? You could've got killed! That car almost hit you!"

The fat man crosses the street muttering, "Stupid drunk old man." The old man looks at him blankly.

"Thank you," I try to tell him, but he doesn't see me. He is lost in his own world. Again turning away, he begins walking past Peter Pan's clothing shop, past the health food store.

The bus pulls up to my stop, so I run across the street wishing I could somehow repay the man that saved my life.

—Alice El Yaman

This next story by a student draws its dramatic force from the writer's evolving contradictory feelings about her cat.

PAWS

At seventeen years plus, she was lying in front of the refrigerator's warm air vent where she spent almost all of her time. Full of dandruff due to a failing kidney, her hind legs atrophying because of nerve damage from the bathroom door I accidentally slammed on her, patches of fur missing from an off-again-on-again nervous condition and diabetes, she lay twitching, dreaming. I bent down to gently awaken her. She didn't respond right away so I increased the pressure a little. When she still didn't wake, I picked her up. Although still twitching, she was completely limp in my hands, her tongue slack. I had given her an insulin injection two hours earlier so she couldn't have needed that.

I quickly, carefully, carried her into the living room and held her on my lap while I dialed the vet. Sunday, I knew he wouldn't be there, but I couldn't think of anything else to do. The recorded message on his phone referred any emergencies to a 24-hour veterinary hospital. The address was fifteen to twenty minutes away from my house. I had no way to get there and didn't want to go alone anyway, so I called my cat friends, Norma and Rich, and asked them for a ride. They arrived ten minutes later.

After putting on my coat, I grabbed a soft pink terry towel to put around Paws. Down the three flights of stairs, briefly out in the cold, then chugging along our way, I was holding her close. She had stopped twitching but her tongue was still hanging out. I kept talking to her, quietly, trying to soothe her. I was wondering if she felt scared.

Rich and Norma went in with me and the doctor saw us right away. When I laid Paws on the steel examining table, the doctor peeled back the towel and I saw that she had lost control of both her bladder and her bowels during the trip. He told me she was in shock but that he might be able to bring her around, or he could give her an injection to put her to sleep. I pictured her "recovered" and told him to go ahead and give her the shot. As he started to pick her up, I asked if he would do it while I was holding her. He told me she didn't know what was going on, that it would only take a minute and that she might lose control of her body functions. Leaving me with instructions to go up front, he told me he would be with me shortly. I felt scared that I wouldn't be able to handle myself if I saw her do something strange and I felt scared to see her die.

I walked to the front desk, and as the receptionist started to explain the $55.00 charge, I was thinking that what the doctor had said didn't make sense. She had already lost control and I had been able to stand it. That's all he could have meant. She and I had been together for over thirteen years and I had turned her over to someone else to let her die alone.

I rushed back to the examining room calling for the doctor, telling him that I had changed my mind; I wanted to hold her. He came out immediately and told me he was sorry—she was already gone.

—Kate Friedlob

The tension in this final passage by a professional writer derives largely from his ironic treatment of the subject matter—the contrasts between what he claims to be true and the real truth of the experience he describes.

MATINEE IDLER

I don't mind admitting that in my gray fedora, I look like Harrison Ford.

My wife and my friends are too shy to point this out to me, but give me a square jaw, hair on the top of my head, and a look in the eye like I know what I'm doing and I could be his double. Yes, I know I look exactly like a middle-class, middle-aged, middle-American dad wrestling candy out of the hands of his sons (ages 5 and 7) at the supermarket checkout counter. But look closer. Don't you see a kind of Indiana Jones charisma? An air of sexy danger?

A psychiatrist might say that I am suffering from a common mental delusion, and that if you scratch beneath the surface of any typical harried father you will find a glamorous alter ego trying to claw its way out.

I don't deny that this syndrome is a problem for many men. My own father was a victim of it. I remember the day, sometime during the 1960s, that he surprised us all by coming home from work sporting what he called his "Rex Harrison hat." I realized with a twinge of boyish embarrassment that my dad actually thought he looked like the distinguished bachelor Henry Higgins in *My Fair Lady*. Now, my dad was a handsome man. But I knew Rex Harrison. I had seen Rex Harrison on TV. Dad was no Rex Harrison.

Fortunately for me, my resemblance to Harrison Ford is a matter of simple fact. Therefore, it seemed only natural that when the opportunity arose last year to be an extra in Ford's movie *The Fugitive*, which was filmed here in Chicago, I would seize it.

On the set, I quickly discovered that in the movie world, the status of extras is roughly equivalent to the status of chairs at a church pancake breakfast—necessary, but ranked far below actual people. My scene, in which I play a guy sitting next to another guy among 200 or so spectators in the courtroom where Dr. Richard Kimble is being tried for the murder of his wife, brought out my most profoundly chairlike qualities. My nuanced performance adds a note of stunning invisibility that is rare in film history.

An extra is just a star with a smaller part.

But that's not really the point. The point is that for a whole day, I worked with Harrison Ford. Like me, Harrison Ford sat. Like me, he had lunch in the cafeteria. Like me, he made wisecracks to break the tedium between takes. Together he and I listened to the state's case against Dr. Richard Kimble. We registered shock, fear, anger, sorrow. We smiled understandingly as an actor flubbed his lines. We looked up in concern when a technician slipped while adjusting a light.

It's true that Harrison leveraged a bit more talent into his role than I did. And yes, he was paid more. But the outline of our day was absolutely identical.

After 12 hours or so of work, I called home to let my wife know that the director planned to film past midnight.

"Past midnight?" In the background I recognized the telltale sounds of barely controlled sibling mayhem.

"I'm sorry, honey, but we're talking Hollywood blockbuster here."

"Okay. But you owe me." She said this playfully, yet with a hint of menace.

As I walked back to the set, I tried to imagine how Harrison Ford would react to the script direction "playfully, yet with a hint of menace." He'd give a sly half-smile followed by a mock-fearful grimace, then move on confidently.

When we get *The Fugitive* on video, I'll hit the pause button when we reach the courtroom scene.

"See, boys, there I am. Next to the fat guy in the tenth row."

"The fat guy near the door, Dad?"

"No, the other fat guy, the one behind the woman in the blue dress next to the man with the plaid sport coat. See, that's me! That's your dad in the same movie as Indiana Jones!"

Then, to avoid the twinge of boyish embarrassment, I'll cock my fedora over my eyes and hit the rewind button for one more glimpse of cinematic glory.

—Robert Hughes

Issues for Investigation and Discussion

1. What is the point of Alice El-Yaman's story? How do oppositions reinforce the point?

2. El-Yaman employs the return-to-the beginning device, in which an action, a detail, a phrase, or an idea at the beginning returns at the end in a different, opposing form or context. What does she repeat, and what is the effect of the repetition?

3. El-Yaman tells her story in the present tense. If she had written in the past tense, how would your reactions to the story change?

4. Kate Friedlob takes us through a number of stages in her feelings toward and expectations about her cat. Identify them.

5. In focusing outwardly on the physical condition of her cat and inwardly on her own thoughts and emotions, Friedlob chooses to include no dialogue. Try adding dialogue to a scene or two. Does the dialogue strengthen the story?

6. What is Friedlob's point? How do oppositions reinforce that point?

7. Much of the humor in Robert Hughes's article arises from the oppositions between his tongue-in-check fantasy world and his actual experiences. Identify several of the oppositions.

8. How does each story establish the setting— the who, what, when, and where issues? What differences in technique do you observe? What similarities?

9. Find words or phrases that signal oppositions in the three stories. Identify as many examples as you can.

10. As a way of summarizing your ideas in response to these stories, turn to your journal and list several common traits of oppositions employed effectively (or create a list with several classmates). Let this list guide you as you compose and revise your own story later.

COMPOSING OPPOSITIONS

Work on composing oppositions, both in your early drafts and in revisions. Gather materials in your journal about opposing events, people, or ideas you encounter or ponder. Explore these contrasts by free writing, brainstorming, or clustering. Compose first drafts in which you write down a phrase or thought and then look for ways of opposing it. Then examine these early drafts. If you find tension and surprise, the draft is potentially strong. If you find very little, you should revise the draft or compose another, this time consciously recording oppositions.

There is tension in the following journal entry by an older student. Note the dialectic between the attitudes of the writer and her daughter—and between the writer's changing attitudes as well.

My daughter had an abortion this weekend. I could never have done that. But I had a husband; she had a boyfriend whom she said was no good. I knew that at the beginning, but she wouldn't listen to me.

She said he never worked, yet she moved out of my house to be with him. She would not help me with any bills, never paid any rent to me, or bought any food. With him, she paid all the bills and did everything financially. He never worked or participated in household work. He wanted to know where she was anytime she was not at work. He was a pig and physically unattractive.

I can understand her ending the pregnancy because she was planning on leaving him. But I was still grieving for my grandchild. I cried in private. I never let her see, because I know these are difficult times. But I suffered in silence for what could have been if only she had listened to me.

How different things would have been if only he had participated in her life.

This journal entry holds potential for a more extended commentary on the relationship between the mother and daughter, or between the mother, daughter, and boyfriend.

The following excerpts from a student's first draft on a controversial subject—racial discrimination—also hold potential for revision. Not only does the draft explore a thesis and antithesis, but it provides a synthesis as well. Note its sharp oppositions within sentences, strengthened by the repetition of words and grammatical structures:

There you have me, as seen through the stereotyped eyes of those who have observed me. Too white to be black, but too black to be white, lost in an oblivious state in between, which I call the Grey Zone.

Because I've never limited myself in thinking and acting, I've developed a personality that will never be held back by boundaries we call society. When people judge me as confused and pity me because I don't know where I belong, I laugh because of the way that they have accustomed themselves to behave: as accepting instead of challenging. I refuse to belong to anything that someone demands me to. I belong only to myself. . . .

Oh, well, such is another day in the Grey Zone. If people must classify me, do it this way: white and black, which makes grey—and add a touch of class to make it silver.

Invention Activity: Exploring Oppositions

Compose several brainstorming lists in which you explore opposite sides of persons, experiences, and/or ideas. Arrange the lists in double columns to help yourself generate opposing traits.

Then select one or more of the lists and explore the oppositions in free writing. Write quickly, letting the ideas flow. You can fashion oppositions in single sentences (for example, "Dad and Mom were poor, but they were rich in their love for us kids") or you may choose to develop an idea more completely before opposing it.

Once you've recorded and judged the worth of your oppositions, you can revise, reorganize, and tighten your early drafts. In the following excerpts from a student's revised story of giving birth to her son, note how tight, fast-paced sentences strengthen the opposition between her expectations about and the reality of events:

I turned over and tried to sleep. After a while, the same tightening woke me again. Could I dare to hope the time had come? No, I shouldn't get my hopes up. The more I told myself to go back to sleep, the less I was able to.

I put down the receiver and felt another weak tightening.

"So that's a contraction," I thought. Since it didn't hurt, I was feeling superior to all the women who complained about birth pains.

I closed my eyes and took a deep breath. The tightening had returned more intensely.

"Fifteen seconds . . . thirty seconds . . . forty-five seconds . . . " Ed counted for me.

I relaxed and smiled weakly. "This is hard work."

Although I didn't allow any anesthetics, I felt that I was drugged. The entire room was floating. My contractions were very intense, with barely enough time in between to recover.

"Now I see why they call it labor," I laughed.

Everything was cloudy, light, a dream. Everything except the powerful motion of my body, slowly opening to unfold life. . . .

With the end of transition, my abdominal muscles were pushing voluntarily. I had no control over my body. As much as I tried to relax, the need to push overwhelmed me.

I pushed and relaxed and pushed again till I felt I would explode. One last push and a sweet relief took over me.

"The hard part is over, " Pat said from somewhere in the room. "The head is out."

Another small push and Ed announced that we had a son. I heard a tiny cough and sneeze.

Pat cleaned our baby and put him on my flabby belly. At last I could see and touch the life that had been growing inside me for so long.

Yousef looked around with large blue eyes, probably wondering about the new colors and sounds. Where was the quiet and darkness he had known?

Ed sat beside me, kissed me, and kissed our child.

"Darling," he hugged me, "we're a family now."

—Alice El-Yaman

Collaborative Activity: Exploring Oppositions Further (25 minutes of class time)

Read one of your free writings aloud twice to a group of several peers: the first time so they may listen, the second so they may suggest where oppositions might be added or shifted from another location. As usual, do not comment on or respond to what they say, but note the group's suggestions in the margins or above the lines of your paper. Some writings will provoke more responses than others, based on the subject matter and the number of oppositions in the original entry.

If the group is struggling to suggest changes, you should play the Devil's Advocate game. Read a line or two of your paper and pause to let group members respond. They should begin each comment with the words "However" or "What if." Continue in this manner until you have read the entire paper.

Conduct these activities with a friend or relative, or by yourself, if you don't meet with a group. In any case, revise the paper afterward to incorporate the advice you find most useful.

COMPOSING A STORY

According to Hegel, oppositions emerge over time and lead to change. One or more events establish the thesis for antithetical events, and the events that provide a synthesis emerge from the conflict. An effective story depicting such change must therefore comprise a series of incidents—smaller stories that together tell a complex tale whose point is often richer and deeper than the sum of its parts.

The following story, written by an older student, illustrates an emerging and changing relationship between the writer and a friend. Note its initial setting of the scene, the links between incidents (each new incident is marked by a line break), and its use of oppositions.

REFLECTIONS

The world of our neighborhood was small and poor. We knew everyone on the block and across the street, their habits, cooking smells, clothing styles and cars. It was a cold day when any bit of gossip took longer than half an hour to get around the block.

My heart was pounding with excitement as I ran up the back stairs to the third floor of our old building. Shaking with impatience, I knocked at the door thinking I must be dreaming. When Donna opened the door my words burst into her face. "Donna! Did you see it? Come on, come with me; they're taking it off the truck in front."

Donna's father owned the building and the new tenants held a mysterious anticipation.

Hand in little hand we stood mesmerized as the muscled men grunted and shouted orders at each other, carrying the beautiful baby grand piano up the flight of outside stairs to the second floor.

We held our breath as a large black car pulled up behind the moving van. Out popped a boy of about twelve or thirteen years old. We felt invaded and betrayed. We were both sure the baby grand would belong to a girl. Our curiosity now defunct, we silently crept into my basement apartment.

"Gloria, do you think we will be allowed to play with him?"

"He is living in our building so it must be okay."

Later that evening, the baby grand roared with classical music. My father was angry at not being able to hear the nightly fights on the radio, my mother's daily headache went migraine and I was in heaven.

The next day we searched at school for our new future friend. We didn't find him. While doing our homework on the front porch, Donna and I watched the yellow school bus pull up in front of our building. Awkwardly he made his way toward us.

"Hello, my name is Gloria and this is Donna." His name was Michael.

Having moved from Michigan, his family planned to stay in our building for about a year until they found a house to buy on the Southwest side. He went to a special school to develop his musical talent.

He let his mom know he was home from school and quickly came back out, struggling with a bicycle built for two. Bouncing it down the stairs, his father angrily shouted behind him, "You know you can't ride your bike until you know every street name and location within three blocks of our house."

"But dad, I am going to take Gloria with me and she could teach me."

"All right Michael, but be back in an hour."

I didn't know how to ride a bike and I didn't want Michael to know. While fear grabbed me tighter than my grip on the handle bars, Michael's soft voice behind me whispered, "Don't be afraid, stay in the middle of the seat and steer. I will pedal and keep our balance." He knew I couldn't ride. I was ashamed. It would be twenty-five years later before I would ask him how he knew.

Pedaling past each house I identified the owners by smell. Mrs. Letto used too much garlic and the Johnsons from the South made wonderful smelling corn bread every night. We rode often that first week, reciting the names of every street. Soon Michael was at home and settled in the neighborhood.

With Michael giggling and nudging me through the door to his apartment I became aware of Michael's reality. Surrounding the piano in the middle of the living room were bumpy sheets of music all around and books of every kind that would have made the library jealous. LP records were piled high in a corner next to the record player. There were no toys, no games. It was a cluttered sanctuary I would soon grow to love.

Michael sat at the piano, with both hands at his sides, closed his eyes, smiled and proudly asked, "What can I play for you?"

"I don't know, Michael, play anything."

His hands stretched, fingers flexed, then gently rested on the keys. He began to play Moonlight Sonata. The last note lingered in the air as Michael turned and calmly asked, "Did you like it?"

"It was beautiful."

The enchantment of the music, the room, and the serenity glowing from Michael's face as he played had created a magical state. At the age of eleven, I was in puppy love.

Donna was uneasy with Michael and left us to our friendship.

In the months that followed, Michael and I became inseparable, and he opened many doors in my mind. He read me stories from different countries; I wrote him poetry. He played and sang for me; I gave him colors. He gave with joy; I gave with gratitude.

As the big black car drove Michael away to his new home, sadness filled me as I knew I would probably never see him again or at least not for a long time.

Many years later I started a new job as a secretary for a fire insurance investigation company. The first duty in the morning was to call the man from whom we would get the fire reports. A soft voice answered, "Hello, it's Mike. How can I help you?"

"Hi, Mike. This is Gloria and I am calling from Freed's office for the fire reports."

As he spoke, my mind strained to recall where I had heard that voice before and why was it having such a strange effect on me.

"Here's one that started at 2:00 AM in my old neighborhood on Cleveland Avenue." Struck numb, I loudly blurted out, "Michael it's Gloria!" Silence met my shouting. Again, but with a quiet knowing confidence, "Michael it's Gloria, Gloria from Cleveland Avenue."

We excitedly made plans to have dinner at my apartment. He arrived by bus at 7:00 PM. As I anxiously opened the door, there stood my childhood friend looking all of fifteen.

"Michael you are disgusting. Will you never grow old?" He laughed, reached out and hugged me, and we cried happy tears of reunion.

Dinner conversation overflowed of our experiences of the last twenty-five years. I had forgotten how fascinating it was to watch Michael eat. Every spoon had a level amount, every fork filled and emptied to the timing of a slowly set metronome.

After dinner we sat on the floor as we did as children. My mind whizzed with the question I had to ask. "Michael, how did you know I didn't know how to ride a bike?"

"I heard you swallow and your breathing changed rhythm."

How simple. Of course, this was a part of Michael's magic.

"Gloria I hope you will want to see me again. You are so beautiful to me and I don't want to lose you again."

Many men will tell you that you are beautiful and it's just a line they think you want to hear. When Michael said it, you would cherish and believe his words because Michael had been blind since birth and could only see with his heart.

—Gloria Udaundo

Udaundo took her time in composing this story. She cared about her subject and wished to convey her feelings effectively to readers. Thus, she worked on the story daily for several weeks, developing each incident fully and then rearranging and revising the incidents to sharpen oppositions and make her point. Undertaking such a large project did not intimidate her, for she knew that a person eats an elephant one bite at a time.

Invention Activity: Getting Started on a Longer Story

In your journal or computer file, list three or four relationships you've had that changed over time. Think about the dynamics between you and another person, place, or institution (such as school, religion, a job, or even the police). Then brainstorm about details that would show opposition and change in each. How did the relationship begin? How did it change—and change again? If it ended, why did it end? What incidents would best oppose others and therefore illustrate stages in the relationship? Jot down whatever occurs to you. (If you can't yet decide on a single topic, explore several.) Perhaps read your notes to a group of three or four classmates to hear what they find interesting and what they'd like to know more about. Their reactions will probably remind you of additional incidents to include.

Take a week or more to compose all the incidents of the full story. Assume that your audience will consist of classmates and that your main purpose will be to entertain. Write a first draft of a different incident daily, but don't revise anything yet. As your work moves along, you may discard some incidents, think of others to include, and rearrange the order in which they occur. Don't worry about composing them in chronological order; essentially, you're playing with pieces in a puzzle. As usual, focus on details, both physical and psychological, and try to generate oppositions in style, fact, and circumstances.

Read your work aloud to the group from time to time. The group members may suggest additions or deletions, and may help you determine the direction of the story.

Follow-Up Activity: Shaping Ideas Around a Point

At some stage in the composing process, ask yourself this question: What main idea is emerging or should emerge? Consider what additional incidents might strengthen that point, and consider—this is painful—which incidents are unnecessary or irrelevant and therefore might be eliminated. Then begin revising your story.

We should be careful to get out of an experience only the wisdom that is in it—and stop there; lest we be like the cat that sits on the hot stove-lid. She will never sit down on a hot stove-lid again—and that is well; but also she will never sit down on a cold one anymore.

—*Mark Twain*

Strengthening Your Story Through Transitions

Any longer story is a series of smaller ones. In novels we call them chapters; in movies we call them scenes. But in either case, the movement from one incident to the next requires that the relationships in time, circumstance, characters, and theme be clear. Successful writers therefore pay special attention to transitions, which serve as road signs along the journey through a story, transitions pointing back to where it has been and forward to where it will be going. Note the transitions between incidents in Uduando's work. The first establishes the shift in the time and location while maintaining the same cast of characters:

> The next day we searched at school for our new future friend.

The second introduces not only a new location but a new dimension of the writer's relationship with Michael:

> With Michael giggling and nudging me through the door to his apartment I became aware of Michael's reality.

Udaundo signals a deepening of their relationship in the next transition, which also indicates the passage of time:

> In the months that followed, Michael and I became inseparable, and he opened many doors in my mind.

And in the final transition, she places the action in a new time and circumstance:

> Many years later I started a new job as a secretary for a fire insurance investigation company.

If you know clearly where your story is heading and how each incident fits into the journey, you'll probably compose transitions automatically. Whatever the case, however, almost every paper benefits when you scrutinize its transitions. Are they logical and clear? Do they explain enough—or explain too much? Establishing the relationship between ideas may require only a single word like *however*, a short phrase like *the next day,* a full sentence, or even a paragraph.

Follow-Up Activity: Adding Transitions and Oppositions

Return to your revised story and look at the breaks between incidents. Are the connections clear? Would a short summary of what happened between events be helpful? Do you need to introduce a new location, time, set of circumstances, or characters? Compose and revise transitions so that they link events gracefully without elbowing the reader in the ribs. You may wish to follow the practice of many professional writers: composing longer transitions on separate pieces of paper and then cutting and pasting them in place. (Of course, you can perform these cut-and-paste functions easily on a computer.)

Also look at the oppositions between incidents, within incidents, and within individual sentences. Are there enough of them? Do they create enough tension? Could you tighten and sharpen them? Make your changes above the lines, on separate sheets of paper, or by cutting and pasting or rearranging your computer file.

Collaborative Activity: Hearing and Reading Responses to Your Story (20 minutes of class time)

Before you start the final revision of your work, exchange papers with a classmate and respond to the papers, guided by the following Postdraft Analysis questions. Later on, note your feelings about the reactions, and consider both before you revise. Let another classmate or friend read your paper if you would like more feedback.

Postdraft Analysis
(To be completed by the writer or peer reader)

1. What is the point of the draft? If the point isn't clear, what would clarify it?
2. How many incidents does the story explore? Would more (or fewer) incidents establish greater tension and movement in the story? What could be added (or removed) and where?
3. What oppositions does the story introduce? Should more be added, deleted, or changed? Indicate with bracketed labels where additions, deletions, or changes might occur.
4. Is there sufficient detail within individual incidents to create a sense of immediacy for readers? If not, identify with brackets where material might be added or expanded.

5. Look at the dialogue in each incident. Should more be included to create a sense of immediacy? If so, indicate where with bracketed notes. Read the dialogue aloud. Does the language seem unrealistic? If so, indicate with bracketed labels where it could be changed.

6. Look at the logical connections between the ending sentence of each paragraph and the beginning of the next. Identify with bracketed labels where connections between ideas could be clarified.

7. Look for places where the language isn't clear, direct, and natural. Indicate with bracketed labels where it should be reworded.

8. Are all the elements of the setting—who, what, where, and when—established at or near the beginning? Are they introduced gracefully? If not, what should be added or made less mechanical? Indicate in brackets.

9. Examine the ending. Is it heavy-handed? Does it continue on unnecessarily? If so, indicate changes in brackets.

10. What other problems, if any, need to be addressed? If so, how might they be addressed?

Concluding Activity: Revising and Editing Your Story

Do a final revision of the story. Strengthen oppositions, make connections clear, sharpen the details, add or change dialogue, tighten and strengthen sentences, and edit the paper carefully for matters of mechanics, grammar, and spelling.

Chapter 6

Telling Another's Story

In our era, even as we separate the functions of language, knowing when we speak scientifically we are not speaking poetically, and when we speak theologically we are not speaking the way we do to each other in our houses, and even as our surveys demand statistics, and our courts demand evidence, and our hypotheses demand proof—our minds are still structured for storytelling.

—E. L. Doctorow

There's another source of experiences you can tap into as you compose: the experiences of others. Sometimes your motivation for seeking out and telling other people's stories is mere curiosity—how did they attain their positions; how do they do their jobs, cope with problems, live their lives? More typically, however, you turn to the experiences to support an *argument*—an attempt to persuade readers to accept your viewpoint, change their attitudes, or take action in response to some issue.

Although the experiences aren't yours, you'll still take ownership of them to support the main points of your argument. During the invention stage of composing, you'll begin with a tentative point of view, seek out stories that confirm or modify it, and solidify that viewpoint in response to what you find. You'll then shape the information to suit your purposes, deciding what to emphasize, what to summarize, what to exclude, and what to include and in what order. The "same" story can be told in a number of ways, each way conveying a different message.

LOOKING AT STORIES

Often the best approach to gathering materials for telling another's story is through a personal interview. Like all invention practices, a successful interview evolves partly from planning and partly from discovery. You consider what to ask beforehand, then alter or abandon those plans as a line of questioning emerges during the interview. Here's a story by syndicated columnist Mike Royko that evolved from a series of interviews. Notice how Royko interweaves the story with his own commentary and interpretation, all of which develops a compelling and disturbing argument.

TEEN GANGBANGERS AN IGNORED ISSUE

If the presidential candidates of both parties want to enliven their debates, they might talk about what they'll do with Jawon.

Jawon, 14, lives on the West Side of Chicago. No permanent address. He and his fellow gang members pick out an abandoned building and call it home.

The cops assume that his source of income is crime. Theft, extortion, maybe drug errands for older gang members. He can barely read or write and doesn't attend school, but he has street smarts.

Lately, he has been showing up around the Herbert Elementary School, 2131 W. Monroe St. But not to learn. Just the opposite. He teaches young kids how to join the gang, what hand signals and gang colors to wear to avoid being shot.

Kids are valuable to gangs. Because of their age, they can shoot someone or run drugs or pull a stickup and get a lighter rap.

Jawon has already learned to handle a gun. He's currently awaiting a hearing for wounding another boy in the face during a gang dispute.

And he can drive a car. Not only drive it but bust in, hot wire the ignition, tear out the radio, and go joy riding.

The police got him for that, too, after he and his pals stole a car belonging to a teacher at the Herbert school. They wouldn't have been caught if they hadn't smashed into another car, injuring a couple of people.

All that, and he's still seven years short of being able to legally buy beer. But there's more.

Recently, a boy's sports jacket was stolen at the school. Jackets are a serious matter. Kids are gunned down for not surrendering them.

When the parents complained to the principal, the suspects were gathered in the school office. One was Jawon's cousin, who brought Jawon for moral support.

The principal describes the meeting:

"I had nine boys in there and the mother of the kid whose jacket was stolen, and I was questioning them. Then I left the room to call in another boy.

"Before I came back, the mother told me that Jawon was intimidating the kids right in front of her.

"His cousin had taken the jacket. We later found out that he had stolen it for Jawon. So Jawon told them: 'You better say that we didn't do it or I'm going to get a Uzi and blow you away.'"

If a 14-year-old in a prep school says he is going to blow you away with an automatic weapon, you might chuckle. But on the West Side and other city neighborhoods like it, there are probably 100 automatic weapons for every tennis racket.

"So I went back in and told Jawon he had to leave," the principal says. "He wouldn't. I told him I was ordering him out. He got out of his seat and started swearing at the kids and threatening them.

"I got up and he starts throwing punches at me. I finally got him off me and out of the office, but as he left, he was swearing and he said he'd be back to blow me away."

There was a time when the principal might have called Jawon's parents in to discuss the boy's behavior. But nobody knows where Jawon's parents are. Maybe Jawon doesn't.

So the principal called the police and filed aggravated battery charges.

That made three criminal charges against Jawon: the earlier shooting of the other kid, which was still pending; the theft of the teacher's car; and the assault on the principal.

When they went to court, the judge continued the case and ordered Jawon to stay away from the school and not to bother the principal or anyone else. The probation officer (Jawon's on probation for the car theft) was told to report any bad behavior.

Jawon nodded and went back to the street, where he will roam until sometime in March when another hearing will be held. Unless he kills someone before then.

That thought has crossed the principal's mind, who was more than a bit upset when Jawon was set free.

"I have to say to you I'm a little angry. No, a lot angry. There's nothing to prevent him from getting a gun and blowing me away. The judge told Jawon that he doesn't want him near the school. What are they going to do if he doesn't obey?

"What's this telling the kid? That he can do anything he wants. It will continue until he murders someone. He's already shown that he has access to guns and that he's willing to use one.

"One of my jobs is protecting students from gang activity. I can't even protect myself. How am I supposed to protect the kids?

"If he comes around and I call the police, what am I going to charge him with—trespassing? Hell, he shot a kid in the face and he's on the streets. Are they going to put him away for trespassing?"

Questions, questions. And who has the answers? We have a kid of 14, no parents, living a gang life. No skills or prospects other than crime. And there are thousands like him.

Is there anything in the president's crime package about that? Not that I've noticed.

A principal fears death. And he's not the only one. What do the candidates propose to do about that sort of educational environment?

An adolescent says he'll get a Uzi. He just might. The gangs now consider a six-shooter an antique. What will the candidates do to keep military hardware out of the hands of the Jawons?

You can rap the judge. But we have a national surplus of young criminals and a shortage of cells. Shall we build more prisons? Sure, and what will you say when the tax bill comes?

Yes, you could devote a speech to Jawon. Or even a State of the Union speech. The silence would be deafening.

Issues for Investigation and Discussion

1. Mike Royko tells Jawon's (and the principal's) story in support of an argument that children like Jawon pose serious, complex, and insoluble problems. What problems does Royko explicitly mention? What others does he imply?

2. Where does Royko summarize events or information? Why? Where does he paraphrase—that is, restate in his own words—the testimony of other people? Why? Where does the specific story about Jawon begin? How does Royko's treatment of the story differ from his treatment of materials leading up to it?

3. Why does Royko quote the principal extensively instead of summarizing his words? How would your reaction to the story change if it were summarized?

4. Royko employs oppositions and comparisons throughout. Cite several, and explain their role in the argument.

5. Royko also examines a number of commonly accepted assumptions—both those of people who don't deal with gangs and those of people who do. Why? How does Royko fit them into his argument?

6. Royko intentionally employs sentence fragments (called "minor sentences" by John Ruskiewitz and Maxine Hairston). What effects do these minor sentences create?

These next examples tell a story in a very different way—through letters—which later became the basis of a column by syndicated writer Bob Greene. You'll see the column later in this chapter. For now, however, read the letters and then respond to the questions that follow.

Ann Meyers
Wilmette, IL 60091

February 24, 1990

Dear Mr. Greene,

I spoke briefly to you on the phone last December about a story for your column and you asked that I write to you.

Last September my father-in-law died of cancer. He had not been sick very long and the illness progressed very rapidly. He entered the hospital for tests, was diagnosed with cancer, Lymphoma, and died within two weeks of the diagnosis.

His death was especially hard on our ten-year-old daughter, Sarah. She had not been able to see or talk to him in the hospital, so she chose her own way of saying good-bye. A few weeks after the funeral she wrote him a letter, placed it in an envelope addressed to Grandpa Bernie in Heaven (she also put her return address on the envelope!), attached the letter to a small helium balloon and released it. I watched with her as the balloon sailed slowly upwards: I feeling quite sure it would get tangled in one of the nearby trees, Sarah equally convinced her grandpa would receive it. After a few minutes we went back inside. Sarah felt much better, and I was touched by her actions.

About two months later Sarah received the enclosed letter and map from a Mr. Donald Kopp of York, Pennsylvania—800 miles away from our home in Wilmette. As he explains, he had found her letter in the woods while deer hunting and felt that Sarah should receive a reply. The quality and sensitivity of his reply I believe speak for themselves.

I look forward to hearing from you. Thank you for your time.

Sincerely,

Dec. 8, 1989

Dear Sarah, Family & Friends

Your letter to Grandpa Bernie Meyers apparently reached its destination and was read by him. I understand they can't keep material things up there so it drifted back to Earth. They just keep thoughts, memories, love and things like that.

I found your letter Dec. 3 while deer hunting on state forest land near PA. Rt. 220 E. between Laporte and Dushore.

Whenever you think or talk about Grandpa, he knows and is very close by with overwhelming love.

Sincerely,
Don Kopp
(also a grandpa)

Issues for Investigation and Discussion

1. Ann Meyers's letter summarizes the events, while Donald Kopp's is a source of specific details. If you were Bob Greene and had decided to write a col-

umn based on these materials, what additional information would you want to know about the situation and the people involved? Whom would you want to interview? List at least three or four questions you'd ask the people involved.

2. What strikes you most about the letters? Which point or points would you therefore emphasize? Which details would you stress?

3. How would you arrange the materials in your column? What information from the letters and the follow-up interviews would you emphasize, deemphasize, or ignore? What might you quote, paraphrase, or summarize?

CONDUCTING AN INTERVIEW

Successful interviews generally begin with careful preparation. Learn what you can about the person you wish to talk to and the topics you'll discuss so you can state your purpose clearly when requesting an interview. Don't be shy about making the request; most people will feel flattered that you asked. Be specific about your intentions, though; tell the person who you are, why you are calling, and how much time you will need (certainly no more than an hour). If the person consents to be interviewed, continue to prepare. Brainstorm or cluster in your journal until you've decided the questions to ask and the order in which to ask them. The comments of the person you interview will prompt you to ask other questions, but you'll probably refer to your list from time to time.

Take notes in your journal on the subject's responses (or tape record them if possible), and write down the most interesting or pertinent ones, but don't attempt to quote every word. Instead, listen carefully while conveying your interest in the subject's story. Begin with factual questions about *who, what, where, why,* and *how* issues; then move on to queries about the subject's feelings and beliefs. Keep your opinions to yourself and let the subject fully explore his or her thoughts. Pose follow-up questions as they occur to you, but don't feel you must cover every question on your original list. Do ask the subject to repeat or clarify a statement, however. Most people want you to quote them accurately and get the facts straight. Also, if your subject's responses are vague, ask questions to elicit more specific responses: "Would you tell me more about that?" "Could you give me an example?" "How did/does that happen?" In any case, keep an open mind, for the person's comments may lead you to entirely different conclusions from those you had prior to the interview.

At the close of the interview, thank the subject and ask if you may call later to clarify or amplify any information. (More questions will probably occur to you when you review the material later.) You might also ask the subject to suggest additional persons to talk to or materials to read. Immediately afterward, you should review, reorganize, and add to your notes. Or listen to the tape recording, transcribe, and then reorganize the most important parts.

While arranging your materials to support the point that emerges, you needn't—and shouldn't—quote every sentence and report on every detail.

Quote only the most important, powerful, or memorable statements, and summarize or paraphrase the less important ideas.

Collaborative Activity: Preparing to Interview Someone Outside Class

In your journal, list two or three issues of concern to the community or the college. Explore your position on each issue, and then brainstorm—either alone or for ten minutes with classmates—about the names or occupations of people who might prove good subjects to interview about the issues. Narrow your choice to a single issue and one (or two) candidates to interview. Then list five or six questions you'd probably ask each subject. (You may wish to solicit your classmates' suggestions about these questions.)

Once you've decided on a subject and a list of questions, call or meet the person or persons to arrange an interview.

Collaborative Activity: Setting Up In-Class Interviews

In addition, or as an alternative to the previous activity, you and a classmate can interview each other. As Ann Meyers did for Bob Greene, write a brief (one- or two-paragraph) summary of one of the following matters so your classmate may prepare for the interview:

1. an unusual job or task that you've performed or witnessed;
2. a time when you or someone else performed an act of heroism or kindness;
3. an exciting or frightening event you either witnessed or experienced.

Compose a first draft of your summary in your journal, and then revise the summary at least once. Don't supply too many details; save them for the interview. Then exchange your summary with a classmate—or let your instructor collect the summaries and distribute one to each member of the class.

Look over the summary you received, consider the most important points it raises, and prepare to interview the author of the summary.

FURTHER EXAMINING STORIES BASED ON INTERVIEWS

After gathering information from the interview, you must decide how to employ it in your story (or, perhaps more accurately, reconsider and modify those decisions throughout the writing process). Here's Bob Greene's column, which he based not only on the letters by Ann Meyers and Donald Kopp, but also on his telephone interviews with them and Sarah Meyers. How do his decisions resemble the ones you contemplated?

FROM A GRANDPA, ABOVE AND BEYOND

When Bernie Meyers, who was 70 years old and who lived in Wilmette, Illinois, went into the hospital last September, his family at first did not know how serious his illness was. Thus his 10-year-old granddaughter, Sarah Meyers, was not taken to see him.

"He hadn't been feeling well for some time," said Sarah's mother, Ann Meyers. "He went into the hospital for some tests. Just to find out what was wrong."

What was wrong was Lymphoma—a cancer of the lymphatic system. In Bernie Meyers' case, the Lymphoma was advanced and irreversible. He died within two weeks.

Sarah Meyers never got a chance to say good-bye to her grandfather.

"Sarah saw him regularly, because we live close to where he lived," her mother said. "This was her first experience with death. We could tell that, as upset as she was, she was additionally upset that she didn't see him in those days before he died. She didn't get to have one last talk with him."

Sarah didn't say much about what she was feeling. But in October she came home from a friend's birthday party. The other children at the party had been given helium balloons as favors. Sarah had hers with her—a bright red balloon.

"She went into the house," her mother said. "When she came back out, she was carrying the balloon—and an envelope."

Inside the envelope was a letter she had written to her grandfather. The envelope was addressed to "Grandpa Bernie, in Heaven Up High." In the letter, Sarah wrote: "Hi Grandpa. How are you? What's it like up there?" The letter ended with Sarah telling her grandfather that she loved him, and that she hoped somehow he could hear what she was telling him.

"I'm not sure what Sarah's concept of heaven is," her mother said. "But I do know that she printed our return address on the envelope. I didn't ask her about it. She punched a hole in the envelope, and tied the envelope to the balloon. Then she let it go.

"That balloon seemed so fragile to me. I didn't think it would even make it past the trees. But it did. We watched the balloon sail away, and then we went back inside."

Two months passed; the weather got cold. Then one day a letter arrived addressed to "Sarah Meyers + Family." The letter bore a York, Pa., postmark, and had been mailed by a man named Donald H. Kopp.

The letter began:

Dear Sarah, Family & Friends—

Your letter to Grandpa Bernie Meyers apparently reached its destination and was read by him. I understand they can't keep material things up there, so it drifted back to earth. They just keep thoughts, memories, love and things like that.

Donald Kopp wrote that he had found the balloon and letter while hunting and hiking in a Pennsylvania state forest near the Maryland border. That is almost 600 miles from Wilmette—the balloon had floated over Illinois, probably parts of Michigan and Indiana, Ohio and all the way across Pennsylvania before settling in the forest.

Donald Kopp's letter to Sarah continued:

Whenever you think or talk about your grandpa, he knows and is very close by with *overwhelming love. Sincerely, Don Kopp. (also a grandpa)*

Sarah said that after she had tied her letter to the balloon and let it float away, "At night I would think about it. I just wanted to hear from Grandpa somehow. In a way, now I think that I have heard from him."

Donald Kopp, who is 63 and retired from his job as a shipping clerk, said the other day that the red balloon, which had almost completely deflated, was resting on a blueberry bush the afternoon he found it.

"That's pretty dense woods," he said. "It was cold and windy that day. I walked over to see what the balloon was. I could tell it was a child's handwriting on the envelope. I didn't have my reading glasses on, and I thought it was addressed to someone at 'Haven High.' A high school or something.

"I put it in my pocket. When I got back home, I saw that it wasn't addressed to Haven High. It was addressed to Sarah's grandfather, in 'Heaven Up High.'"

So he decided to write his letter to Sarah. "It was important to me that I write to her," he said. "But I'm not very good at writing; I don't do it that often. It took me a couple of days to think of what to put in the letter. Then I mailed it.

"Like I said in the letter—I'm a grandfather, too."

Greene's column was later abridged and adapted for inclusion in *Reader's Digest*. See if it tells the same story.

LOVE FINDS A WAY

When 70-year-old Bernie Meyers of Wilmette, Ill., died suddenly of cancer, his ten-year-old granddaughter Sarah Meyers didn't have a chance to say good-by to him. For weeks Sarah said little about what she was feeling. But then one day she came home from a friend's birthday party with a bright-red helium balloon. "She went into the house," her mother recalls, "and came out carrying the balloon—and an envelope addressed to 'Grandpa Bernie, in Heaven Up High.'"

The envelope contained a letter in which Sarah told her grandfather that she loved him and hoped somehow he could hear her. Sarah printed her return address on the envelope, tied the envelope to the balloon and let it go. "The balloon seemed so fragile," her mother remembers. "I didn't think it would make it past the trees. But it did."

Two months passed. Then one day a letter arrived addressed to "Sarah Meyers & Family" and bearing a York, Pa., postmark.

"Dear Sarah, Family & Friends: Your letter to Grandpa Bernie Meyers apparently reached its destination and was read by him. I understand they can't keep material things up there, so it drifted back to Earth. They just keep thoughts, memories, love and things like that. Sarah, whenever you think about your grandpa, he knows and is very close by with overwhelming love. Sincerely, Don

Kopp (also a grandpa)."

Kopp, a 63-year-old retired receiving clerk, had found the letter and the nearly deflated balloon while hunting in northeastern Pennsylvania—almost 600 miles from Wilmette. The balloon had floated over at least three states and one of the Great Lakes before coming to rest on a blueberry bush.

"Though it took me a couple of days to think of what to say," Kopp notes, "it was important to me that I write to Sarah."

Says Sarah, "I just wanted to hear from Grandpa somehow. In a way, now I think I *have* heard from him."

Issues for Additional Investigation and Discussion

1. Does Bob Greene change or omit any facts from the original materials? If so, why? What does he add to the original materials? Why?

2. Unlike Royko, Greene handles his materials much more like a story. He shapes the materials to make a point—actually several points—but doesn't state a thesis or map out his journey. What points does Greene make or suggest?

3. Greene relies heavily on quoting to tell this story. Why doesn't he use Ann Meyers's original letter?

4. Greene also chooses to paraphrase part of Kopp's letter before returning to quote its ending. Why?

5. Donald Kopp tells Greene, "I'm not very good at writing. . . . It took me a couple of days to think of what to put in the letter." That may be true, but Kopp probably had other reasons for deliberating so long over what to say. What were these reasons?

6. In condensing the original article, what does *Reader's Digest* omit or change?

7. The two treatments also differ in organization and structure. How? What effects do the changes have on your reactions? Is the point of the two treatments the same? (Look especially at the endings.)

8. All three versions of the story—Ann Meyers's, Greene's original column, and the abridgment in *Reader's Digest*—are treated more or less objectively, relying heavily on facts and dialogue. Yet the three versions differ in their organization, emphasis, and message. Can writing therefore ever be completely "objective"? What subjective decisions must a writer make when he or she gathers and organizes information?

9. As a way of summarizing your ideas in response to these questions, or to any other matters you observe in Royko's column earlier in the chapter, turn now to your journal. List a dozen or so common traits for the effective retelling of another person's story to support an argument. Alternatively, you might create a list with several classmates. Let this list guide you as you compose and revise your own story later.

Follow-Up Activity: Conducting the Interview

Meet with the subject of your interview and explore the questions you've prepared and any others that arise during the meeting. Take notes or tape record the subject's responses. Look over or transcribe your notes afterward, and see what leading ideas emerge. Brainstorm, cluster, or loop until you've clarified the main points of your argument based on the subject's story, and then shape the materials from the interview to develop the argument.

COMPOSING THE STORY

After completing your interview, you can begin to compose your story. You'll need to decide which of your subject's comments (and any written material you may have gathered) to quote directly, which to summarize, and which to paraphrase.

Summarizing

A story shouldn't be any longer than it has to be. Its length depends in part on the writer's purpose, audience, or limitations of the medium in which it will be told. Ann Meyers, for example, intended to summarize the story so Bob Greene—a busy man—could judge its worth, and *Reader's Digest* lacked the room to include every detail. Furthermore, a story shouldn't contain details that don't develop its central point. Thus, writing an effective summary means distilling the essence of the material into a few words, sentences, or paragraphs. You must thoroughly understand your subject matter, locate and articulate the main point or idea, and discuss important supporting points but no specific details or examples. As you compare the full version of Lincoln's Gettysburg Address with the summary that follows, note that the summary also departs from the original arrangement of ideas.

Original: Four score and seven years ago our fathers brought forth onto this continent a new nation, conceived in liberty, and dedicated to the proposition that all men are created equal.

Now we are engaged in a great Civil War, testing whether that nation, or any nation so conceived and so dedicated, can long endure. We are met on a great battlefield of that war. We have come to dedicate a portion of that field, as a final resting place for those who here gave their lives that a nation might live. It is altogether fitting and proper that we should do this.

But, in a larger sense, we can not dedicate—we can not consecrate—we can not hallow—this ground. The brave men, living and dead, who struggled here have consecrated it far above our poor power to add or detract. The world will little note nor long remember what we say here, but it can never forget what they did here. It is for us the living, rather, to be dedicated here to the unfinished work which they who fought here have thus far so nobly advanced. It is rather for us to be here dedicated to the great task remaining before us—that from these honored dead we take increased devotion to that cause for which they gave the last full measure of devotion—that we here highly resolve that these dead shall not have died in vain—that this nation, under God, shall have a new birth of freedom—and that government of the people, by the people, for the people, shall not perish from the earth.

Summary: In his Gettysburg Address, delivered at the dedication of a cemetery on the battlefields of Gettysburg, President Abraham Lincoln begins by asserting that the real goal of the Civil War is to preserve our country and maintain its commitment to liberty and equality. He also states that the Civil War will show the world whether such high ideals can be maintained. While acknowledging that the dedication is indeed an appropriate act, he emphasizes that the deaths of the men on the battlefield speak far more eloquently than his or anyone's words; their actions will be remembered through posterity. The only appropriate way to honor their deaths, he concludes, is to continue the fight to renew the government's promise of a free and representative democracy.

Composing Activity: Writing a Summary

Compose a two- or three-paragraph summary of Mike Royko's article at the beginning of this chapter, discussing its central ideas and its major supporting ideas. Begin by rereading the article and taking notes about its main points. Then write your summary without looking back at the article too often, lest you allow Royko's words or sentence structure to sneak into your work. You may wish to do some looping (see Chapter 2) to arrive at a clear statement of Royko's main idea.

Spend fifteen minutes comparing your version with those of several classmates, suggesting to each other how to clarify the summaries. Then, if necessary, revise your summary outside of class.

Composing Activity: Summarizing the Materials from Your Interview

Now write a single-paragraph summary of the information you gathered in the interview. Follow procedures similar to those discussed in the last activity: look over your notes several times prior to composing the summary, and consult your notes as you compose and revise. Use looping if necessary.

When you finish, put the summary away. Later, you may wish to incorporate parts of it in the story based on the interview.

Quoting

Quote the subject of your interview directly, but not needlessly. Include only his or her most important, memorable, or dramatic statements exactly as they were said—or at least as how they appear in your notes. You can shorten, but not change, a quotation, provided you don't distort or confuse its meaning.

How often misused words generate misleading thoughts.

—*Herbert Spenser*

Follow the same guidelines for quoting as you did in Chapter 3. Here are a few additional reminders:

- Place periods, commas, and question marks inside the end quotation marks.
- You can identify the speaker before, after, or in middle of a quotation— but don't place quotation marks around the identification. And use commas, not periods, to set quotations off.

Wilson said, "Immediately after the accident, I was too busy helping my wife and kids to think about myself."

"Immediately after the accident, I was too busy helping my wife and kids to think about myself," *Wilson said.*

"Immediately after the accident," *Wilson said,* "I was too busy helping my wife and kids to think about myself."

- When a quotation continues over several paragraphs, begin each paragraph with a quotation mark, but place an end quotation mark only in the last paragraph:

"One of my jobs is protecting students from gang activity. I can't even protect myself. How am I supposed to protect the kids?

"If he comes around and I call the police, what am I going to charge him with—trespassing? Hell, he shot a kid in the face and he's on the streets. Are they going to put him away for trespassing?"

—Mike Royko

Paraphrasing

Paraphrasing means retelling a speaker's or writer's ideas in your own words and sentence structure. Unlike a summary, a paraphrase retains most of information and examples of the original. But like a summary, it does not employ any of the original language.

Paraphrasing is difficult; it taxes the limits of your vocabulary and knowledge of syntax. You must compose and then continue to revise your version until it clearly and gracefully captures the meaning of the original without parroting its word choice or word order. A speaker's or writer's words belong to him or her, so a paraphrase must avoid plagiarism—the (illegal) presentation of another's language as your own. Compare the opening sentence of Lincoln's Gettysburg Address with two paraphrases, one effective, the other bordering on plagiarism:

Original : Four score and seven years ago our fathers brought forth on this continent a new nation, conceived in liberty, and dedicated to the proposition that all men are created equal.

Effective Paraphrase: In his Gettysburg Address, President Abraham Lincoln said that, eighty-seven years earlier, the fathers of our country had established its government based on two principles: liberty and equality of opportunity.

Poor Paraphrase: In his Gettysburg Address, President Abraham Lincoln said that eighty-seven years earlier the founding fathers created a new country on this continent, based on the concept of liberty and the belief that all men are created equal.

When including some language from the original—either because you cannot think of an alternative or because you wish to retain a memorable phrase—quote the language exactly, as in the following example:

Paraphrase and quotation: In his Gettysburg Address, President Abraham Lincoln said that the fathers of our country had established government based on two principles: liberty and "the proposition that all men are created equal."

Accurate paraphrasing will become even more important in later chapters, when you'll incorporate material from written sources into your arguments. But even when you paraphrase the comments of someone you interview, you still must preserve the speaker's meaning.

Composing Activity: Writing a Paraphrase

Paraphrase three quotations of the principal from Royko's article at the beginning of this chapter. Exchange your paraphrase with a classmate's, examining each other's work for clarity, grace, and the absence of plagiarism.

Composing Activity: Writing a First Draft of Your Story

Compose a first draft of a story based on your interview with a member of the community or a classmate. Shape the materials to support each point you wish to make. Assume that your audience will be classmates who are familiar with the issues you discuss, but not with the story itself.

Decide whether to interpret and comment on events as Royko did, or to let the events speak for themselves as Greene did. Decide what to include or exclude, what to quote, what to summarize, and what to examine in detail. Also look over your notes for a strong quotation for closing the story.

Follow-Up Activity: Consulting with the Subject of Your Interview

If you've based your paper on a classmate's story, let him or her read the draft and suggest ways to strengthen the story or add information that wasn't mentioned in the initial interview.

Collaborative Activity: Eliciting Responses to Your Story (30 minutes of class time)

Before revising your paper in the final stages of composing, read it aloud to your group twice as you have done in past instances. Record (or let someone else record) the group's responses to the following Postdraft Analysis questions. Look at their responses later and note your reactions. Do you agree or disagree, or has another idea occurred to you? Consider these reactions when you revise.

Postdraft Analysis
(To be completed by the writer or peer reader)

1. What is the point of the draft? If the point isn't clear, what would clarify it? Does anything need to be added? If so, where would you place the new material?

2. Is the organization of the draft clear? If not, how might ideas be rearranged? Where might connections between ideas be clarified? Identify those places with bracketed labels.

3. Examine the detail in each incident. Is there enough detail to create a sense of immediacy for readers? If not, where might it be added or expanded? Identify those places with bracketed labels.

4. Examine the use of quotations in individual scenes. Is the quoting sufficient, insufficient, or unnecessary in places? Where should quotes be added or changed? Identify those places.

5. Where does paraphrasing occur? Is the paraphrasing appropriate and clear? If not, identify with bracketed labels where it should be reworded.

6. Where are summaries used? If they are too general or unclear, identify where more detail could be included.

7. Are all the elements of the setting—who, what, where, and when—established at or near the beginning? Is the subject of the interview identified? If not, what should be added or made less mechanical? Indicate in brackets.

8. Examine the ending. Is it heavy-handed? Does it continue on unnecessarily? If so, indicate changes.

9. Do any other problems need to be addressed? If so, how might they be addressed?

Concluding Activity: Revising and Editing Your Story

Consider the responses to the Postdraft Analysis questions, and then do a final revision of the story—adding or changing quotations, paraphrases, and summaries, clarifying connections between ideas and events, and editing the paper carefully for matters of mechanics, grammar, and spelling.

Chapter 7

Making a Meaningful Point

In your writing you must go over your material in your mind, trying to find the focus, the perspective, the angle of vision that will make you see clearly the shape of whatever it is you are writing about. There has to be a point that is sharply in focus, and a clear grouping of everything else around it. Once you see this clearly, your reader will see it too. And that, the shape of your ideas, is usually all [he or she] is going to carry away from his reading.

—Rudolf Flesch

Both writers and readers construct meaning in a text, the writers by composing experiences through words, and the readers by interpreting those words. Readers are not mere passive consumers of content; they actively engage themselves in making sense of the words on the page. They try to draw a coherent mental picture of your ideas and how your thoughts relate to each other. They sketch the outlines of that picture from what you tell them in the first paragraph, then fill in the details and redraw the outlines later as you tell them more. Thus, your opening paragraph (or the first two or even three paragraphs) is crucial to the success of your paper. The beginning must not only engage your readers' interest, but must also guide them along their intellectual journey through your text.

The opening paragraphs aid your readers' search for coherence in two ways: (1) by making a point and establishing the key issues they'll encounter, and (2) by relating these matters to the readers' own lives and work. A reminder here, however: we're talking about final—not first—drafts. Only through multiple revisions will such a strong beginning to your paper emerge. We'll return to this issue later, after examining two essays by professional writers.

LOOKING AT ESSAYS

In this first example, the late Sydney J. Harris, a syndicated newspaper columnist, addresses his audience as "we" and quotes a doctor's words to make his point. As you read the selection, think about whom Harris means by "we" as well as his purpose in writing the argument.

DELINQUENCY COULD BE WORSE

We are concerned, as we should be, about the delinquency problem. It is growing every year, and its prevalence and intensity threaten the whole fabric of society.

But it is also wise to keep in mind the words of Dr. Lauretta Bender of New York University. Dr. Bender said in a speech some years ago:

"Far more children should be delinquent than actually are. They have an amazing capacity to tolerate bad parents, poor teachers, dreadful homes and communities."

As we look around at our disrupted social order, with its corruption, its fierce competitiveness, its nervous instability, its tremulous existence under the cloud of atomic catastrophe—it can then be seen, more coolly and clearly, that young people do have an astonishing tolerance for growing up under adverse conditions.

For how can we compare the world today with the world in which we experienced our childhood? Within one generation, the world has moved a thousand times faster than in all the previous generations since Adam. Most of the familiar landmarks have disappeared—not only the physical ones, but the psychological, social and moral landmarks as well.

It is hard to believe that when I was a little boy, 40 years ago, there were virtually no automobiles, few telephones, the radio had barely been born, and the child's world was utterly divorced from the adult's world.

My playmates and I moved in a separate sphere; indeed, until the Great Depression of 1929, we were not aware of the adult world. Our diversions were different, the things we heard and saw were designed for children, the activities we engaged in were sharply marked off. There was no such thing as a "teen-ager" in my day.

Now, of course, children are exposed to the adult world from the earliest age. The auto, the telephone, television, impinge upon their senses from the time they can walk and talk. Crime, war, calamities of all sorts are now part of their natural environment. There is no longer a "world of children"; the ages have blurred together into one long continuum.

This fearful acceleration in the physical world has made for an equal acceleration in the emotional world: children become sophisticated before they become wise, cynical before they become knowing, jaded before they become satisfied, ambitious before they become able and sometimes decadent before they become civilized. The real wonder and delight is that so many of them survive and flourish as decent human beings in the setting we have provided them.

In this next example, Ellen Goodman, another syndicated newspaper columnist, writes to achieve a far different purpose than does Harris. Consider that purpose as you read.

DIVINING THE STRANGE EATING HABITS OF KIDS

As a parent who works with words for a living, I have prided myself over many years for a certain skill in breaking the codes of childspeak. I began by interpreting baby talk, moved to more sophisticated challenges like "chill out" and I graduated with "wicked good."

One phrase, however, always stumped me. I was unable to crack the meaning of the common cry echoing through most middle-class American households: "There's Nothing to Eat in This House!"

This exclamation becomes a constant refrain during the summer months when children who have been released from the schoolhouse door grow attached to the refrigerator door. It is during the summer when the average taxpayer realizes the true cost-effectiveness of school: It keeps kids out of the kitchen for roughly seven hours a day. A feat no parent is able to match.

At first, like so many others, I assumed that "NETH!" [as in "Nothing to Eat in This House"] was a straightforward description of reality; if there was NETH, it was because the children had eaten it all. After all, an empty larder is something you come to expect when you live through the locust phase of adolescence.

I have one friend with three teen-age sons who swears that she doesn't even have to unload her groceries anymore. Her children feed directly from the bags, rather like ponies. I have other friends who buy ingredients for supper only on the way home so that supper doesn't turn into lunch.

Over the years, I have considered color-coding food with red, yellow and green stickers. Green for eat. Yellow for eat only if you are starving. Red for "touch this and you die."

However, I discovered that these same locusts can stand in front of a relatively full refrigerator while bleating the same pathetic choruses of "NETH! NETH!" By carefully observing my research subjects, I discovered that the demand of "NETH!" may indeed have little to do with the supply.

What then does the average underage eater mean when he or she bleats "NETH! NETH!" You will be glad to know that I have finally broken the code for the "nothing" in NETH and offer herewith, free of charge, my translation.

NETH includes:

1. Any food that must be cooked, especially in a pan or by convectional heat. This covers boiling, frying or baking. Toasting is acceptable under dire conditions.

2. Any food that is in a frozen state with the single exception of ice cream. A frozen pizza may be considered "something to eat" only if there is a microwave oven on hand.

3. Any food that must be assembled before eaten. This means tuna that is still in a can. It may also mean a banana that has to be peeled, but only in extreme cases. Peanut butter and jelly are exempt from this rule as long as they are on the same shelf beside the bread.

4. Leftovers. Particularly if they must be reheated [See 1].

5. Plain yogurt or anything else that might have been left as a nutrition trap.

6. Food that must be put on a plate, or cut with a knife and fork, as opposed to ripped with teeth while watching videos.

7. Anything that is not stored precisely at eye level. This includes:

8. Any item on a high cupboard shelf, unless it is a box of cookies and:

9. Any edible in the back of the refrigerator, especially on the middle shelf.

While divining the nine meanings of "NETH!" I should also tell you that I developed an anthropological theory about the eating patterns of young Americans. For the most part, I am convinced, Americans below the age of 20 have arrested their development at the food-gathering stage.

They are intrinsically nomadic. Traveling in packs, they engage in nothing more sophisticated than hand-to-mouth dining. They are, in effect, strip eaters who devour the ripest food from one home, and move on to another.

Someday, I am sure they will learn about the use of fire, not to mention forks. Someday, they will be cured of the shelf-blindness, the inability to imagine anything hidden behind a large milk carton. But for now, they can only graze. All the rest is NETHing.

Issues for Investigation and Discussion

1. Both Harris and Goodman write "about" teenagers, but for very different purposes. Who are Harris' readers, and what does he want them to do with his information?

2. Harris and Goodman also express very different points. What sentence near the beginning states Harris's main point, and where does he reiterate the point?

3. Does Harris back up his main point and supporting points mostly with facts and figures or mostly with personal experiences and observations?

4. How might Harris have changed his argument if he had addressed it to children instead of adults?

5. Who is Ellen Goodman's audience, and what does she expect them to do with her information? Where does she state her point, and what is it?

6. After listing the nine meaings of NETH, Goodman makes several other observations. Are they irrelevant to her point? Compare the ending of her argument to the ending of Harris's. What traits do they have in common?

7. As way of summarizing your ideas in response to these questions, or to any other matters you observe in Harris's and Goodman's writing, turn to your journal or computer file and list several common traits of effective beginnings to arguments. Note especially how these beginnings account for purpose, subject matter, and audience. Alternatively, create a list with several classmates. Let your list guide you as you compose and revise your own paper later.

MAKING A POINT

For readers to make the sense of your argument, they need to understand your point. Also called a *thesis*, the point is the central message you want to convey. The point isn't the "topic," what the writing is "about." It's what the writing *says* about the topic. Nor is the point or thesis some vague notion that readers may excavate from the writing after much hard digging. Instead, a point is often stated in an actual sentence (or two or three) that readers can recognize and identify. It's the hook on which everything hangs, the message inside the greeting card, the moral of the story. A statement of point answers the central question: "So what?" Readers should understand *why* they are reading an argument, what message it will deliver, and what they will do with that message when they finish.

Therefore, many writers choose to state the point up front, in or near the first paragraph, to help readers search for coherence among the materials they'll later encounter. Occasionally you may defer the statement of point to the end of an argument when you wish to show readers how you arrived at the point. We'll examine this approach in Chapter 11, but we'll concentrate here on stating the point early.

Not only should your statement of point be clear, but everything you say throughout your paper should support the statement. If you stay on the topic but stray off the point, you risk confusing or misleading readers. They may reinterpret the point to account for your digressions, thereby misunderstanding a message they could otherwise have easily understood. You should thus experiment with and explore your ideas in the early drafts of your paper until you see a point emerging. Then revise and reshape your materials until the final draft makes and sticks to that point.

I don't like to decide too quickly . . . I like to have it happen, just like our own lives. We don't always know where we're going, and if we make formal decisions on a given night, if we sit down and put a list of things we're going to do on a piece of paper, they almost never work out right.

—Norman Mailer

Expressing an Attitude

The statement of point should also express or imply a *judgment* about or *attitude* toward the subject. Compare these statements of point:

Poor: There were three types of teachers I had in elementary and high school. They were the charismatic types, the lecturers, and those who taught me to teach myself. *(So what?)*

Better: The elementary and high school teachers *I've come to appreciate most* weren't necessarily the most charismatic personalities or the best lecturers. They were the ones who taught me to teach myself. *(Judgment: Teaching self-reliance is more important than entertaining students.)*

Poor: In this paper, I will compare and contrast dormitory life with life at home. (Why? And who cares?)

Better: Living in a dormitory has *forced* me to be more self-reliant than I ever was at home. *(Implied Attitude: I may not like it, but dorm life is a valuable experience.)*

The two nonattitudinal or nonjudgmental statements go nowhere. Both would probably lead writers to compose a paper following a "what-next?" strategy: characterized by random claims "about" the subject, a lot of head scratching and gazing out the window, and very little real development of ideas. Readers might find neither point nor interest in the materials and therefore toss the paper aside. The writer and reader wouldn't engage in purposeful and useful communication. Conversely, the statements of attitude or judgment—whether written early or late in the composing process—would probably impel writers to support claims. They'd compose and revise with a goal in mind and a sense of the logical connections between ideas. Readers would probably recognize that goal and find coherence in the composition.

Invention Activity: Gathering Materials for an Argument

1. Brainstorm, free write, or cluster in your journal or a computer file for fifteen minutes about two or three possible topics for papers in which you discuss an experience or experiences—yours or someone else's—that connect in some way to a subject discussed or debated publicly. The subject needn't be profound and shouldn't lead to moralizing (remember Ellen Goodman's column), but should potentially support a stated or implied attitude or judgment. Write on the left-side pages only, reserving the right-side pages for recording later comments and ideas. If you use a computer file, create separate columns or sections for later comments.

2. Begin to explore each topic by jotting down (or circling in a cluster diagram) a rough idea of your point. You needn't write a complete sentence or be too precise. Then list or generate details of the experience or experiences.

3. Next, if possible, meet with several classmates to exchange ideas, discuss which topics have the most potential, and select one topic for your writing. Let the group tell you what they find most interesting, what parts of the topic they'd like to see expanded (or summarized or dropped), and how the material might be organized. Then turn to your journal for five minutes and use the right-hand pages to record notes and ideas on the topic.

4. Away from the group, explore and develop your ideas further. Draft a preliminary statement of your point. Consider where to comment on the material, how to show the connections between and significance of each part, and how to show the relevance of each part to your point. Additional brainstorming or clustering may help you generate ideas, and looping may help you focus on the point.

Constructing or Identifying a Problem for Readers

You can't ignore the concerns and interests of your audience when stating your point. People understand the unfamiliar by relating it to the familiar. If readers see the relevance of your point to what they believe and value, they'll most likely find meaning in the issues you discuss. Your task, therefore, is also to frame your point as a problem that affects your audience. Merely naming the problem—especially in a single word ("pollution," "racism," "poverty") or a short phrase ("failure in school," "world starvation")—won't suffice. Compare these examples:

> *Poor:* One important kind of water pollution is the high levels of lead in drinking water.

> *Effective:* High levels of lead in the water your young children drink can cause them permanent brain damage.

The first example simply announces the point without addressing a specific audience, and only hinting at an answer to their "So what?" question. The second example constructs *a problem for parents* who will probably want to hear a solution to (or at least become better acquainted with) the problem. They might expect to learn why lead threatens their children, how the threat can be eliminated, what the solution will cost, and so on.

If you were to address your argument to people without young children, however, you'd have to construct the problem differently:

> High levels of lead in the water that children drink can cause permanent brain damage, hindering their ability to learn and therefore to become fully productive members of our society.

This audience would relate the problem to their concerns about the human and economic costs to the larger society.

Thus, a well-written statement of point constructs or identifies a difficult or troublesome issue for readers who care (or can be made to care) about its direct or indirect costs on them. Constructing a problem for readers will become increasingly important in Unit II of this book, where you'll make more sophisticated arguments.

Invention Activity: Analyzing Your Audience and Purpose

Constructing a problem effectively requires that you think about who your readers are—as well as your intentions for them. Either prior to or after composing an early draft of your argument, you should consider whom you are addressing: Parents? Business people? Young adults? Suburbanites? Republicans? Smokers? Poor people? Also consider your purpose in writing the argument—to inform, to persuade, or to entertain. The following planning questions should help you analyze your audience's needs and interests.[*]

Planning or Revising Questions
1. Who are the members of your audience? How old are they? Where do they live? What kind of clothes are they wearing? What kind of jobs do they have? How well-educated are they?
2. What do they already know about the subject? (List as many ideas as you can.) How do they feel about it?
3. What new information will you be providing the audience?
4. What would you like the audience to do with your information? Would you like to influence their behavior, and, if so, how?
5. How do you want your audience to feel after reading your paper?

Roadmapping

The arguments by Sydney J. Harris and Ellen Goodman you read earlier are fairly short. But when you compose a longer and more complex argument, you can guide readers on their journey through your ideas if you draw them a map at the onset—that is, a brief outline of what you'll be saying. The map helps them anticipate and find coherence among the major parts. Here's the beginning of a student's argument which emerged after multiple revisions. (That is, the student revised this opening paragraph after composing the body of the paper.) The roadmapping words are in italics:

> What images come to mind when you think of a drug abuser? A sweaty coke fiend? Or a heroin addict with her dirty needles? How about a high school kid that spends more time smoking pot than attending class? These are, in general, the depictions of the drug abuser we get from the media. As a result, we see the drug abuse problem centering on illegal drugs. Unfortunately, illegal drug abuse is just the tip of the iceberg. What about the seven-tenths we don't see—legal drug abuse? Because coke is illegal, when you use it you abuse it, but *what about non-prescription -, prescription-drugs, tobacco, and alcohol? To answer these questions, we first need to define drug abuse and its effects, and then examine drug abuse as it applies to a variety of widely used drugs.*

The map helps readers predict that the writer will first define drug abuse, and then apply that definition to non-prescription-, prescription-drug, tobacco, and alcohol use in that order. The writer does indeed do precisely that, and backs up his analysis with stories about his own experiences with prescription drugs to treat epilepsy and the (hypothetical) experiences of other people with drugs.

[*]These questions are based on a similar list prepared by Roland K. Huff in "Teaching Revision: A Model of the Drafting Process," *College English*, December 1983, 806–807.

Signposting

Readers can also recognize each stop along their journey through a complex argument if you put up signposts. These are terms repeated from the map in your first paragraph, or transitional expressions showing the relationships between ideas. Here are the beginnings of body paragraphs in the student's argument, with the key signposting terms in italic:

1. Let's look at both words: *drug and abuse.* A drug changes the way your body works and how you feel. *For example,* the Phenobarbital I take every night slows my heartbeat and makes me sleepy.

2. Having seen some of the warning signs and *effects of drug abuse, let's look at some examples.* . . .

3. *In the first example,* Ezra is eighty and his legs bother him constantly. He's been taking *non-prescription drugs,* but the dosages don't seem to be helping him. . . .

4. Mary has been feeling very tense lately. . . . So her doctor writes her a *prescription* for valium. . . .

5. The responsibility for misusing *other legal drugs* lies with the user, for your doctor can advise you *not to smoke or drink,* but it's up to you whether to quit.

6. *For instance, Jerry has smoked* three packs of cigarettes a day for the past twelve years. . . .

Readers can easily follow the writer's progression of ideas because he's repeated the key mapping terms from the opening paragraph. He also uses the term *example* or *for instance* to label all but one of his examples. These signposts aren't accidental; the writer added several while revising the argument—and then revised further to make the writing graceful and clear.

Follow-Up Activity: Shaping Ideas Around a Point and Examining Your Organization

Take a few days to experiment with composing and revising a draft of your argument, especially if you need to develop the thesis by exploring more than one experience or interviewing another person. At some stage in the process, compose a statement of the central point, a road map of your main ideas, and signposts throughout your paper. (You'll probably add or revise several or all of these matters numerous times later.) Decide at least tentatively what parts of the experiences you include to summarize, what to develop through specific facts and quotations, and what to exclude altogether.

Collaborative Activity: Reconsidering and Revising Your Argument (30 minutes of class time)

Before composing the final draft of your paper, read it aloud twice to a group of several classmates—or to a single partner. Record (or let someone else record) the group's or partner's responses to the following Postdraft Analysis questions. Look at the listeners' responses later, record your own, and consider these reactions when you revise.

Postdraft Analysis
(To be completed by the writer or peer reader)

1. Reread the first paragraph of the argument, and then stop to let your audience (or yourself) predict what will come. List those predictions. Now read the remainder of the paper, putting a check mark next to the predictions it fulfilled. If any predictions weren't fulfilled, consider whether they should be.

2. What problem does the first paragraph construct for its intended audience? If the problem is not clear, how might it be better constructed?

3. What roadmapping of the argument does the first paragraph provide? Identify the main points of the journey throughout the paper. Are they clearly indicated? Do they follow the roadmap in the first paragraph? If there are any problems, indicate them with bracketed notes in the margins of the paper.

4. Would the progression of your argument benefit from a change in the sequence of ideas? If so, indicate the new order by numbering the ideas in brackets.

5. Underline the first and last sentences of each paragraph and then examine these sentences carefully. Are the connections between the ideas of paragraphs unclear in any places in the draft? If so, add words that explain the relationships. Are additional signposts needed in spots? If so, indicate where with bracketed labels.

6. Look again at the main ideas throughout the paper. Are there places in the draft where you should elaborate upon ideas or add examples? Identify these places with bracketed labels.

7. Does the conclusion let readers know what you expect them to do or think? Are these expectations realistic? If not, how might the conclusion be changed? Note these changes in brackets on the paper.

8. Examine the paraphrases, quotes, and summaries. Are they placed effectively? If not, identify with brackets the places where they should be changed, expanded, shortened, or reworded.

Concluding Activity: Revising and Editing Your Story

Consider the responses to the Postdraft Analysis questions, and then do a final revision of the story. Add and rearrange material, reword ideas, clarify connections between ideas and events, and edit the paper carefully for matters of mechanics, grammar, and spelling.

UNIT II

Writing from Expanded Experience

Chapter 8

Making and Supporting Claims

By now, you've strengthened your writing voice while composing from experience—yours or another's, but in either case first-hand encounters with what you've done, seen, or heard. You've enlivened your writing with pertinent facts, dialogue, oppositions, and fast-paced, tight sentences. You've shaped your writings around a central point that constructs a problem for readers. You've learned to anticipate and respond to the concerns of your readers, and you've employed roadmapping techniques that help readers navigate the journey your writing will take. You've reported on the experiences of others, and you've written summaries of their ideas.

But not all writing relies on personal experience. In school or at work, you must also write explanatory or persuasive themes, letters, articles, or memos on subjects outside your immediate experience, based in part on material drawn from books, articles, and research. Although such objective writing is both necessary and important, many students encounter temporary paralysis of mind and voice in their first attempts. They may revert to old bad habits of writing "about" a subject but making no point, of assembling quotes and data for no apparent reason. Their writing may even deteriorate into a series of awkward, sweeping generalizations in underdeveloped paragraphs as they pursue a "what-do-I-say next?" strategy.

These problems needn't persist, however, if you take ownership of the subject matter. You should read, discuss, and challenge other people's ideas and data—integrating or contrasting them with your own—until you form a viewpoint you can articulate and develop confidently, gracefully, and specifically. You needn't abandon narration, either, for you can still employ stories to support your claims. (You'll see examples of such narrative support later in the chapter.)

In short, you can comfortably compose an argument—an attempt to influence others to accept your claims or act as you recommend. Indeed, all writing, including narration, is argument to some degree. Even the old clichéd topic of "what I did on my summer vacation" typically makes (or implies) the claim that the vacation was fun, then backs up the claim with facts, examples, and explanations. Any argument is also a dialogue with an audience. You support and explain your claims in response to objections, counterarguments, demands for proof, and questions you anticipate from readers. As in a well-written story, the implicit dialogue in argument creates tension from the interplay of the thesis, antithesis, and synthesis discussed in Chapter 5, as well as creating suspense. How will the argument come out, and who will win? Objective writing should be neither abstract nor dull. It's a spirited attempt to express your personal viewpoints and influence your readers to accept them.

Where there is much desire to learn, there of necessity will be much arguing, much writing, many opinions; for opinion in good men is but knowledge in the making.

—*John Milton*

LOOKING AT THE TOULMIN MODEL

Probably the most useful model for understanding and constructing arguments was introduced in 1958 by Stephen E. Toulmin, a British mathematician and professor of philosophy. In his view, an argument consists of five major parts: the claim, its qualifiers, the support for the claim, the reasons behind it, and the rebuttal of counterarguments. We'll examine most of Toulmin's model here but postpone the discussion of the rebuttal until a later chapter.

The Claim

The claim is an assertion or conclusion you need to prove. There are three basic types: *fact, value,* and *policy.*[*] The claim of *fact*—that something does, did, or will exist—is often supported by other facts that readers probably wouldn't challenge. Here are some examples from writings you'll read later in this chapter:

I know lots of men who are full-time lawyers, doctors, editors, and the like.

—Anna Quindlen

There seems to be something about sports that causes grown men to lose their maturity.

—Sidney Porter

---

[*]These terms come from Annette T. Rottenberg's adaptation of Toulmin in *Elements of Argument,* 3rd Edition (New York: Bedford Books, 1991) pp. 10–11.

The second type is a claim of *value*—that one thing is better or worse than another, morally right or wrong, worthless or worthwhile. These examples are also taken from the writings you'll see later:

> I think women are superior to men.
>
> —Anna Quindlen

> The rivalry is good for college basketball.
>
> —Sidney Porter

> Gene Keady. . . is looking at a well-deserved suspension. . . .
>
> —Sidney Porter

The third is a claim of *policy*—a suggestion or recommendation on how to solve a problem. This claim typically employs the verb *should, must,* or *ought to,* as in, for instance, "Good, affordable health care ought to be available for all citizens." A rhetorical question—that is, a question to which the answer is obvious—can also argue for a policy, as in this example:

> Why not let the players have a say in this matter?
>
> —Sidney Porter

The Qualifiers

Since many issues are too complex to be covered by a blanket statement of right versus wrong or good versus evil, claims often include *qualifiers*—acknowledgments of exceptions. For instance, a claim that college tuition should be lowered might cite as exceptions the tuition fees of students from families with very high incomes. Or a claim that no one should be allowed to carry handguns would probably exempt the police in high-crime areas. Here's another example from Anna Quindlen's argument for the "natural" superiority of women you'll read later. She begins by claiming that men should be eligible for the same jobs as women, backs up the claim with an example, and then qualifies (or at least states her reservations about) the example:

> I would fight for the right of any laid-off sanitation man to work, for example, at the gift-wrap counter at Macy's, *even though any woman knows that men are hormonally incapable of wrapping packages or tying bows.*

Similar to qualifiers are *reservations*—special instances in which the claims would not apply. Quindlen, for instance, acknowledges the following reservation:

> I keep hearing that there's a new breed of men out there who don't talk about helping a woman as though they're doing you a favor and who do seriously consider leaving the office if a child comes down with a fever at school, rather than assuming that you will leave yours.

But she then quickly refutes the reservation by asserting that it rarely applies:

> But from what I've seen, there aren't enough of these men to qualify as a breed, only as a subgroup.

The Support

I'm not the one for putting off the proof.
Let it be overwhelming.

—Robert Frost

The *support*—or backing—for claims is the proof you furnish: facts, figures, experiences (often little stories), the opinions of experts, and even appeals to the attitudes and values of readers. Here are examples of claims and their support:

> There seems to be something about sports that causes grown men to lose their maturity. [claim] *How many times have we seen or heard head coaches having a fit over a blown call, a missed play, or lack of fan support?* [support]

—Sidney Porter

> Come to think of it, I can't think of any job women don't do. [claim] ... *I know lots of women who are full-time lawyers and part-time interior decorators, pastry chefs, algebra teachers, and garbage slingers.* [support]

—Anna Quindlen

The Warrant

The warrant is a statement of *why*. It shows how the evidence supports the claim, especially if the connections between claim and support aren't clear.[*]

---

[*]Thus, police seek a *search warrant* when some evidence that a crime was committed justifies the search. And we say a claim that cannot be supported is *unwarranted*.

For instance, you might cite statistics on the numbers of infant deaths in this country to back up the claim, "We must lower the infant mortality rate." But for those statistics to be meaningful—to warrant (or justify) our concern—you probably should compare them to the much lower rates of infant deaths found in most other industrialized countries.

The more that readers don't understand an issue—or hold views contrary to yours—the more you must explain the connections between your claims and support. A familiar and controversial topic should illustrate the point. Writers who advocate outlawing abortions often cite the growing numbers of abortions performed as evidence of the problem. But these numbers are meaningless unless skeptical readers can be persuaded to accept (1) that life begins at conception; (2) that ending such life is therefore murder; and (3) that government must prevent this rapidly increasing murder rate. Conversely, supporters of abortion rights should probably attempt to convince opponents (1) that life begins only at birth (or at a late stage of development of the fetus); (2) that ending a pregnancy is a personal choice and private matter; and (3) that government should not interfere with people's rights to choice and privacy. However, these warrants are also claims—and controversial ones at that—so they may also require backing (a medical definition of when life begins, for example).

Since our purpose is not to argue about abortion but to examine the nature of warrants, let's look at warrants for less controversial claims. These examples also show that the order of claim, warrant, and backing can vary. A writer may make a claim and then support and explain it, or she may present and explain some information that leads into the claim.

Scheffler leads the nation in field goal percentage. [evidence] *Because of his physical strength, he so dominates opposing centers and maintains position so close to the basket,* [warrant] how could he not make 75% of his shots? [claim]

—Sidney Porter

The other day a very wise friend of mine asked: "Have you ever noticed that what passes as a terrific man would only be an adequate woman?" [evidence] A Roman candle went off in my head; she was absolutely right. [claim] *What I expect from my male friends is that they are polite and clean. What I expect from my female friends is unconditional love, the ability to finish my sentences for me when I am sobbing, a complete and total willingness to pour their hearts out to me, and the ability to tell me why the meat thermometer isn't supposed to touch the bone.* [warrant]

—Anna Quindlen

The following clustering diagram should help you visualize the relation-ships among the parts of the Toulmin model:

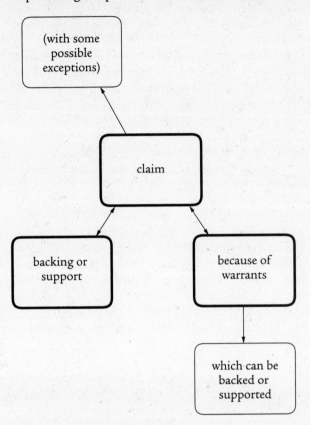

LOOKING AT ARGUMENTS

Here are the full texts of the arguments you've already read in bits and pieces. The first, written by a student, establishes a familiar relationship with us through his informal yet authoritative voice, his use of the first-person-plural *we*, and his frequent questioning of us. That informal context allows him to support many of his claims with short stories.

THE CRYING GAME

Forget athletic shoes, car dealerships, or supermarkets. The only true product for coaches to endorse is tissue. How about this? Purdue basketball coach, Gene Keady, is in the midst of one of his many tirades over an official's call, when just as he is about to lose it all, one of his players hands him a Kleenex and tells him everything will be all right.

Now that is reality. When we view a commercial, we look for sincerity from the product and spokesperson. What would be more real than a commercial for tissue featuring the biggest crybabies of all, head coaches?

There seems to be something about sports that causes grown men to lose their maturity. How many times have we seen or heard head coaches having a fit over a blown call, a missed play, or lack of fan support? How coaches make it from game to game without a heart specialist by their side is a miracle. Lucky there are not microphones placed on the sidelines, dugouts, and benches. Seeing these guys pitch-a-bitch alone is enough to get sporting events an R-rating (R for ridiculous).

Gene Keady, already reprimanded once this year for senseless tirades over officials' calls, is looking at a well-deserved suspension, not for his predictable and immature behavior during a game between his Purdue team and Illinois, but what happened after.

Keady confronted the Illinois assistant coach, Mark Coomes, in the tunnel leading to the teams' locker rooms. Keady, who did not care for the physical play of Illini center, Rodney Jones, against Purdue center, Steve Scheffler, reportedly told Coomes: "You'd better kick Jones' _ _ _, because if you don't, I will!"

Little did mean Gene know that Rodney Jones was standing right behind him. No punches were thrown, luckily for Keady or he would have gone from living legend to a dead one!

With this second infraction of the Big Ten's "unsportsmanlike conduct" clause, Keady is a sure bet for some type of suspension. What makes this incident more ridiculous is the fact that Keady was crying over the physical treatment that Scheffler received.

If you are unfamiliar with Mr. Scheffler, let me introduce you. Scheffler stands about 6'9" and weighs 250 pounds, 250 pounds of muscle. If for some reason Scheffler does not make it in the NBA, any NFL team would welcome him with open arms.

Scheffler leads the nation in field goal percentage. Because of his physical strength, he so dominates opposing centers and maintains position so close to the basket, how could he not make 75% of his shots?

With Jones finally giving Scheffler the kind of physical match he needed, he was less effective; thus Purdue lost the game. If I were Gene Keady, I would hope that none of the other Big Ten coaches took notice of this.

Then there is the case of Arizona's Lute Olson, front runner for the 1992 Olympic basketball coach's position and widely recognized as a winner. But before we christen him with sainthood, let's discuss the matter of UNLV (the University of Nevada Las Vegas).

It seems that Olson's Arizona team has endured one too many butt kickings by UNLV. After the most recent whipping, Olson had a tantrum and said he was ending the series between the teams. When asked why (as if it wasn't obvious) Olson said he did not have to give a reason.

Doesn't this sound like a child on the playground who, when he does not win at a game, would threaten to take his ball and go home if he is not allowed to win? The rivalry is good for college basketball. Arizona and UNLV are, without a doubt, the top two programs year after year in the West.

Why not let the players have a say in this matter? Correct me if I am wrong, but isn't it the players who are putting it on the line by playing UNLV? This appears to be another case of a coach thinking he is the team. Lute, buddy, can you honestly say that if your team had beaten UNLV in last year's tournament or in last week's game, you would still want to end the series? Be a big boy, go regroup the troops, and say yes to another series that will further expose just how weak you really are.

—Sidney Porter

The second argument, by syndicated columnist Anna Quindlen, is unabashedly personal, although it addresses an important national issue. Writing informally in the first person, she employs humor to gain our allegiance and supports many claims with stories from her own experience.

———

WOMEN ARE JUST BETTER

My favorite news story so far this year was the one saying that in England scientists are working on a way to allow men to have babies. I'd buy tickets to that. I'd be happy to stand next to any man I know in one of those labor rooms the size of a Volkswagen trunk and whisper, "No, dear, you don't really need the Demerol; just relax and do your second-stage breathing." It puts me in mind of an old angry feminist slogan: "If men got pregnant, abortion would be a sacrament." I think this is specious. If men got pregnant, there would be safe, reliable methods of birth control. They'd be inexpensive, too.

I can almost hear some of you out there thinking that I do not like men. This isn't true. I have been married for some years to a man and I hope that someday our two sons will grow up to be men. All three of my brothers are men, as is my father. Some of my best friends are men. It is simply that I think women are superior to men.

There, I've said it. It is my dirty little secret. We're not supposed to say it because in the old days men used to say that women were superior. What they meant was that we were too wonderful to enter courtrooms, enjoy sex, or worry our minds about money. Obviously, this is not what I mean at all.

The other day a very wise friend of mine asked: "Have you ever noticed that what passes as a terrific man would only be an adequate woman?" A Roman candle went off in my head; she was absolutely right. What I expect from my male friends is that they are polite and clean. What I expect from my female friends is unconditional love, the ability to finish my sentences for me when I am sobbing, a complete and total willingness to pour their hearts out to me, and the ability to tell me why the meat thermometer isn't supposed to touch the bone.

The inherent superiority of women came to mind just the other day when I was reading about sanitation workers. New York City has finally hired women to pick up the garbage, which makes sense to me, since, as I've discovered, a good bit of being a woman consists of picking up garbage. There was a story about the hiring of these female sanitation workers, and I was struck by the fact that I could have written that story without ever leaving my living room—a reflection not upon the quality of the reporting but the predictability of the male sanitation workers' responses.

The story started by describing the event, and then the two women, who were just your average working women trying to make a buck and get by. There was something about all the maneuvering that had to take place before they could be hired, and then there were the obligatory quotes from male sanitation workers about how women were incapable of doing the job. They were similar to quotes I have read over the years suggesting that women are not fit to be rabbis, combat soldiers, astronauts, firefighters, judges, ironworkers, and President of the United States. Chief among them was a comment from one sanitation worker, who said it just wasn't our kind of job, that women were cut out to do dishes and men were cut out to do yard work.

As a woman who has done dishes, yard work, and tossed a fair number of Hefty bags, I was peeved—more so because I would fight for the right of any laid-off sanitation man to work, for example, at the gift-wrap counter at Macy's, even though any woman knows that men are hormonally incapable of wrapping packages or tying bows.

I simply can't think of any jobs any more that women can't do. Come to think of it, I can't think of any job women don't do. I know lots of men who are full-time lawyers, doctors, editors and the like. And I know lots of women who are full-time lawyers and part-time interior decorators, pastry chefs, algebra teachers, and garbage slingers. Women are the glue that holds our day-to-day world together.

Maybe the sanitation workers who talk about the sex division of duties are talking about girls just like the girls that married dear old dad. Their day is done. Now lots of women know that if they don't carry the garbage bag to the curb, it's not going to get carried—either because they're single, or their husband is working a second job, or he's staying at the office until midnight, or he just left them.

I keep hearing that there's a new breed of men out there who don't talk about helping a woman as though they're doing you a favor and who do seriously consider leaving the office if a child comes down with a fever at school, rather than assuming that you will leave yours. But from what I've seen, there aren't enough of these men to qualify as a breed, only as a subgroup.

This all sounds angry; it is. After a lifetime spent with winds of sexual change buffeting me this way and that, it still makes me angry to read the same dumb quotes with the same dumb stereotypes that I was reading when I was eighteen. It makes me angry to realize that after so much change, very little is different. It makes me angry to think that these two female sanitation workers will spend their days doing a job most of their co-workers think they can't handle, and then they will go home and do another job most of their co-workers don't want.

Issues for Investigation and Discussion

1. Sidney Porter begins his argument with a story about a coach being given a tissue by one of his players. What is the point of this story—that is, what

claim does it support?

2. Cite three or four claims made by Porter. What kind of backing does he provide for each?

3. Although Porter probably assumes that his audience is familiar with college basketball, he doesn't assume complete familiarity. When does he explain and support his claims with background information and warrants?

4. At several points, Porter compares college basketball coaches to children. Where? Why?

5. Late in his argument, Porter mentions that the reason behind Lute Olson's behavior is "obvious." What is that warrant?

6. Unlike Porter, who implies his point through rhetorical questions, Anna Quindlen states hers directly. What is her point and where does she state it?

7. Quindlen claims that she is angry. Is that how you would characterize her tone? What evidence would suggest that she makes some claims with tongue in cheek?

8. The two writers often back up their claims with short narratives, but the nature, source, and treatment of the material differ. Compare and contrast these differences. How is each writer's choice of support appropriate to his or her argument?

9. Based on your answers to these questions and any other matters you observe, turn to your journal or computer file and list six or more common traits of effective arguments (or create a list with several classmates). Let this list guide you as you compose and revise your own argument later.

GENERATING YOUR OWN ARGUMENT

Here's how you might utilize Toulmin's scheme during the invention stage of composing an argument. Suppose that faculty and students at your college are debating whether to abolish required courses. You want to argue your case for eliminating such courses in a letter to the editors of the college newspaper. Before composing a first draft, you could explore your reasoning through a clustering diagram. For example, your research into the issue might have suggested to you that many students soon forget information from courses outside their majors or fields of interest. You could make that claim and back it up with statistics and stories from your own and other people's experience:

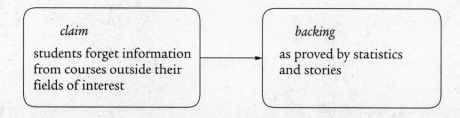

claim

students forget information from courses outside their fields of interest

backing

as proved by statistics and stories

However, since you realize that college administrators won't necessarily understand *why* students might forget such information, you might also consider the warrant behind the claim—your assumption that people retain only what they want or need to know. Thus:

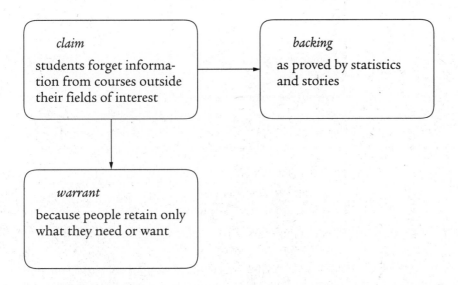

If you think that administrators won't accept this warrant (which is also a claim), you might look for additional backing—perhaps further statistics and stories. Now your clustering diagram will look like this:

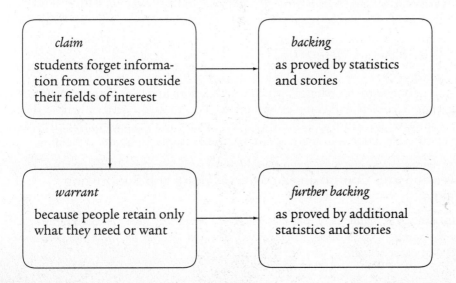

After further consideration, you may think of exceptions to your arguments. For example, some students—geniuses and highly motivated persons—retain much of anything they learn. By predicting and acknowledging this objection, you may be able to soften your audience's resistance to your argument:

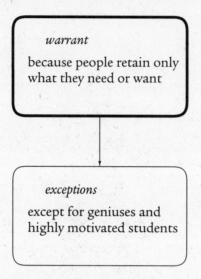

warrant

because people retain only what they need or want

exceptions

except for geniuses and highly motivated students

Fine. You've outlined a neat, logical argument—which persuades your fellow students who, for example, hate physical science anyway. But the Board of Governors at your college might reply like this:

1. Shouldn't we seek ways to better motivate students so they retain what they learn?

2. How can students know what they want until they've been exposed to a variety of subjects?

3. And what do we do with all the professors we've hired to teach the required courses, and how can we staff our college when we can't predict what students will want to learn?

These are issues for rebuttal, which you'll explore in a later chapter that deals with more complete and complex arguments. For now, you need only note that the rebuttal requires further backing of claims, explanation of reasoning, and backing of the explanations—in short, additional thinking, planning, and explaining.

Invention and Composing Activity: Making and Supporting Claims

(Alternatively or additionally, you may follow the procedures found in the Writing in a Social Context section that begins on p. 107. These procedures will help you here and with subsequent activities.)

Choose two or three issues of national concern with which you've had some first-hand experience or know about from the experiences of others. These topics might address access to health care; effects of TV violence, guns, and drug use; problems in education (from elementary school through college); problems of single-parent households; problems with jobs; problems with money; role models for children; or women's or men's roles. Do free writing, brainstorming, or looping (or simply think about the issue) until you've arrived at the central point you'd make about each issue.

If possible, meet with several classmates and do the following:

- Take turns reading each statement of point aloud, solicit each other's opinions about the ideas you find most interesting, and select one to explore fully. (Choose by yourself if you cannot meet with classmates.)
- Then turn to your journal for ten minutes and list four or five claims (with qualifiers) that develop the point. List one or more examples to support or illustrate each claim.
- When you've finished, read your work aloud to members of your group, and listen to their suggestions concerning (1) the clarity and validity of your point; (2) the relevance of your claims to the point; (3) the qualifiers to your claims; (4) the examples to support or illustrate each claim; (5) the inclusion of additional claims; and (6) the order in which they might be presented. (Short predicting sessions following the reading of each claim might be useful here.) Record the suggestions of your group members in your journal without responding or trying to defend yourself. (Examine your paper for these matters by yourself if you cannot meet with your group.)
- Finally, spend a few more minutes with your journal, jotting down ideas about additional claims that develop your main point and the backing you'll use for each of these claims.

With or without the group's help, consider further ways of supporting your claims. Look for specifics: personal experiences, the experiences of others, stories or events in the news, and whatever facts you can supply without library research. Record your notes of these investigations in your journal also. Then compose a first draft of the argument. If the writing becomes too difficult, take some time off to contemplate your ideas, or consider choosing another topic from your initial list.

Before composing the first draft, you may wish to explore your ideas through a clustering diagram like the ones illustrating the Toulmin model earlier in the chapter. Begin with a claim and then draw lines to indicate the backing, warrants, backing for the warrants, and exceptions to the claim. Each claim and its support may require a separate diagram.

Collaborative Activity: Providing Warrants

Play the "Why?" or "Yes-but-*why?*" games with your group (or by yourself), challenging the claims and backing you produced in the first collaborative activity. In the "Why?" game, demand a warrant (a *because* statement) for each claim. In the "Yes-but-*why?*" game, probe further, demanding an explanation of the underlying assumptions for a claim that the writer might otherwise take for granted. (You might challenge claims even further in the "Says-who?" and "How-do-I-know-it's true?" games, each testing the validity of and connections between the supporting material and the claims.) Each game should take no more than ten minutes.

Record your responses to the games in your journal, and decide which matters you must address in your argument.

Composing Activity: Writing Your Argument

After organizing your ideas through whatever invention techniques you choose, write a first draft of your argument and read it to your group. As usual, read the paper twice, record the responses of the group on the following Postdraft Analysis questions, and respond to the group's responses later. Take additional notes, and consider what changes to make as you revise. Then write a second draft of the paper.

Postdraft Analysis
(To be completed by the writer or peer reader)

1. Locate the sentence or sentences that establish a problem for the intended audience. Is the problem clearly established? Valid? If not, how might this material be revised?

2. Look at each major claim. Is each sufficiently backed by relevant facts, examples, or incidents? If not, identify with bracketed labels where additional backing might be supplied. Do any claims need further qualification? If so, indicate where in brackets.

3. What are the warrants for each claim? Do any need further explanation or development? If so, identify with bracketed labels where warrants might be added or expanded.

4. Who seems to be the intended audience for this argument? What reasonable questions of that audience does the argument address? Should it address any others? Are the responses to the questions effective and clear?

5. Identify the main outlines of the argument. Are they logical and clear? If not, how might ideas be rearranged? Identify with bracketed labels where connections between ideas might be strengthened.

6. Is the language clear, direct, and natural? If not, identify with bracketed labels where it should be reworded or tightened.

7. Do any other problems need to be addressed? If so, how?

Concluding Activity: Revising and Editing Your Argument

Assemble all your notes and then rewrite your argument, establishing a logical structure; roadmapping the structure in the opening paragraph; showing the connections between all the parts by repeating key mapping terms throughout; tightening the sentences; sharpening the details; and editing it carefully for matters of mechanics, grammar, and spelling.

WRITING IN A SOCIAL CONTEXT: DEALING WITH URBAN RENEWAL

The following activity is the first of many you'll find in each of the remaining chapters of this book. The activity simulates a real situation in which you and your classmates can gain first-hand experience, devise arguments, debate the issues, and then communicate your ideas in writing. You'll read the material provided before coming to class, choose one of four roles to play, and then present your case in an open meeting. The entire activity should require no more than forty-five to seventy-five minutes, divided as follows:

- five minutes for choosing roles
- ten to fifteen minutes for determining strategy
- twenty to forty minutes to present arguments
- ten to fifteen minutes for rebuttal

After choosing or being assigned to a group representing one of the four roles, you and the other group members will meet to discuss the claims, backing, and reasoning you'll present, based on the materials provided and any stories (real or imagined) you devise. Then your instructor will convene the whole class, first allowing each group five to ten minutes to make its case, followed by ten minutes or so of give-and-take among the groups. (You needn't negotiate and resolve the conflict in this instance, but you will do so in activities in later chapters of this book.) Finally, again within your role, you will compose a written argument addressed to a specified audience.

Alternatively, you may simply read through the materials and discuss them in class before composing an argument within one of the four roles.

The Context

Until a few years ago, Lakeside, an inner-city neighborhood in a large American city, was teeming with unemployment, poverty, gang membership, crime, burned-out buildings, and large numbers of welfare recipients, many of whom were single parents. However, after developers began to renovate and "gentrify" the buildings in the Lakeside neighborhood—replacing current residents with middle- to upper-middle-class tenants who pay much higher rents and create stability—conditions have gradually improved. Among the prime candidates for renovation is the Marlboro, a privately-owned, government-subsidized apartment complex. Once an elegant collection of three hundred spacious and stately apartments, the complex has deteriorated so badly that the owners want to sell it to developers who would modernize and gentrify it. Because of the government subsidy, city officials must approve the sale.

The Marlboro's current residents—all poor or working class—welcome the renovation plans, but strongly oppose any attempt at gentrification. Many displaced families would have difficulty finding new apartments in the area, which already suffers from a shortage of low-income housing. These families have tales to tell about past struggles to find decent, affordable places to live.

Two community groups have lined up on either side of the issue: one group (mostly poor and working-class people) proposing that government-sponsored and private programs provide the opportunity for tenants to purchase and renovate the property themselves; and the other group (mostly middle-class or upper-middle class people) supporting the gentrification and displacement effort.

Because the developers are seeking waivers of some requirements concerning government subsidies and relocation of low-income residents, the City Housing Commission has jurisdiction over the issue. Furthermore, because the issue has already generated a great deal of publicity, the Commission has called a special public meeting at the local YMCA at which all parties will present their cases. The Commission has also asked that, following the meeting, all participants submit written arguments to the Commission, although many participants plan to write directly to the mayor as well.

The Participants

The Developer.   You would like to purchase, refurbish, and then rent the three hundred apartments in the complex at rates that would yield a reasonable profit. Well aware that such projects have not succeeded everywhere, you are nevertheless willing to accept the risk, for you are an entrepreneur who believes in free enterprise. While you are somewhat sympathetic to the plight of the current residents, you believe that gentrification is both worthwhile and necessary as it revitalizes the inner city. And, of course, you invite any of the current residents to remain, provided they can pay the rent.

Resident of the Apartment Complex.   Although poor or working class, you'd of course like to live in clean, safe, and stable conditions. Thus, you welcome the attempt to refurbish the apartment complex but fear for your family's welfare if you must move. Your life has not been easy, and you have already suffered frequent dislocations. You would like to be part of a group that buys and revitalizes the complex but have no idea how to do so.

Member of Community Group 1.   A young professional with a family, you support the efforts of the developers, for you recently took the risk of renting or buying an apartment in Lakeside and would like to see further improvements in safety, schools, retail stores, and basic services. You are committed to living in the city, but fear to walk in your own neighborhood at night.

Member of Community Group 2.   Like the members of the first community group, you also are committed to living in the city, but you are poor or working class. Unwilling to sit by idly while the three hundred families are exiled from their apartments, you not only oppose the developers but are willing to support any community-based effort to buy and renovate the buildings.

The Facts

1. Only ten minutes by car or public transportation from the downtown area, Lakeside attracts professionals who work downtown. Furthermore, although gentrification would at least double the rents in the complex (currently $350 for a two-bedroom apartment), they would still average far less than in the more fashionable neighborhoods of the city.

2. Many of the deteriorated apartments in Lakeside, which was once an upper-class residential community, have architectural and historical significance.

3. A single parent of two children receives approximately $500 a month in welfare payments and food stamps worth an additional $150.

4. In other renovated and gentrified buildings in Lakeside, the population is racially and ethnically mixed, unlike most buildings in this highly segregated minority neighborhood. Many middle-class African Americans and Hispanics who had previously left Lakeside have returned.

5. Other cities (Portland, Minneapolis, and Denver) have successfully stabilized and rehabilitated formerly deteriorating neighborhoods through programs of subsidized housing and community-based projects to improve education, family services, public safety, and other key services. These programs, which have not displaced poor residents, have been supported both by governmental and private organizations.

6. Since 1973, South Shore Bank of Chicago has made loans to poor and working class families to buy and renovate their buildings and apartments. The bank has enjoyed substantial profits and serves as a model for programs throughout the country.

7. The formerly seedy Amsterdam Avenue in New York's Upper West Side has been gentrified; it now houses a mix of middle-class residents from all ethnic groups and contains thriving supper clubs, children's stores, and family restaurants. Rent and other prices are moderate.

8. The gentrification of Brooklyn's Park Slope area has failed. Crime, high taxes, urban problems, and recession have caused a number of refurbished buildings to be auctioned at half their original purchase prices.

9. In 1993, a tenant group in Chicago contracted to buy the 27-story Carmen-Marine Apartments in the Uptown neighborhood for approximately $10 million under terms of the 1990 National Affordable Housing Act. The purchase, the first of its kind in the country, was overseen by the United States Department of Housing and Urban Development (HUD). The building had originally been constructed as subsidized housing for

low- and moderate-income families and was about to become gentrified, thus doubling or tripling the $300–$400 rents. Under HUD's supervision, the building would first be rehabilitated and then converted to a co-op (in which all tenants are co-owners). Tenants purchased a share to the co-op for the equivalent of two months' rent, and their monthly payments toward the mortgage would equal their current rental payments.

10. Homelessness increased dramatically in the United States throughout the 1980s as the stock of affordable low-income housing declined. Among the homeless are many children who have been shunted from place to place as they seek food and shelter.

11. The rates of unemployment, school dropouts, drug abuse, prostitution, gang membership, robbery, burglary, and murder in Lakeside are among the highest in the city.

Short Composing Activity: Summarizing Other People's Arguments

Not everyone from your group was able to attend the meeting, so you promised to report on what the other groups discussed. Take minutes of the meeting, summarizing each important point the groups have presented, and then write a single-page summary of their main arguments and the support they offered. Be concise but clear while emphasizing the issues that are most important to members of your group.

Main Composing Activity: Writing Your Argument

Compose a letter to the City Housing Commission or the mayor, in which you reiterate your argument and support its claims with relevant facts and short stories. Don't try to rebut the arguments of the other groups; just make a straightforward and clear presentation of your side of the issue. At various stages in the composing and revising process, discuss your paper with members of your group. Follow the procedures (including the use of the Postdraft Analysis questions) introduced in this chapter.

Follow-Up Activity: Examining the Coherence of Your Argument

Read only the first sentence of your argument to your group members—and the mapping phrasing, if you've provided any. Then take notes of their predictions of what will follow. Repeat this procedure with the first sentence of every paragraph. Alternatively, simply write out the first sentence of each paragraph and conduct the examination yourself.

Also underline the first and last sentence of every paragraph and then examine whether the links between paragraphs are clear (that is, whether you've established a logical and coherent progression of ideas).

Chapter 9

Reporting on a Problem-Solving Process

A writer is not so much someone who has something to say as he is someone who has found a process that will bring about new things he would not have thought of if he had not started to say them.

—William Stafford

Report writing is an essential skill. Teachers report on students progress, scientists on experimental results, recording secretaries on committee actions, government officials on legislative changes, investment fund managers on profits or losses, census officials on societal trends, and so on. Readers of reports—whether corporate directors, doctors, lawyers, students, or interested lay people—are primarily information seekers. They appreciate a lively style but expect—even demand—clear, accurate summaries and explanations. Your task as a report writer, therefore, is to maximize the opportunity for your audience to acquire the information they seek.

That does not mean, however, that you must abandon narrative form in composing reports. Many reports tell a story of what people discovered, learned, or decided in an experiment, lecture, or meeting—emphasizing not only the solution to a problem but also the process involved in arriving there. The story begins by defining a problem, continues by exploring for a solution, and ends with the discovery of the solution itself. The exploration moves from question to answer to question until all the questions are answered. And along the way it helps readers comprehend the nuances of a complex issue that a simple summary of results cannot. Indeed, teachers of courses in mathematics and the sciences are increasingly assigning such reports to see how their students approach problem solving: what avenues they considered, abandoned, and followed.

LOOKING AT REPORTS

Here are two examples of problem-solving narrative reports. In the first, an article that appeared in *Harper's* magazine in 1975, Dr. Roy C. Selby, Jr., tells a lay audience the story of an operation—an attempt to solve a patient's medical problem. He describes a series of decisions and actions, each one in response to a further (and often unexpected) aspect of the problem and solution. Because he writes for nondoctors, Selby must not only narrate what he did and thought, but must also explain and define many terms and procedures.

A DELICATE OPERATION

In the autumn of 1973 a woman in her early fifties noticed, upon closing one eye while reading, that she was unable to see clearly. Her eyesight grew slowly worse. Changing her eyeglasses did not help. She saw an ophthalmologist, who found that her vision was seriously impaired in both eyes. She then saw a neurologist, who confirmed the finding and obtained X-rays of the skull and an EMI scan—a photograph of the patient's head. The latter revealed a tumor growing between the optic nerves at the base of the brain. The woman was admitted to the hospital by a neurosurgeon.

Further diagnosis, based on angiography, a detailed X-ray study of the circulatory system, showed the tumor to be about two inches in diameter and supplied by many small blood vessels. It rested beneath the brain, just above the pituitary gland, stretching the optic nerves to either side and intimately close to the major blood vessels supplying the brain. Removing it would pose many technical problems. Probably benign and slow-growing, it may have been present for several years. If left alone it would continue to grow and produce blindness and might become impossible to remove completely. Removing it, however, might not improve the patient's vision and could make it worse. A major blood vessel could be damaged, causing a stroke. Damage to the under-surface of the brain could cause impairment of memory and changes in mood and personality. The hypothalamus, a most important structure of the brain, could be injured, causing coma, high fever, bleeding from the stomach, and death.

The neurosurgeon met with the patient and her husband and discussed the various possibilities. The common decision was to operate.

The patient's hair was shampooed for two nights before surgery. She was given a cortisone-like drug to reduce the risk of damage to the brain during surgery. Five units of blood were cross-matched, as a contingency against hemorrhage. At 1:00 P.M. the operation began. After the patient was anesthetized her hair was completely clipped and shaved from the scalp. Her head was prepped with an organic iodine solution for ten minutes. Drapes were placed over her, leaving exposed only the forehead and crown of the skull. All the routine instruments were brought up—the electrocautery used to coagulate areas of bleeding, bipolar coagulation forceps to arrest bleeding from individual blood vessels without damaging adjacent tissues, and small suction tubes to remove blood and cerebrospinal fluid from the head, thus giving the surgeon a better view of the tumor and surrounding areas.

A curved incision was made behind the hairline so it would be concealed when the hair grew back. It extended almost from ear to ear. Plastic clips were applied to the cut edges of the scalp to arrest bleeding. The scalp was folded back to the level of the eyebrows. Incisions were made in the muscle of the right temple, and three sets of holes were drilled near the temple and the top of the head because the tumor had to be approached from directly in front. The drill, powered by nitrogen, was replaced with a fluted steel blade, and the holes were connected. The incised piece of skull was pried loose and held out of the way by a large sponge.

Beneath the bone is a yellowish leather-like membrane, the dura, that surrounds the brain. Down the middle of the head the dura carries a large vein, but in the area near the nose the vein is small. At that point the vein and dura were cut, and clips made of tantalum, a hard metal, were applied to arrest and prevent bleeding. Sutures were put into the dura and tied to the scalp to keep the dura open and retracted. A malleable silver retractor, resembling the blade of a butter knife, was inserted between the brain and skull. The anesthesiologist began to administer a drug to relax the brain by removing some of its water, making it easier for the surgeon to manipulate the retractor, hold the brain back, and see the tumor. The nerve tracts for smell were cut on both sides to provide additional room. The tumor was seen approximately two-and-one-half inches behind the base of the nose. It was pink in color. On touching it, it proved to be very fibrous and tough. A special retractor was attached to the skull, enabling the other retractor blades to be held automatically and freeing the surgeon's hands. With further displacement of the frontal lobes of the brain, the tumor could be seen better, but no normal structures—the carotid arteries, their branches, and the optic nerves—were visible. The tumor obscured them.

A surgical microscope was placed above the wound. The surgeon had selected the lenses and focal length prior to the operation. Looking through the microscope, he could see some of the small vessels supplying the tumor and he coagulated them. He incised the tumor to attempt to remove its core and thus collapse it, but the substance of the tumor was too firm to be removed in this fashion. He then began to slowly dissect the tumor from the adjacent brain tissue and from where he believed the normal structures to be.

Using small squares of cotton, he began to separate the tumor from very loose fibrous bands connecting it to the brain and to the right side of the part of the skull where the pituitary gland lies. The right optic nerve and carotid artery came into view, both displaced considerably to the right. The optic nerve had a normal appearance. He protected these structures with cotton compresses placed between them and the tumor. He began to raise the tumor from the skull and slowly to reach the point of its origin and attachment—just in front of the pituitary gland and medial to the left optic nerve, which still could not be seen. The small blood vessels entering the tumor were cauterized. The upper portion of the tumor was gradually separated from the brain, and the branches of the carotid arteries and the branches to the tumor were coagulated. The tumor was slowly and gently lifted from its bed, and for the first time the left carotid artery and optic nerve could be seen. Part of the tumor adhered to this nerve. The bulk of the tumor was amputated, leaving a small bit attached to the nerve. Very slowly and carefully the tumor fragment was resected.

The tumor now removed, a most impressive sight came into view—the pituitary gland and its stalk of attachment to the hypothalamus, the hypothalamus itself, and the brainstem, which conveys nerve impulses between the body and the brain. As far as could be determined, no damage had been done to these structures or other vital centers, but the left optic nerve, from chronic pressure of the tumor, appeared gray and thin. Probably it would not completely recover its function.

After making certain there was no bleeding, the surgeon closed the wounds and placed wire mesh over the holes in the skull to prevent dimpling of the scalp over the points that had been drilled. A gauze dressing was applied to the patient's head. She was awakened and sent to the recovery room.

Even with the microscope, damage might still have occurred to the cerebral cortex and hypothalamus. It would require at least a day to be reasonably certain there was none, and about seventy-two hours to monitor for the major postoperative dangers—swelling of the brain and blood clots forming over the surface of the brain. The surgeon explained this to the patient's husband, and both of them waited anxiously. The operation had required seven hours. A glass of orange juice had given the surgeon some additional energy during the closure of the wound. Though exhausted, he could not fall asleep until after two in the morning, momentarily expecting a call from the nurse in the intensive care unit announcing deterioration of the patient's condition.

At 8:00 A.M. the surgeon saw the patient in the intensive care unit. She was alert, oriented, and showed no sign of additional damage to the optic nerves or the brain. She appeared to be in better shape than the surgeon or her husband.

In this second example, paleontologist and professor of geology Stephen Jay Gould also tells a nonscientific audience the story of his attempt to solve a life-threatening medical problem, this time his own. But Gould's purpose goes far beyond explaining procedures.

THE MEDIAN ISN'T THE MESSAGE

My life has intersected, in a most personal way, two of Mark Twain's famous quips. One I shall defer to the end of this essay. The other (sometimes attributed to Disraeli) identifies three species of mendacity, each worse than the one before—lies, damned lies, and statistics.

Consider the standard example of stretching truth with numbers—a case quite relevant to my story. Statistics recognizes different measures of an "average," or central tendency. The *mean* represents our usual concept of an overall average—add up the items and divide them by the number of sharers (100 candy bars collected for five kids next Halloween will yield 20 for each in a fair world). The *median,* a different measure of central tendency, is the halfway point. If I line up five kids by height, the median child is shorter than two and taller than the other two (who might have trouble getting their mean share of the candy). A politician in power might say with pride, "The mean income of our citizens is $15,000 per year." The leader of the opposition might retort, "But half our citizens make less than $10,000 per year." Both are right, but neither cites a statistic with impassive objectivity. The first invokes a mean, the second a median. (Means are higher than medians in such cases because one millionaire may outweigh hundreds of poor people in setting a mean, but can balance only one mendicant in calculating a median.)

The larger issue that creates a common distrust or contempt for statistics is more troubling. Many people make an unfortunate and invalid separation between heart and mind, or feeling and intellect. In some contemporary traditions, abetted by attitudes stereotypically centered upon Southern California, feelings are exalted as more "real" and the only proper basis for action, while intellect gets short shrift as a hang-up of outmoded elitism. Statistics, in this absurd dichotomy, often becomes the symbol of the enemy. As Hilaire Belloc wrote, "Statistics are the triumph of the quantitative method, and the quantitative method is the victory of sterility and death."

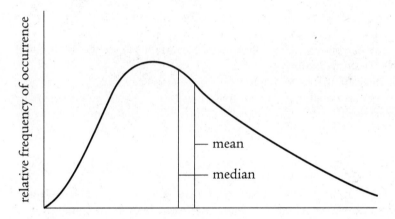

A RIGHT-SKEWED distribution showing that means must be higher than medians, and that the right side of the distribution extends out into a long tail. BEN GAMIT.

This is a personal story of statistics, properly interpreted, as profoundly nurturant and life-giving. It declares holy war on the downgrading of intellect by telling a small story to illustrate the utility of dry, academic knowledge about science. Heart and head are focal points of one body, one personality.

In July 1982, I learned that I was suffering from abdominal mesothelioma, a rare and serious cancer usually associated with exposure to asbestos. When I revived after surgery, I asked my first question of my doctor and chemotherapist

"What is the best technical literature about mesothelioma?" She replied, with a touch of diplomacy (the only departure she has ever made from direct frankness), that the medical literature contained nothing really worth reading.

Of course, trying to keep an intellectual away from literature works about as well as recommending chastity to *Homo sapiens,* the sexiest primate of all. As soon as I could walk, I made a beeline for Harvard's Countway medical library and punched mesothelioma into the computer's bibliographic search program. An hour later, surrounded by the latest literature on abdominal mesothelioma, I realized with a gulp why my doctor had offered that humane advice. The literature couldn't have been more brutally clear: Mesothelioma is incurable, with a median mortality of only eight months after discovery. I sat stunned for about fifteen minutes, then smiled and said to myself: So that's why they didn't give me anything to read. Then my mind started to work again, thank goodness.

If a little learning could ever be a dangerous thing, I had encountered a classic example. Attitude clearly matters in fighting cancer. We don't know why (from my old-style materialistic perspective, I suspect that mental states feed back upon the immune system). But match people with the same cancer for age, class, health, and socioeconomic status, and, in general, those with positive attitudes, with a strong will and purpose for living, with commitment to struggle, and with an active response to aiding their own treatment and not just a passive acceptance of anything doctors say, tend to live longer. A few months later I asked Sir Peter Medawar, my personal scientific guru and a Nobelist in immunology, what the best prescription for success against cancer might be. "A sanguine personality," he replied. Fortunately (since one can't reconstruct oneself at short notice and for a definite purpose), I am, if anything, even-tempered and confident in just this manner.

Hence the dilemma for humane doctors: Since attitude matters so critically, should such a somber conclusion be advertised, especially since few people have sufficient understanding of statistics to evaluate what the statements really mean? From years of experience with the small-scale evolution of Bahamian land snails treated quantitatively, I have developed this technical knowledge—and I am convinced that it played a major role in saving my life. Knowledge is indeed power, as Francis Bacon proclaimed.

The problem may be briefly stated: What does "median mortality of eight months" signify in our vernacular? I suspect that most people, without training in statistics, would read such a statement as "I will probably be dead in eight months"—the very conclusion that must be avoided, both because this formulation is false, and because attitude matters so much.

I was not, of course, overjoyed; but I didn't read the statement in this vernacular way either. My technical training enjoined a different perspective on "eight months median mortality." The point may seem subtle, but the consequences can be profound. Moreover, this perspective embodies the distinctive way of thinking in my own field of evolutionary biology and natural history.

We will carry the historical baggage of a Platonic heritage that seeks sharp essences and definite boundaries. (Thus we hope to find an unambiguous "beginning of life" or "definition of death," although nature often comes to us as irreducible continua.) This Platonic heritage, with its emphasis on clear distinctions and separated immutable entities, leads us to view statistical measures of central tendency wrongly, indeed opposite to the appropriate interpretation in our actual world of variation, shadings, and continua. In short, we view means and medians as hard "realities," and the variation that permits their calculation as a set of transient and imperfect measurements of this hidden essence. If the median is a reality and variation around the median just a device for calculation, then "I will probably be dead in eight months" may pass as a reasonable interpretation.

But all evolutionary biologists know that variation itself is nature's only irreducible essence. Variation is the hard reality, not a set of imperfect measures for a central tendency. Means and medians are the abstractions. Therefore, I looked at the mesothelioma statistics quite differently—and not only because I am an optimist who tends to see the doughnut instead of the hole, but primarily because I know that variation itself is the reality. I had to place myself amidst the variation.

When I learned about the eight-month median, my first intellectual reaction was: Fine, half the people will live longer; now what are my chances of being in that half. I read for a furious and nervous hour and concluded, with relief: damned good. I possessed every one of the characteristics conferring a probability of longer life: I was young; my disease had been recognized in a relatively early stage; I would receive the nation's best medical treatment; I had the world to live for; I knew how to read the data properly and not despair.

Another technical point then added even more solace. I immediately recognized that the distribution of variation about the eight-month median would almost surely be what statisticians call "right skewed." (In a symmetrical distribution, the profile of variation to the left of the tendency is a mirror image of the variation to the right. Skewed distributions are asymmetrical, with variation stretching out more in one direction than the other—left skewed if extended to the left, right skewed if stretched out to the right.) The distribution of variation had to be right skewed, I reasoned. After all, the left of the distribution contains an irrevocable lower boundary of zero (since mesothelioma can only be identified at death or before). Thus, little space exists for the distribution's lower (or left) half—it must be scrunched up between zero and eight months. But the upper (or right) half can extend out for years and years, even if nobody ultimately survives. This distribution must be right skewed, and I needed to know how long the extended tail ran—for I had already concluded that my favorable profile made me a good candidate for the right half of the curve.

The distribution was, indeed, strongly right skewed, with a long tail (however small) that extended for several years above the eight-month median. I saw no reason why I shouldn't be in that small tail, and I breathed a very long sigh of relief. My technical knowledge had helped. I had read the graph correctly. I had asked the right question and found the answers. I had obtained, in all probability, that most precious of all possible gifts in the circumstances—substantial time. I didn't have to stop and immediately follow Isaiah's injunction to Hezekiah—set thine house in order: for thou shalt die, and not live. I would have time to think, to plan, and to fight.

One final point about statistical distributions. They apply only to a prescribed set of circumstances—in this case to survival with mesothelioma under conventional modes of treatment. If circumstances change, the distribution may alter. I was placed on an experimental protocol of treatment and, if fortune holds, will be in the first cohort of a new distribution with high median and a right tail extending to death by natural causes at advanced old age.*

It has become, in my view, a bit too trendy to regard the acceptance of death as something tantamount to intrinsic dignity. Of course I agree with the preacher of Ecclesiastes that there is a time to love and a time to die—and when my skein runs out I hope to face the end calmly and in my own way. For most situations, however, I prefer the more martial view that death is the ultimate enemy—and I find nothing reproachable in those who rage mightily against the dying of the light.

The swords of battle are numerous, and none more effective than humor. My death was announced at a meeting of my colleagues in Scotland, and I almost experienced the delicious pleasure of reading my obituary penned by one of my best friends (the so-and-so got suspicious and checked; he too is a statistician, and didn't expect to find me so far out on the left tail). Still, the incident provided my first good laugh after the diagnosis. Just think, I almost got to repeat Mark Twain's most famous line of all: The reports of my death are greatly exaggerated. **

Issues for Investigation and Discussion

1. Although Roy C. Selby, Jr., clearly is narrating his personal experiences, he chooses to discuss them in the third person—probably a result of his training in "objective" report writing. Does he express any subjective reactions, though? How might your perceptions of the experiences have changed if Selby had related them in the first person?

2. Stephen Jay Gould, writing in *Natural History,* a scientific magazine intended for nonscientists, tells his story in the first person. Why?

3. What is the purpose of each report? What problem does each construct for its readers? Discuss the tone of each writer as it relates to his purpose and audience.

4. Most of Selby's readers wouldn't understand medical terms. How has Selby dealt with this problem? Gould also defines terms for his nonscientific audience. How does his method of defining terms differ from Selby's? Why are Gould's definitions longer?

5. Selby takes readers step by step through the process of an operation. The details could have been dry and unexciting to nonscientists. How does he create tension?

---

*So far so good.

**Since writing this, my death has actually been reported in two European magazines, five years apart. *Fama volat* (and lasts a long time). I squawked very loudly both times and demanded a retraction: guess I don't have Mr. Clemen's *savoir faire.*

6. Only in the fourth paragraph does Gould begin his personal story. Why does he delay? Then at several points in the narrative Gould digresses from the story to discuss other matters. Why?

7. Since the primary purpose of a report is to convey information, many reports reveal their main findings or conclusions in the opening paragraph. Where do Selby and Gould discuss their main findings? Why?

8. Based on your answers to these questions and any other matters you observe, turn to your journal or computer file and list at least six common traits of reports on a problem-solving process (or create a list with several classmates). Let this list guide you as you compose and revise your own report later.

COMPOSING A PROCESS REPORT

Although process analysis often tells readers how to *do* something (make lasagna, or operate a VCR, for example), your goal is to help readers *understand* the process of solving a problem. You do not expect them to perform the process themselves. Whether you announce the solution at the beginning or end of your final draft is less important than your explanation of how you reached the solution. Your report will probably address the following issues, based on your audience's knowledge of and familiarity with the subject:

- constructing the problem (and perhaps summarizing the solution)
- backgrounding the problem
- defining unfamiliar terms
- describing the steps toward reaching the solution
- showing the relationship among the steps
- describing the solution

We'll address each of these in turn.

Invention Activity: Exploring Topics for Your Report (10 minutes of class time)

(Alternatively or additionally, you may follow the procedures of this and subsequent composing/revising activities to compose your argument in the Writing in a Social Context section that begins on p. 124.)

In your journal or computer file, list three or four problems you've solved—whether personal, job-related, or school- and learning-related—that might prove interesting or useful to readers. For example, have you made a major decision after much thought or soul-searching? Eliminated some danger or threat? Discovered something significant? Isolated the cause of a malfunctioning machine and repaired it? Improved procedures at work? Increased your performance or efficiency at school or at work?

If possible, meet with several classmates and share your lists, exchanging opinions about the topics you'd enjoy reading. Choose one topic and begin the process of examining your ideas in a double-entry format in your journal or computer file. Use one set of entries for generating the content of your report, perhaps through brainstorming, clustering, free writing, and/or looping. If you discover any gaps in your knowledge about the topic, fill those gaps through library research or interviewing, and record your findings in your journal.

Use the second set of entries to examine your thoughts about organizing and developing the materials. Begin to think about the topic from the point of view of the audience—your classmates and instructor. What do you know that they don't—and what, therefore, must you explain? Where should you explain what you know?

Return to your journal or computer file whenever additional ideas occur to you.

Constructing a Problem

Forget your generalized audience. In the first place, the nameless, faceless audience will scare you to death and in the second place, unlike the theatre, it doesn't exist. In writing, your audience is one single reader. I have found that sometimes it helps to pick out one person—a real person you know or an imagined person and write to that one.

—*John Steinbeck*

A solution depends on how and for whom you construct the problem. Laying off several high-paid, middle-level managers presents one problem to the company's board of directors, quite another problem for the managers themselves. The final draft of your paper must therefore take into account the concerns, interests, and knowledge of your audience: Do they understand the problem? How do they feel about it? If they're indifferent to the problem, how can you make them care? In the example you read earlier, Roy C. Selby knows his readers aren't doctors, so he maps out the dangers of the operation (a stroke, memory impairment, a coma, fever, abdominal bleeding, even death) and appeals to his audience's curiosity by constructing the problem as a drama: Can he remove the patient's brain tumor without injuring or killing her?

Stephen Jay Gould also tells the story of attempting to save a life—in this case, his own—but wishes to construct a larger problem for readers: the real, physical dangers involved in divorcing the intellect from emotions. He spends the opening four paragraphs of his essay introducing the general problem and solution, while suggesting but not explicitly roadmapping his journey toward a solution (the specifics of which he won't disclose lest he diminish his readers' curiosity about the journey):

This is a personal story of statistics, properly interpreted, as profoundly nurturant and life-giving. It declares holy war on the downgrading of intellect by telling a small story to illustrate the utility of dry, academic knowledge about science.

Here's a different example from a student's paper, in which the writer constructs the problem as a warning to his readers:

> My struggle to extricate myself from credit card debt should serve as a cautionary tale for anyone who is tempted by the buy-now-pay-later mentality. Not only did I pay later, but I paid twice as much.

Invention Activity: Constructing the Problem

A useful starting point for constructing the problem may be to consider the significance of the problem to you. What difficulties, obstacles, dangers, or threats did it present? Then consciously turn your attention outward, toward your audience. How can you communicate that significance to them? Explore your ideas either through free writing, looping, or both—or simply compose a first-draft statement of the problem.

You may feel most comfortable deferring the exploration until after you've written the first draft. (See the Composing Activity on p. 123.) Read through the draft to see if a problem is emerging, and then compose a statement or let one evolve through free writing and/or looping. No matter what your approach, however, expect to revise the statement later.

Providing Background Information and Definitions

Without background on a problem's history, terminology, or underlying assumptions, readers may not fully understand the problem or solution. Selby therefore begins his story with background information on the causes of his patient's failing eyesight, and thus reveals the reason for the brain surgery. Gould begins his article with quite different backgrounding information: extended definitions of *median* and *mean*—terms that play a central role in the tale he wants to tell—and an argument for not divorcing the intellect from the emotions.

Backgrounding almost always requires definitions of terms, but how and where you define them depends on your purpose. Gould addresses them first because of their importance to his point, but Selby's main concern is to tell the story of the operation. For this reason, he defines terms in short phrases without interrupting the narrative:

> . . .angiography, a detailed X-ray study of the circulatory system, . . .

> Beneath the bone is a yellowish leather-like membrane, the dura, that surrounds the brain. . . . clips made of tantalum, a hard metal, were applied. . . .

At some point in the composing and revising process, you must consciously address what background information and definitions of terms your audience needs. If you can do so comfortably before composing a first draft, fine. Otherwise, write the draft, read it through, and make notes for changes in the margins.

The first thing writers look for in their drafts is information. *They know that a good piece of writing is built from specific, accurate, and interesting information. The writer must have an abundance of information from which to construct a readable piece of writing.*

Next writers look for meaning *in the information. The specifics must build to a pattern of significance. Each piece of specific information must carry the reader toward meaning.*

—*Donald Murray*

Invention Activity: Shaping Your Message Around Purpose and Audience

Consider your intended audience and purpose in writing the report. The following questions may guide your considerations, which you may make either prior to or after composing the first draft.

Planning or Revising Questions

1. What is your primary purpose in writing the report? That is, what do you expect your readers to do with its information?

2. Who is your audience? That is, who would most benefit from reading the report?

3. What don't your readers know about this issue? In other words, what background or history should you supply?

4. What terms do you need to define for readers? (You'll probably add or discard terms when composing the paper.) Do any terms require extensive definition and illustration? If so, where should you define them?

Tracing the Steps in the Process

As you guide your readers along the journey through which you solved the problem, you'll need to establish how each step determined the direction of the next. If one step uncovered some surprising information, show what you decided to do with that information. If a step revealed a partial solution, explain how you attempted to find the remainder of the solution. If a step disclosed a further problem, show how you tried to resolve that problem.

Consider the case of Stephen Jay Gould. When he learns of his cancer, his first problem is to locate literature on the disease. The literature discloses another problem: that the median life expectancy of those with the illness is eight months after diagnosis. He resolves that problem by recovering his composure and beginning to interpret the data. The interpretation yields a partial solution: his personality and medical profile place him on the "right-skewed" part of the distribution curve; therefore, he should live beyond eight months. The next problem—predicting how long he'll live—leads him to further analysis that reveals a happy solution: he should live for quite a while. Gould's final solution to the problem is to undergo a new treatment for the disease, and the solution seems to be working.

The student with the bank-card difficulties resolved his problems by (1) deciding to borrow money to erase his revolving-credit debt and significantly lower his interest payments, (2) investigating where he could borrow the money, and (3) borrowing it by establishing a line of credit with a large bank.

Invention Activity: Analyzing the Steps in the Process

Use a double-entry format in your journal, list all the steps in the process on the left-hand page (adding further steps to the list as they occur to you), and analyze the reasons you pursued each step on the right-hand page. Did you need to answer a question, gather information, solve a problem? Did the answer, information, or solution necessitate further action? Include this additional action in the list on the left-hand page if you haven't already done so. You may return to this journal entry periodically as new ideas and insights occur to you.

If you're using a computer for journal keeping, establish two files or two columns—whatever your word processing program handles most easily.

Composing Activity: Writing and Revising the Paper

Compose and revise a first draft of the paper. Establish the problem at the beginning, narrate each step you took to overcome an obstacle, explain the consequences of that step, define important terms as necessary, and reach a conclusion. Don't merely summarize your thoughts and actions; explain them in detail. Decide whether you wish to roadmap your paper's journey in the opening paragraph. (You can defer this decision until the revising stages of composing—even until the late stages of revising.) In any case, be sure to construct signposts at key points in the journey so that readers can see how each point relates to what precedes and follows. (These signposts can and probably should be added during revisions.)

Collaborative Activity: Evaluating the Paper (25 minutes of class time)

With several classmates, take turns reading your drafts of the papers. Stop at the end of the first paragraph and periodically throughout the paper so that listeners can predict what will follow. Then test their predictions against what you say. The questions that follow may also facilitate your discussion.

Postdraft Analysis
(To be completed by the writer or peer reader)

1. Read aloud the opening paragraph(s) that establish the problem; then stop to let your audience (or yourself) predict what will follow. List those predictions. Now read the remainder of the paper and put a check mark next to the predictions it fulfilled. If any predictions weren't fulfilled but should have been, indicate where in bracketed notes in the margins of the paper.

2. Locate the sentence or sentences that construct a problem for the intended audience. Is the problem clearly established? Is it valid? If not, how might this material be revised?

3. Locate any terms that might be unfamiliar to the intended readers. Does any term require a definition? Do any definitions require clarifying examples? If so, indicate where in brackets in the margins.

4. What are the important steps in the process? Have any been omitted? If not, are the steps explained fully and clearly? Is the writer's reasoning and motivation behind each step clear? If not, indicate in brackets in the margins where further explanation, amplification, or examples might be added. Should any steps, details, or definitions be eliminated? If so, bracket them.

5. Underline the first and last sentences of each paragraph and then examine these sentences carefully. Are the connections between the ideas of paragraphs unclear in any places in the draft—where ideas are related in ways you haven't shown? If so, add the words that explain the relationships. Are additional signposts needed in spots? If so, indicate where in brackets.

6. Does the conclusion resolve the problem? If not, how might the conclusion be changed?

Concluding Activity: Revising and Editing Your Report

Consider the responses to the Postdraft Analysis questions, and then do a final revision of the story—adding and rearranging material, rewording ideas, clarifying connections between ideas and events, and editing the paper carefully for matters of mechanics, grammar, and spelling.

WRITING IN A SOCIAL CONTEXT: HOUSING THE DISABLED

The following activity simulates a real situation in which you and your classmates can gain first-hand experience, devise arguments, debate the issues, and then communicate your ideas in writing. You'll read the material provided before coming to class, choose one of five roles to play, and then meet with your classmates who share your role. The entire activity should require no more than fifty minutes, divided as follows:

- five minutes for choosing roles
- forty-five minutes for discussing how to define and solve the problem

Alternatively, you may simply read through the materials and discuss them in class before composing an argument within one of the five roles.

The Context

A controversy has developed in Maple Grove, a quiet, integrated middle-class suburb. Maple Grove Care, a not-for-profit organization that serves the mentally handicapped and mentally ill in Maple Grove, would like to purchase two houses on residential streets to establish two group homes for its clientele. Maple Grove Care would like each home to house eight mentally handicapped or mentally ill adolescents and adults, along with a licensed mental health worker. Currently, the town's zoning ordinances don't permit such homes, so a new ordinance would have to be passed by the City Council, which might change the terms requested by Maple Grove Care.

Many residents of the community support the ordinance, either because of its benefits to their own families or for humanitarian reasons. But approximately the same number of residents oppose the ordinance; they fear that group homes could endanger people in the community, create an unpleasant atmosphere in the area immediately surrounding the homes, and lower property values in the area.

The City Council is asking that all interested parties submit written reports on ways to resolve the issue. Among the problems are these: Are such homes the best solution to the problem? How will they benefit the community (or harm it)? Which people—and how many—should be allowed to live in them? What kinds of housing—single family, townhouse, multifamily buildings—should be made available for group homes, and how far apart must the group homes be spaced? Reports should define the problems, explore solutions (and cite backing for these solutions), and arrive at a recommendation.

The Participants

Parents of Residents with Down's Syndrome.   Down's syndrome is a form of mental retardation that occurs primarily in children born to women over thirty-five years of age. Up to now, most of these children have lived at home and attended special education classes in the community's elementary schools, but as adolescents or adults, they require skilled supervision and training that their parents cannot provide. All would be attending special classes or working during the day and returning to the homes in the late afternoon. They would be free to walk in the neighborhoods.

You'll be reporting on your "family's" current difficulties and on the benefits that group homes will bring to your family and others like it. Support your claims with data and examples from the fact sheet included later in this chapter.

Parents of Mentally Disabled Residents. These adolescents or adults either have a history of mental illness—primarily manic depression or schizophrenia—that can be controlled by drugs, or they are recovering drug or alcohol abusers. Their behavior is considered low risk by psychiatrists and psychologists. Like the parents of the Down's syndrome children, you will be defining the problems of your "family" and other families like yours, reporting on how group homes would solve the problems, and supporting your claims with material from the fact sheet.

Community Members Who Oppose the Group Homes. You are afraid that the residents will commit crimes (including rape), endanger or harass children, and cause a decline in property values. You also oppose placing ten people in a house, for they may cause problems with maintenance, sanitation, excessive noise, and traffic. You believe that no matter how carefully the community restricts the use of group homes, once the ordinance is approved, the state or federal government will impose its own rules on the homes. Although you sympathize with the plight of your neighbors, you feel that group homes cause too many problems in a community.

You'll be reporting on the problems group homes would create, supporting your claims with material from the fact sheet, and recommending that Maple Grove prohibit group homes.

Community Members Who Support the Homes. Some of you favor the homes because you are friendly with the parents of the residents; others support the homes on humanitarian grounds. You are convinced that the experiences of other communities have proven that the fears about such homes are groundless. You will define the problems as you see them and explore the process that led you to conclude that group homes would be the best solution to the problems.

Representative of Maple Grove Care. You will define and illustrate the problem, explain your reasoning in proposing the ordinance, and recommend its passage. You'll cite hypothetical examples from the experiences of families with mentally handicapped or mentally ill adolescents or adults, and you'll discuss the experiences of other communities with group homes (found on the fact sheet).

The Facts

1. Mix of homes in Maple Grove is 75 percent single family, 10 percent townhouses (the average number of homes in a townhouse development is eight) and 15 percent apartments, including some high rise.
2. Very low crime rate in community, especially for violent crimes. Only one murder in the last five years. Main crimes: burglaries, bicycle thefts, drunken driving, and drug use.
3. Nearest group home is fifty miles away. Most mentally handicapped or

mentally ill people confined to county or state institutions because of a shortage of group homes.

4. Average house in Maple Grove has 3.2 residents. Proposed ordinance would allow nine per group home, in addition to a full-time staff supervisor.

5. In one wealthy suburb in another state, one such home began operating in 1992. Soon after the home first opened, a man appearing to be lost knocked on a neighbor's door, a "peeping Tom" was reported but never caught, and a bicycle was stolen. Police have received some complaints, but claim they are typical of problems in any neighborhood: garbage being dumped on a lawn, and a puddle of gasoline burning in the street.

   Mixed reaction from neighbors. One said that although some "goofy" things happened at first, "nothing major" has occurred since, and her children now walk by the house "just like any other." Another neighbor claims a family moved from the neighborhood because of the home.

   In 1989 in another suburb, scores of angry residents gathered at city hall to oppose issuing a permit for mentally handicapped adults. Their arguments: the home unsuitable for residential community and would harm property values. Three years after home was built, there have been no serious problems.

6. Currently, 231 homes housing 5,506 mentally ill or developmentally disabled adults exist throughout the state. Law limits number of residents in each to sixteen.

7. Many residents who had lived in large institutions enjoy the smaller environments and independence. At one home, residents eat breakfast and dinner together but work at nearby skills development center during day, watch television or engage in art projects, or take walks in neighborhood.

8. Many neighbors of one group express worry about possible changes in the type of residents allowed. "We're just concerned that it doesn't become a home for drug addicts or kids with criminal records," said elderly neighbor.

9. The supervisor of one group home said, "These people generally have a difficult time relating to others. The idea that they would be harmful to anyone is not so. The nature of their disabilities causes them to be withdrawn."

10. Costs to hospitalize a mentally ill person: $60,000 to $300,000 a year, but costs are far less at a group home.

11. Opponents contend standards needed to determine who can live in the homes. "If this type of housing is allowed, any other group can claim discrimination," and the city could not reject other types of group living arrangements—like the Branch Davidians outside Waco, Texas. "We are afraid that we'll never be able to sell our home. When people buy a home in a residential area, they expect the area to remain residential."

12. Alderman in one community complained about size of group homes: "I

don't know how many people here have ten or twelve children, but there aren't too many. You're creating a small hotel."

13. People in one community where a group home was to be placed—including psychiatrist and two clinical psychologists—complained about absence of laws for monitoring and keeping the home safe. Ordinance doesn't specify how residents are to be medicated or establish clear standards concerning who is eligible to live there.

14. The United States Fair Housing Act, as amended in 1988, prohibits practices that discriminate against all physically, mentally, and developmentally disabled people. However, a city ordinance may limit the number of people who can live in a house based on its size, no matter what their physical condition.

Composing Activity: Writing Your Argument

Within your role, compose a letter to the City Council. In your letter, define the problem, examine your reasoning and steps you took in solving it, and propose your solution. Consider what tone to adopt in the letter. Should you sound angry? Impatient? Insistent? Pleading? Calm and reasonable? Refer to the invention, composing, and revising activities throughout the chapter for guidance. And do not merely copy the facts supplied. Paraphrase or quote them.

Follow-Up Activity: Writing an Ordinance

Meet with several classmates who will serve as members of the Maple Grove City Council, examine several reports from the five groups supporting or opposing the ordinance (your instructor may provide these for you), and then compose an ordinance that solves the problems these reports discuss. The ordinance should carefully stipulate the type and number of people who may live in group homes, the number of homes that will be allowed in any given area, the type and number of supervisory personnel who must be present, and the conditions under which a permit for a group home will be granted.

Here's a sample of part of an ordinance permitting group homes for elderly people. The complete ordinance, which stipulates all the procedures for licensing of the homes and applying for permits, is much longer. (You may omit most of the WHEREAS clauses from the ordinance you write; the residents of Maple Grove won't mind.)

AN ORDINANCE PROVIDING FOR THE LICENSING AND REGULATION OF GROUP HOMES IN MAPLE GROVE

WHEREAS, there is need for Group Homes for the Elderly, and
WHEREAS, the Fair Housing Act Amendments of 1988 and the Community

Residence Location Planning Act require the City of Maple Grove to recognize and accommodate the need for Group Homes for the Elderly, and

WHEREAS, Group Homes are authorized under provisions of the Maple Grove Zoning Ordinance, and

WHEREAS, it is in the best interest of the City of Maple Grove and elderly persons that Group Homes for the Elderly be licensed and regulated by the City of Maple Grove,

NOW, THEREFORE, BE IT ORDAINED BY THE MAYOR AND BOARD OF THE CITY OF MAPLE GROVE THAT SUCH HOMES BE ESTABLISHED AS PERMITTED USES IN THE CITY Of MAPLE GROVE UNDER THE FOLLOWING TERMS AND CONDITIONS:

PART 1: DEFINITION:

Group Home for the Elderly. A dwelling shared by two to five unrelated persons who are 62 years of age or more, who live together as a single housekeeping unit, and who require and receive supervision or care by staff to live in a family setting. A group home for the elderly may be located in a dwelling unit in (1) a detached dwelling; (2) a dwelling unit in a two-flat dwelling in a zoning district where two-flat dwellings are allowed, provided that both units in the two-flat dwelling are operated as group homes for the elderly by the same operator; (3) a townhouse in a zoning district where townhouses are allowed. The term group home for the elderly shall not include an alcoholism or drug treatment center, a work-release facility for convicts or ex-convicts, or any other housing facility serving as an alternative to incarceration. Nothing in this definition shall affect the right of persons who satisfy the definition of "family" to live as a family in appropriate zoning districts. . . .

PART 2: "R" SINGLE-FAMILY DETACHED RESIDENCE DISTRICT

The R District is established to protect, promote, and maintain the development of single-family detached housing and limited public and institutional uses that are compatible with the surrounding residential neighborhood. The development standards and range of allowable uses for this district are designed to maintain a suitable environment for family living at the low density of development characteristic of the current pattern of development in the district, which consists of large lots with abundant open space.

The following uses may be established as permitted uses in the R District:
  (a) Detached dwellings.
  (b) Group homes for the elderly, provided that:
    (1) The use is licensed by the city; and
    (2) First preference for occupancy in the home is accorded to persons who currently reside in the city, to the extent permissible under applicable state and federal laws and regulations; and
    (3) The home is located no closer than____feet to any other group home for the elderly.

Follow-Up Activity: Defending the Ordinance

Write a position paper in which you explain the reasons for your ordinance. You will have two audiences for this paper: (1) those who opposed the ordinance, and (2) those who feel the ordinance doesn't go far enough.

Chapter 10

Reporting Results

The most important things, I told [my students], were observation and consciousness. Keep your eyes open, see clearly, think about what you see, ask yourself what it means.

—Francine Prose

Many readers turn to reports with one objective in mind: What's the bottom line? "Don't tell me a story," these busy people would say. "Just let me know the ending." For these readers, you need to compose a straightforward report of results, not a narrative of how those results were learned or achieved.

Each industry, profession, or community employs its own jargon for such reports. Doctors communicate in a specialized vocabulary, accountants in another, and school administrators in yet another. Membership in a profession requires learning the lingo. Nonetheless, all bottom-line reports employ virtually the same strategy for conveying information directly and succinctly: They state the most important findings or generalizations first—that is, they begin by making their most important claims—then explain and back them up, and then examine the less important ideas. In a sense, therefore, the reports incorporate some elements of arguments, as the examples that follow demonstrate.

LOOKING AT REPORTS

The following two reports differ greatly in audience, purpose, and tone but share a similar organization. The first example, from *Consumer Reports* magazine, recounts the results of research. Like most scientific reports, it deals with first-hand information; the same group both researches and discloses its findings. The researchers also describe their research design: that is, the procedures they followed in gathering and evaluating data. (The ellipses marks [. . .] indicate where specific recommendations have been omitted.)

CHOCOLATE-CHIP COOKIES

Be it ever so humble, there's no chocolate-chip cookie like a homemade one. Served warm, when it's at its best, the cookie is crisp on the outside but chewy within, and the silky chips melt in your mouth. For this sensory pleasure, you pay about a fifth what you would for cookies bought at a specialty store. And if you're concerned about saturated fat, you can tinker with the ingredients, creating a custom cookie that better fits your diet.

Some people don't have the time or patience to get out bowls, measure ingredients, and mix and beat. They satisfy their cookie craving with one of the ready-to-eat, packaged brands. Consumers spend almost $700-million a year on packaged chocolate-chip cookies.

What we looked for

An excellent cookie must be full of the flavor of browned grain, possibly with hints of butter, vanilla, and brown sugar. Its ingredients should taste fresh. The cookie's surface and edges should be crisp and crunchy; its insides should be moist and chewy.

As for chips, the more chocolatey, the better. The makers of some packaged brands suggest they bake as many chips as they physically can into the cookie, as if to turn the confection into a chocolate bar with dough chips. But loading up with chips is no good if the chocolate doesn't measure up. It should be soft, melt smoothly in the mouth, and provide a "hit" of chocolate flavor. All the cookies we tried list some type of chocolate in their ingredients. Some chips contain cocoa or chocolate liquor, a liquid extract of the cocoa bean, and some have artificial flavor. We discovered that a chip's ingredients don't give a clue as to its taste.

Lower-quality cookies lack the appropriate just-baked flavor and may taste of artificial vanilla, fruit, or raw dough. A really bad cookie may taste stale or medicinal or be extremely dry, crumbly, tough, or gritty.

Where the chips fell

Our trained tasters sampled 10 fresh-baked and 25 packaged brands of chocolate-chip cookie. The fresh-baked cookies are homemade from recipes, dry mixes, or raw dough, or are sold by cookie shops; the packaged cookies are both hard and soft types. Among the attributes panelists noted were the intensity of the chocolate pieces, the crispness or chewiness of the cookies, and whether there were hints of staleness or inappropriate flavors. To level the playing field, we served the fresh-baked cookies at room temperature.

Fresh-baked cookies led the Ratings, with two made-from-scratch recipes earning excellent scores. One of them, a recipe reportedly devised by Hillary Rodham Clinton, was published in *Family Circle* magazine. Her recipe calls for rolled oats, which gave the cookies a delicate, crisp, chewy texture. The other top recipe: the *Original Nestlé Toll House* version found on packages of *Nestlé Semi-*

Sweet Chocolate Morsels. Those old favorites were chewy, buttery, and crisp on their surface. . . .

Some other fresh-baked cookies from mixes, doughs, and cookie shops did nearly as well. *Mrs. Fields* and *David's*—the store-bought product as well as its dough brandmate—tasted fresh but were buttery to the point of greasiness. . . .

The best of the packaged cookies had at least a hint of fresh flavor and lots of high-quality chocolate chips or chunks. Generally, hard-style cookies tasted better than soft, though, as might be expected, they were somewhat dry and weren't chewy. Highest-rated of the packaged brands were *President's Choice, Pepperidge Farm American Collection Nantucket,* and *Sam's American Choice.*

Soft-baked packaged cookies try to match the texture of the fresh types. They're made with invert sugar, a mixture of glucose and fructose that keeps them soft. Although they were appropriately moist, the soft cookies didn't have the crisp shell of a fresh-baked cookie. Many also lost points for bland chips and flavors reminiscent of raisins, figs, or apple juice. . . .

Nutritious?

In a word, no. The rule of thumb for cookies is that rich taste equals poor nutrition.

To compare the cookies nutritionally, we first had to decide on a standard serving. We couldn't use "one cookie," because the size of the cookies varies greatly. We chose to look at 30 grams (1.06 ounces) of cookie, the Food and Drug Administration's proposed serving size. To put it in perspective, that's less than one whole *David's* cookie-shop cookie and more than a *Pepperidge Farm Nantucket.* The Ratings show, for each brand, how many cookies you get in a 30-gram serving.

Most of the cookies have 140 to 160 calories per serving, with 6 to 8 grams of fat—about 39 to 49 percent of their calories. Eat four *Toll House* cookies, which have more than 7 grams of fat each, and you're up to almost half the recommended limit for fat in a 2000-calorie daily diet. . . .

You can buy a dietetic cookie, but we wonder if you'd want to. The four we tasted—*Weight Watchers Soft and Chewy* and *Nabisco SnackWell's* with only 2 grams of fat in a serving, and *R W. Frookie* and *Estee,* sweetened primarily with fructose—didn't taste much like chocolate-chip cookies. . . .

Cookie costs

Generally, the more work you do the less you'll pay. A 30-gram serving of homemade cookies costs about a dime, as does a serving from the *Stop & Shop* mix. Other mixes and raw doughs may cost a bit more.

The price of packaged cookies runs from about 10 cents to 50 cents a serving. You can find a good cookie at the low end of that range: Highly rated *President's Choice* cost 21 cents per serving; *Sam's American Choice,* nearly as good, cost only 16 cents.

Most expensive of all, besides *Weight Watchers,* are the cookie-shop cookies. *Mrs. Fields* cost 58 cents per serving, and that buys only part of a cookie; a whole cookie will set you back 98 cents.

—Consumer Reports

This next report, adapted from a suburban community's bi-yearly newsletter, discusses the results and implications of a governmental action. Its authors are not the same people who took the action, so their reporting is secondhand. Furthermore, as you'll soon discover, their purpose goes beyond merely conveying information.

TOUGHER ON TEEN-AGE DRINKING

The Newfield Village Board of Trustees has become increasingly concerned over underage drinking parties which are occurring in this area. These parties not only violate the law but endanger our youth. **Alcohol is the number one cause of death among youth.** The Board has taken action against this problem by unanimously passing tougher laws and by asking all parents of the high school youth in the area to join in the fight.

Underage drinking parties are a serious problem in Newfield and in all of the adjoining towns. This was revealed by the recent survey conducted among the youth of Newfield and five surrounding communities. Among the alarming results of this survey are these:

- 60% of high school juniors used alcohol within thirty days of the survey, mainly at parties.
- One-third of juniors consumed five or more drinks in one sitting within two weeks of the survey.
- More than 20% of juniors drove a vehicle after drinking within twelve months of the survey.

The results of this survey do not surprise parents who know about the social life of many high school students in this area, which centers not around traditional high school activities like football games, clubs, dances, and dates, but around private drinking parties in homes. These parties occur every Friday and Saturday night.

This underage drinking culture did not develop overnight. A variety of factors contributed to it: the poor example provided by some parents, the media's glamorization of alcohol, the drug culture of the 1960s, the increased stress on today's youth, the lack of wholesome alternatives, the greater freedom of youth (or, said another way, the reduced supervision by parents), and widespread ambivalence on the part of parents as to whether underage drinking is something they can or should prevent.

The consequences of underage drinking may not be fully known for years, but intuition tells us that every parent must be concerned. It is clear that youthful drinkers become addicted to alcohol faster than adults. They are also at an age where they believe they are invincible. This belief, combined with a few beers and a car, can be deadly. And the victims of underage drinking sometimes are totally innocent and uninvolved persons—our relatives and friends who just happened to be on the wrong road at the wrong time. At a minimum, the underage drinking culture distracts our youth from wholesome activities which are important to their normal development.

The Newfield Village Board recently adopted an ordinance which gives our Police Department new weapons to address this problem. This ordinance is not a solution. Other communities will have to adopt and enforce similar ordinances. Parents Against Drunk Driving and school officials will have to continue their educational efforts. Most important, more parents will have to get on board with the program—parents who knowingly allow underage drinking to occur, parents who send mixed messages about whether it's okay to drink, parents who naively assume that underage drinking is not a problem which will affect their children, parents who negligently leave their minor children on weekends with no supervision.

Newfield's new ordinance does two things. First, it adds a civil remedy to the existing parental responsibility ordinance. It gives a person who is injured because of a minor's intoxication a right of action against any person who contributed to the intoxication by furnishing alcohol or by allowing a home to be used for an underage drinking party.

The new ordinance also requires package liquor stores to document the sale of kegs and to place identification tags on the kegs which they sell. The idea is that kegs are often the container-of-choice for underage drinking parties, and if the kegs can be tied to their purchaser, the police will be able to determine who unlawfully furnished the beer for the party.

Parents of high-school-age students have good reason to be outraged at the small group of parents who permit underage drinking parties in their homes. No matter what message you communicate to your children in your home, you are undermined when these parents allow the underage drinking culture to persist because of their permissiveness or carelessness. These parents are arrogating your parental rights unto themselves.

Please join us in fighting underage drinking parties. Be vigilant to assure that these parties do not occur in your home. Call the police when you become aware of an illegal party. Send a strong message to your children that underage drinking is wrong and that you do not condone it.

—The Communicator

Issues for Investigation and Discussion

1. Who is the audience for each report? What problem does each report construct (or tacitly acknowledge) for the readers? What is the purpose of each report—that is, what do the authors expect readers to do with its informa-

tion? Does either report reflect a bias—that is, does the report interpret the data in order to argue for a particular point of view?

2. How would you characterize the tone of each report? (Chatty? Formal? Humorous? Angry? Pleading?) Is this tone appropriate for the audience and purpose of the report?

3. Despite the differing purposes of the reports, their first paragraphs share a number of important traits. What are these traits, and why are they similar?

4. What are the most important conclusions of each report, and where are they stated? Where are less important conclusions stated?

5. What backing does each report provide for its conclusions? What warrants?

6. Does either report explain how the data were gathered? If so, where and why?

7. Where do the authors of *Tougher on Teen-Age Drinking* explain the provisions of the new ordinance? Why do the authors place them there?

8. Why does the report on drinking employ the first-person-plural *(we, our, us)* throughout? It also asserts that "Parents of high-school-age students have good reason to be outraged at the small group of parents who permit underage drinking parties in their homes," and accuses them of "permissiveness or carelessness." How might this "small group of parents" react when they read the report?

9. As a way of summarizing your ideas in response to these questions, or to any other matters you observe in the two reports, turn to your journal or computer file and list several common traits of effective reports. Let this list guide you as you compose and revise your own report later.

COMPOSING A REPORT IN INVERTED PYRAMID FORM

The organization of your bottom-line report will depend on your purpose, audience, and subject matter, as well as your own invention and composing practices. But that organization will probably take on some characteristics of what L. Sue Baugh calls an inverted pyramid, with the heaviest information first and the lightest last. The beginning states the most important conclusion or finding; the middle section backs up, explains, or interprets it (and thus is the longest section of the report); and the end discusses additional findings or details.* In other words, the report helps readers extract information quickly by presenting conclusions before discussions, generalizations before exceptions, summaries before details, and answers before explanations.

While the model is useful, don't attempt to follow it slavishly. Depart from it any time you feel your audience needs some background information before you introduce a finding or conclusion. Or compose a modified version of the report

---

Handbook for Memo Writing (Lincolnwood, IL: NTC Business Books, 1990), pp. 44–45.

discussed in Chapter 9, narrating the process involved in reaching the main find-ings—but this time summarizing those findings in the opening paragraph.

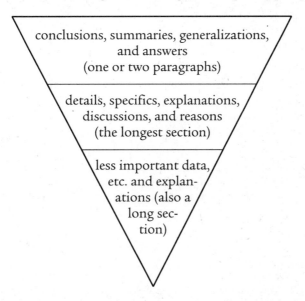

Collaborative Activity: Analyzing Reports (25 minutes of class time)

With a group of several classmates or by yourself, examine the two reports from the beginning of the chapter to test whether they follow the inverted-pyramid structure. If either report departs from that structure, discuss why.

Invention Activity: Gathering and Organizing Information for Your Report

(Alternatively or additionally, you may follow the procedures of this and subsequent composing/revising activities to compose your argument in the Writing in a Social Context section that begins on p. 144.)

Assume that your college is planning to publish a supplemental booklet of lecture notes for a course you're taking, and that you've volunteered or have been chosen to compose a 500-word report (approximately two double-spaced, typewritten pages) on one or more lectures comprising a unit of instruction. The purpose of the booklet is to help students learn the material, and it should be detailed enough so that students who miss an occasional class can keep up with the instruction. The report should state the main points of the lecture, illustrate and explain them, and then discuss the less important points.

Perhaps you and one or more colleagues from your English class can attend the same lecture and then compare notes as well as early drafts of your reports—although that may not be possible. In any case, the following procedure may be helpful:

- Attend the lecture(s) and take notes, but don't try to transcribe every word. You may wish to tape record the lecture for later reference if your instructor permits.

- Immediately after the lecture(s), thoroughly familiarize yourself with the materials. Spend two or three minutes listing the major ideas, in your own words. If you can explain the ideas clearly at that point, you'll probably feel comfortable explaining them later.

- Begin to organize your materials by determining the main ideas and minor details. Use whatever invention activities you wish: free writing, brainstorming, clustering, looping, or placing details within a pyramid. Then put the materials away for later use.

Alternative Invention Activity: Gathering and Shaping Data for a Laboratory Report

If you're conducting an experiment in a laboratory science course, compose a report on your findings for inclusion in a supplemental-instruction booklet. The report should state the main findings of the experiment, describe the experimental design, examine and interpret the data, and then discuss any other findings. Scientific reports customarily avoid the first-person pronoun *I*, saying, for example, "The experiment demonstrated" instead of "I learned" or "I discovered." Scan a few scientific journals in your library to learn more about their format, including their use of headings.

Again, you may be able to work collaboratively with one or more of the people in your English class, following procedures similar to those described in the previous invention activity:

- Prepare by making notes on the data and the conclusions they suggest.
- Use free writing, brainstorming, clustering, looping, or pyramid drawing to help you organize the data, describe the experimental design, and decide what terms you must define for students.
- Put your materials away for later use.

Forming the Base of the Pyramid: Constructing and Resolving a Problem

As in most kinds of writing, the beginning of your report should construct a problem for your audience, so you should consider what will motivate them to read the report. Are they interested in profit, savings, convenience, pleasure, prestige, safety, health, or freedom from fear—or are they merely curious? The answer will help you determine the findings or conclusions to emphasize. For example, the readers of the *Consumer Reports* article on chocolate-chip cookies probably care most about pleasure and less about convenience and savings. Thus, the report discusses the pleasure issue first—homemade cookies taste best—and the other issues later.

Here's the beginning of a report in *Newsweek* magazine. It constructs the problem: perhaps readers may not read or compute as well as they think; and American education may be even less effective than they suspected. Then it summarizes the most important findings from a new study of the country's literacy and mathematical ability:

DUMBER THAN WE THOUGHT

Literacy: A new study shows we can't cope with everyday life

Just because you can make out this sentence isn't proof that you're literate. And just because you shelled out the correct $2.95 for this issue of NEWSWEEK doesn't mean you've got satisfactory arithmetic skills. The better measures: can you reach our offices using a Manhattan subway map, [or]write us a letter about a billing error. . . ?

So concludes the most comprehensive study of literacy ever done of Americans. Released last week by the U.S. Department of Education, the report offers an appalling portrait of the population's proficiency with words and numbers. It, too, seems to confirm some of the worst fears of business leaders and educators: American workers—and not just the latest wave of immigrants—appear ill-equipped to compete globally, and high schools are hardly helping by awarding degrees to students barely able to read or write. "This should be a wake-up call," says Education Secretary Richard Riley. "The vast majority of Americans do not know that they do not have the skills to earn a living in our increasingly technological society and international marketplace."

Notice that the second paragraph of the report begins to interpret the conclusions of the study. They're "appalling," the authors say, a confirmation of "some of the worst fears of business leaders and educators." And they quote the U.S. Secretary of Education as further support. These interpretations reflect the authors' biases, which we probably don't object to (or even notice) because of the authoritative tone and fast-paced writing style of the authors. You too can write authoritatively once you feel comfortable with the information and your reactions to it. Take ownership of the material you discuss; assimilate it into your experience—whether first-or second-hand—by studying it carefully and continually revising your drafts with an eye toward clarity and economy. If you don't understand the material yourself, you can't explain it to your readers.

Invention Activity: Analyzing Your Audience and Materials

The problem you construct for your audience, as well as the findings you emphasize at the beginning of the report, is based in large part on who you perceive your audience to be. At some point in (or throughout) the composing and revising process, you must address the following issues:

- Who is your audience? How similar are their interests in and attitude toward the subject matter?
- How important is this issue to them? What would make it important? In other words, what problem can you construct for them? (You may approach this question by examining what you personally find most interesting and important.)
- What do they probably know about your subject? What don't they know?
- Based on your answers to the previous questions, make some tentative decisions about the findings to emphasize at the beginning of your report, as well as the minor findings to include later.

Explore these issues through notes in your journal before composing the first draft. But don't be surprised if additional—or better—ideas occur to you during composing and revising.

Building on the Base of the Pyramid: Adding Data and Interpretation

After composing a statement of the main findings or conclusions at the beginning of your report, you can attempt to explain, back up, or interpret them, as the middle paragraphs of the *Newsweek* article illustrate. Note what they tell you about the design of the study, and consider the kinds of backing and warrants they provide. Also look for words or phrases revealing the writers' biases—or the biases of the experts they quote.

Sure, Johnny can read simple prose. And Mary can add a couple of integers all right. The problem is their inability to make practical use of those skills in everyday life. Nearly half of the nation's 191 million adults, the study says, cannot do such tasks as fill out a bank-deposit slip, compute the cost of carpeting a room or translate information from a table to a graph. And heaven help them if they need to find a Saturday departure on a bus schedule. Despite those facts, most of the 26,000 randomly selected participants in the literacy study said they were able to read and write English "well" or "very well." "Yeah, we're dumber than we thought we were," says William Bennett, secretary of education under President Reagan and current conservative activist.

The last major federal study on literacy was in 1975. It concluded that roughly 25 million American adults were functionally illiterate—far below the numbers revealed in last week's landmark report. Part of the reason for the increase is that the definitions have been changed. Traditionally, illiteracy has referred only to folks who signed their names "X" or hadn't graduated at least from a low grade. Now the net has been cast wider. "This test revealed that many people can read in the technical sense that they can decode the words," says Irwin Kirsch, project director for the $14 million Education Department survey, which Congress commissioned five years ago. "But they lack the strategies and skills needed to use the information." Case in point: half of the individuals scoring in the lowest 20th percent graduated from high school. "Does a high school diploma mean anything today?" asks Bennett. "No. Zero."

Completing the Pyramid: Examining Secondary Findings

After stating and interpreting the most important findings or conclusions, your report can explore the less important ones. The *Newsweek* article lists several and examines their implications for businesses:

> Among the report's other findings:
>
> • Literacy among 21- to 25-year-olds is dropping, when compared with a similar study from 1985. The likely cause is the dramatic increase in young Hispanics in the population, many of whom were born in other countries and are learning English as a second language. They might do better if the test were given in other languages, but the study only set out to measure English literacy, and those who conducted the study point out that American commerce is still primarily done in English. . . .
>
> • Men did about as well as women in reading skills but were better at math and interpreting documents. . . .
>
> • Individuals with higher literacy more often were employed and earned higher wages. Those with the lowest test scores earned an average of $230 a week; those with the highest, about $680.
>
> • Of course, the more education a person had, the better he or she did. Nonetheless, 4 percent of college graduates tested at the lowest levels.
>
> The survey results are especially worrisome because many employers now need workers with higher math and reading skills. "During various transition periods of our history, society's demands outstrip the skills of the people," Kirsch says. "We're now moving away from a manufacturing society to an information society." That means workers will need more interpretative abilities and less of the rote skills prized on the assembly line. Kirsch and others, including President Clinton, have long urged redoubled efforts to educate and train Americans. By some estimates, employers are spending as much as $50 billion to try to eliminate the kind of practical illiteracy that the new study describes.

The final paragraph then discusses a further implication before ending with an ironic punch line.

The alarm sounded by American business, of course, raises again the specter of the United States being overtaken by the more qualified work forces of other Western nations. Maybe so, but they're about to get the treatment as well. The literacy test is being exported to eight other countries—Germany, Canada, Mexico, Ireland, France, Poland, Switzerland and the Netherlands—with a report due out in 1995. They, too, could be in for a few surprises.

—Newsweek

A reminder: this article is the final product of professional reporters and editors; it reveals nothing about the process that produced it. Like them, you'll compose many drafts before arriving at a logically organized and gracefully written report. But keep at it. Challenge your work; continually ask yourself (and others who read it) if you can express your ideas more clearly, directly, interestingly. Revise until the ideas flow from one to another.

Do you revise? Is the sun going to set today? One of the great pleasures of writing is revision, the second and third and fourth chance you hardly ever get in any other area of your life. . . .

—Hilma Wolitzer

Invention and Composing Activity: Planning and Drafting Your Report

Return to the materials you've compiled and consider them with the following questions in mind.

1. Do your earlier decisions about the major and minor findings still hold? If not, what should you change?
2. What backing—statistics, examples, or explanations—would support or illustrate your major conclusion or finding? (You may wish to supply examples of your own.) Where should you provide the backing?
3. What warrants, if any, would show the connection between the backing and claim?
4. What other findings should you discuss later in the report?
5. And what backing and warrants does each finding require?

Use whatever invention techniques (free writing, brainstorming, clustering, looping, pyramid drawing) you need to resolve these issues at least tentatively, and then compose a first draft of your report. Or reverse this procedure: compose a first draft, look it over, and then organize the materials. In either case, expect to revise and reorganize the first draft later, perhaps extensively. Outlining your ideas prior to or after the drafting process may also prove useful.

Collaborative Activity: Improving the Clarity of Your Report (25 minutes of class time)

Take turns with several classmates reading a draft of your reports aloud. Stop at the end of the first paragraph and periodically throughout the report to allow listeners to predict what you'll say next. If your report doesn't meet their reasonable expectations, add bracketed notes for changes in the margins of your paper.

The following Postdraft Analysis questions should also guide you during the revision process.

Postdraft Analysis
(To be completed by the writer or peer reader)

1. Locate the sentence or sentences that construct a problem for the intended audience. Is the problem clearly established? Is it valid? If not, how might this material be revised?

2. What major finding or conclusion is stated at the beginning? Is the statement clear? If not, indicate in brackets how it might be revised.

3. Locate the other important findings or conclusions stated later. Are these statements clear? Are they presented in a logical order? If not, make bracketed notes of organizational changes in the margins of the paper.

4. Examine the backing for each main point. Does each provide sufficient relevant facts, examples, explanations, or interpretations? Is some backing irrelevant or unnecessary? Indicate in bracketed notes where backing could be expanded or cut.

5. If the report discusses four major findings, could it manage with three—or does it need a fifth? What should be cut or added?

6. Examine each claim and backing again. Are connections (warrants) between each claim and backing clear? If not, identify with bracketed labels where warrants might be added or expanded.

7. Do any terms need to be explained? Indicate where in bracketed labels.

8. Look at the ending and beginning sentences of each paragraph. Will the transitions between paragraphs be clear to your audience? If not, which might be strengthened or made more explicit? Indicate these in bracketed notes.

9. What should be the tone of your report: impersonal? casual? formal? even

angry? alarmed? Does your language consistently develop that tone? Is it also clear, direct, and graceful? If not, identify with bracketed notes where it should be reworded or tightened.

10. Do any other problems need to be addressed? If so, how might they be addressed?

Concluding Activity: Revising and Editing Your Report

Assemble all your revision notes and then revise your report. Be sure to clarify the transitions between sentences and paragraphs, tighten the sentences, sharpen the details, and edit carefully for matters of mechanics, grammar, and spelling.

WRITING IN A SOCIAL CONTEXT: MODERNIZING A COMPANY

The following activity simulates a real situation in which you and your classmates can gain first-hand experience, devise reports, discuss and question them, and then communicate your ideas in writing. You'll read the material provided before coming to class, choose one of four roles to play, and then present your report in an open meeting. The entire activity should require no more than forty-five to seventy-five minutes, divided as follows:

- five minutes for choosing roles
- ten to fifteen minutes for determining strategy
- twenty to forty minutes to present reports
- ten to fifteen minutes for rebuttal

After choosing or being assigned to a group representing one of the four roles, you and the other group members will meet to discuss the claims, backing, and warrants you'll present, based on the materials provided and any others you devise. *(Don't attempt to use all the facts provided—only those that are most relevant to your role and the claims you make.)* Then your instructor will convene the whole class, first allowing each group five to ten minutes to make its report, followed by ten minutes or so of give-and-take among the groups. Finally, again within your role, you will compose a written report outside of class addressed to a specified audience.

Alternatively, you may simply read through the materials and discuss them in class before composing a report within one of the four roles.

The Context

Columbia Motors, the fourth largest automobile-manufacturing company in the United States, has long been unable to compete effectively with foreign manufacturers and with the big three auto makers (General Motors, Ford, and Chrysler). Last year, the company lost $1.4 billion, and its market share—the percentage of total sales from all companies—declined from its highs of 18 percent in the United States and 5 percent abroad to 10 percent and 2 percent respectively. Its traditional assembly-line manufacturing process has incurred far greater costs than those of other auto makers, and the reliability and quality of its cars have suffered in comparison to competitors. Each 100 cars that Columbia Motors manufactures average 168 defects, far above the industry-wide average of 111, and more than double the 76 defects per 100 cars of the industry leader, a Japanese firm.

After many years of attempting minor adjustments in planning, manufacturing, and marketing, the company has proposed a complete overhaul of its operations, modeled after the practices of GM's Saturn and Chrysler's Neon subcompact-car manufacturing divisions. Like GM and Chrysler, it wishes to produce an entirely new automobile, utilizing the best designing, manufacturing, and management practices available. To start the process, it has asked outside consultants, mid-level managers, automobile designers, and assembly-line workers to conduct preliminary research into the company's current practices and those of competitors. Then at an open meeting, they will report their findings and make recommendations, as well as explore ideas for change or further investigation.

The Participants

Mid-Level Managers. You have concluded that assembly-line procedures and union work rules at Columbia Motors are inefficient and costly. You also feel that mid-level managers are virtually powerless to make day-to-day decisions because of the unrealistic and inflexible policies of the top-level management, who are far removed from the actual process of producing automobiles.

Assembly-Line Workers. You feel that your company's manufacturing practices are outmoded and inefficient. Workers frequently experience fatigue that leads to errors; repairs or adjustments to machinery often halt the assembly line for long time periods; and workers—who know first-hand the problems in the assembly and design of the car—are given no voice in solving these problems. However, you also fear that radical changes may eliminate your job.

Automobile Designers. You are convinced that your company can produce a reliable and attractive product, but you feel hamstrung by the lack of input you receive from management and workers. You want more research into product design and cost, more consulting with the people who build and market the cars, and more flexibility in making changes in design and procedures.

Outside Consultants. You have studied the design, manufacturing, and management practices of Columbia Motors, as well as of the Saturn and Neon companies, and would like to suggest a number of changes based on the Saturn and Neon models.

The Facts

About Columbia Motors

1. Founded in 1932, Columbia uses the mass-production methods introduced at the turn of the century by Henry Ford and modified over the years. Assembly line performs many of its operations robotically. Workers still walk or run alongside the line while performing repetitive tasks. Assembly of automobile requires over 1,800 separate operations over almost 48 consecutive hours (in three eight-hour shifts).

2. Over 70 percent of the components of the cars manufactured by outside contractors. Parts transported over great distances at great cost, then unloaded at main dock to be warehoused until needed. Defects often not discovered until the parts are removed from the warehouse and brought to the assembly site. Management must then decide to delay production until new parts can be located in the warehouse (or can be shipped from the contractors) or to use the defective parts.

3. Benefits for assembly-line workers, all union members: high hourly pay, high overtime pay, and excellent insurance. But job satisfaction is low, absenteeism high, and layoffs frequent when car sales decline. (Laid-off workers receive almost full pay from unemployment insurance and union reserve funds, but in some cases may be unable to work for months or years, or not at all.)

4. Cumbersome and expensive billing and accounting practices, involving the transmission and filing of orders, confirmations, invoices, receipts, and inventory reports.

About the Automobile Market

1. According to a study from the Massachusetts Institute of Technology, Japanese car plants in America are as productive as car plants in Japan. Manufacturing a car in Japan requires 20.3 hours, but only 19.6 hours in America.

2. Research and development engineers in American companies have traditionally designed cars without consulting production engineers, workers, or parts makers. Japanese engineers continually receive suggestions from everyone involved throughout the design, manufacturing, and marketing processes.

3. Successful modern company must stress efficiency in how cars are built and in basic structure of the organization. Must employ fewer workers and use the most up-to-date technology and practices.

About the Saturn (General Motors)

1. Workers, all veteran GM employees, volunteered to work for the company without promise of a bonus, but for the opportunity to participate in designing cars.

2. Union contract allows great worker participation in running the plant. For example, assembly-line workers visited machine tool builders in the United States and in Japan to learn production equipment they would be using to build Saturn.

3. "Just-in-time" delivery of parts and materials from suppliers reduces warehousing costs.

4. Height of the engine assembly line rises and falls at various stations to optimize specific operations.

5. Most parts produced on site, not by suppliers. However, start-up costs of the project, including building a state-of-art manufacturing facility, were $3 billion.

6. All Saturn employees receive salary—not hourly wage—and eat in the same cafeterias. Starting pay is 20 percent less than pay of other auto workers, but employees can earn more pay than at other factories by meeting or exceeding productivity goals.

7. All workers trained in interpersonal skills, and the applicants, whether for blue- or white collar jobs, required approval of joint union-member and management panel. Employees learn teamwork and consensus building. Also undergo 100 to 750 hours of additional training, including learning to understand a balance sheet. All employees expected to examine the company's books and know how much their operations add to production costs.

8. Union members gave up all seniority rights, but labor agreement protects them from layoffs, except for "unforeseen or catastrophic events or severe economic conditions."

9. Parts made outside the plant go directly to docks closest to where they will be used. Line workers unload cases and spot defects immediately.

10. The final assembly line made of wood, reducing strain on the feet. Car rests on wooden pallet that can be raised or lowered for convenience. And workers remain with car on platform; they don't walk alongside moving car body.

11. Saturn's financial system virtually paperless, and all information is stored in a single computerized database, greatly decreasing administrative costs.

12. Mid-level managers closest to the production process decide goals and business plans, streamlining time needed to make decisions.

About the Neon (Chrysler Corporation)
1. Uses new concept called "concurrent engineering," in which engineering, marketing, purchasing, and financial people work together.

2. Engineers measured precisely how foreign and domestic subcompacts are handled. Also tore the cars apart, weighed each component, and computed manufacturing costs.

3. Result of engineers' survey of owners of subcompact cars: most important features were reliable, safe car that felt like a big one and was fun to drive.

4. Outside manufacturers of component parts involved in designing and planning process early. Told the targeted costs for components, and were asked to share financial data. Some higher component costs actually lowered final cost of the car. For example, one supplier designed a fold-down rear seat that could be installed in every model in the same way. Design will save Chrysler up to $1 million by simplifying the final assembly.

5. Assembly-line workers worked with engineers to streamline production methods, make car easy to build, and minimize defects. Suggested more than 4,000 changes in the car's design and manufacturing process; many have been implemented.

6. Final design cut costs where customers wouldn't notice, or wouldn't care. Power windows and a four-speed automatic transmission unimportant, so neither was offered.

7. Conversely, company spends more money on the safety features small-car owners want: standard dual airbags and reinforced doors that meet 1997 federal crash-impact standards.

Composing Activity: Writing Your Report

Within your role, write a report to the top management of Columbia Motors, in which you reiterate your argument and support and explain its claims. Don't attempt to use all the facts supplied, just those that are most relevant to your findings. At various stages in the composing and revising process, discuss your paper with members of your group. Follow the procedures (including the Postdraft Analysis questions) introduced in this chapter. You may also wish to examine the coherence of the report by using the procedures discussed at the end of Chapter 8.

Additional Composing Activity: Reporting on the Report

Write a press release in which you report on the main points raised in the meeting. Don't attempt an elaborate discussion of each group's findings or recommendations; just summarize and explain them briefly.

Chapter 11

Taking a Critical Journey

To criticize is to appreciate, to appropriate, to take intellectual possession, to establish . . . a relation with the criticized thing and to make it one's own.

—Henry James

You read a criticism or review—be it of a book, movie, poem, play, exhibit, piece of art, or public performance—for two reasons: (1) to help you decide whether to spend your time and money on the subject criticized; and (2) to help you understand and appreciate its themes, ideas, and achievements. Too often, however, students' attempts at criticism degenerate into long plot summaries that teach nothing and, by disclosing everything that happens in the work, even dampen the readers' motivation to see or hear the original.

Why do reviews from novice critics fall into the plot-summary trap (and are often badly written summaries at that)? Perhaps partly because of students' experiences with grammar-school (and even high-school) book reports that were heavy on plot, light on insight. But the main reason goes deeper and is tied to the writers' fears that they have nothing to say. Intimidated by their lack of familiarity with both the subject and the field, the writers resort to what they can discuss: the plot. Moreover, their discomfort with the materials often reveals itself in awkward and confusing language.

These problems needn't occur, however, if you write about what you know through training or experience or love. Whatever your background, you're "expert" enough about *some* field—popular or classical music, soap operas, movies, detective stories, science fiction novels, painting, college basketball, or music videos—to share honest reactions to a particular work or performance. And you can probe your background for experiences, information, and insights that enrich that reaction.

When you write, you lay out a line of words. The line of words is a miner's pick, a wood-carver's gouge, a surgeon's probe. You wield it, and it digs a path you follow. Soon you find yourself deep in new territory. Is it a dead end, or have you located the real subject? You will know tomorrow, or this time next year.

—Annie Dillard, The Writing Life

Furthermore, you needn't worry about the quality of your observations. Good critics write with authority but not infallibility; they're thoughtful and knowledgeable, but above all human and honest. Your readers will make their own judgments about the work you discuss; they don't expect you to provide the final word on the subject. So relax and share your biases, experiences, and feelings with readers while taking them along the journey through your responses to some performance or work of art—and then arrive at some conclusion. Don't let plot summary enslave you; enlist the summary to support your claims instead.

LOOKING AT CRITICISMS

Each of the following criticisms tells the story of a writer's evolving responses to a work or performance. In the first example, a naturalized American of Chinese descent reacts to a movie about China from a unique viewpoint that broadens our understanding of the thematic elements of the movie.

When I first saw the title of the movie, I had no idea about it at all. "Iron and Silk"—what is the relationship between these two? My curiosity compelled me to go to the cinema.

My first surprise was that the movie tells a story closely relating to China; actually it is based on an American's experience in China. The author of the book upon which it is based, Mark Salzman, portrays himself in the movie. He has been invited to teach English in one of the colleges in Hangzhon, China. He teaches middle-aged teachers who are much older than he is, learns martial arts from a famous master who has won a championship, and meets a Chinese girl who knows more English poetry than he does. He works and lives among common people. However, it is through their lives that he recognizes the spirit of the Chinese.

At the beginning I thought that the movie would be ridiculous because foreigners could hardly understand the thoughts of Chinese people. As it goes on, though, I found myself greatly fascinated by every detail. There is no lecturing, no commentary, no artificiality—just the facts. For example, once in Mark's class in conversational English, a student says that she has watched "Tess" and considers the actress, Nastassja Kinski, not beautiful because of her full mouth. Mark is astonished. "You can't be serious. A full mouth is good." "Good for what?" the students ask. "For kissing," Mark answers without hesitation. This comment arouses a laugh and one of the students tells Mark that people never kiss in China. It may seem unbelievable to Americans, but it is true. Even young lovers rarely kiss, whether in front of or away from others. They express their love through holding another's hand or through their eyes—a kind of implicit communication. Different from American's frankness, it is the usual manner by which Chinese display their feelings: love or hatred, sadness or happiness, contempt or respect. I was amazed at how accurately Mark soon figures out the difference between these two cultures after a simple conversation.

In addition to the cultural differences Mark encounters in his teaching experiences, the story goes on to explore two further intertwining themes. One involves his learning of martial arts. "What you have learned is garbage," Mark's martial arts instructor tells him. "You have to relearn everything." So Mark practices hours on end, trying to master skills that would give him the look and power of a tiger crashing down a mountainside. But that's not the only learning he experiences. Each day brings a new clash between Mark's Western ways and the age-old traditions of the Orient. Martial arts is one of many precious cultures that have a long history. To imitate its surface actions is easy, but he can never master the sport without understanding its underlying essentials. The movie tries to tell those in Western countries that martial arts not only train your body but also your willpower. That is what "eating bitter" means. To be a master you should have both iron fists and iron will.

The third theme also reveals a big difference between Western and Oriental culture. Love in China is not two people's business; it is everyone's business. Although love between Mark and a Chinese girl is pure as silk, it is also prevented by a tradition as old as the history of silk.

Since I came from China and am now an American, I recognize the many differences between the two cultures. I know that people from the two cultures can hardly understand each other because they lack knowledge of these differences. Therefore, I was really touched by this movie because it speaks out my thoughts, not by words, but through facts. I consider it the first step in our getting to know each other, and I hope it won't be the only step.

—Hua Yan

Criticism needn't be directed only at movies or books. This next example, by a student who knows and appreciates Italian food, takes us on a journey through her experiences with a carry-out restaurant.

"A Menu You Can't Refuse!" That's what it says on a flyer from Mulberry St., N.Y.-N.Y., a new Italian restaurant in the Lincoln Park area. I found their carry-out and delivery menu stuffed in my front door the other day and, intrigued, decided to order up a little Italian food fest.

The person who answered the phone spoke in a clear, fluent English voice. If you are a delivered-food junkie as I am, you will certainly appreciate talking to someone who doesn't ask for your address four times, and who leaves you with the impression that your dinner will indeed arrive.

On this first Mulberry adventure, I was delighted to have another food aficionado join me, thus creating more to taste. We decided on the House Specialty: Arincini. This translates to an appetizer consisting of rice balls stuffed with ricotta cheese along with herbs and spices rolled in bread crumbs, and deep fried. They were quite yummy and large, so one for each of us was sufficient.

We also ordered two different chicken dishes. The first was Pollo Alla Latanzi. It featured a chicken breast that was sautéed in wine with plenty of mushrooms and artichoke hearts. We favored this one over the Pollo Alla Vesuvio, which was breaded in a sauce with vegetables. Both dinners came with a small salad, complete with those funny garbanzo beans.

Our one disappointment on this first encounter with Mulberry St. was minor: Even though the menu listed beer and wine, none was available. More than compensating for this failing was the service, which was fast and friendly and included no delivery charge.

On another occasion, I dined on ravioli with meat sauce. It was great! My friend's spinach salad also proved to be an economical and tasty meal at only $3.50. The tomato bread, a half loaf of crusty Italian bread spread with marinara sauce and then baked, was provided with each meal at no extra charge.

The Super Thin Crust Pizza we ordered in our third foray into Mulberry St.'s offerings proved to be a culinary disappointment, however. Maybe we Chicagoans are just spoiled by ample, bready-heavy crust oozing with melted cheese and lots of sauce. A pale, thin piece of flat dough with an anemic looking sauce didn't tantalize my taste buds much. It was possibly developed as pizza for anorexics.

Mulberry St. is open seven days a week from 11:00 A.M. to 1:00 A.M. You will find the service excellent and most of the food scrumptious. Get out the china, a few candles, and your wine glasses. Let Mulberry St. bring you some fine Italian cuisine, and you'll have a romantic dinner for two without having a sauce pan to scrub.

—Virginia Ray

A final example, by professional film critic Roger Ebert, brings a level of expertise and experience to his review that most student writers cannot match. Nonetheless, his approach to his subject matter is similar to Hua Yan's and Virginia Ray's. Like them, Ebert probes his background and experiences to help us understand the achievement of the film he reviews. And also like Yan and Ray, he takes us on a journey through his personal reactions toward (and biases about) the movie until he arrives at his recommendation.

OLD MEETS NEW: STEAMY "HOT SPOT" BLENDS B MOVIE, FILM NOIR

A guy comes in from out of town. He doesn't have a past—at least not one he wants to talk about. He gets a job in a used-car lot. It's one of those typical small towns from the movies of the 1940s and 1950s, the kind of backwater where the other guy on the job is a nerd, and the boss is a blowhard with a bum ticker—but the boss' wife is this great broad with blond hair and big eyelashes and when she gets up in the morning she puts on her negligee just when the other women in town are taking theirs off. Oh, and the bookkeeper at work is this innocent young girl who is intimidated, for mysterious reasons, by the vicious creep who lives in a shack outside of town.

I feel at home in movies like "The Hot Spot." They come out of that vast universe formed by the historic-meeting of B movies and the idea of film noir—films about the soft underbelly of the human conscience. There are certain conventions to be observed, and "The Hot Spot" knows them and observes them. The hero has to smoke and look laconic and be trying to suppress something in his past. It helps if he drives a Studebaker. The boss' wife has to have learned all of her moves by studying old movies. The plot has to provide that the bad guys don't commit all of the crimes; the hero, for example, robs the bank.

Dennis Hopper, who directed "The Hot Spot," grew up in the movies at a time when films like this were familiar—back in the days when there was time for luxuries like a supporting cast and a plot, back before high-tech violence and machinegun editing came to dominate crime movies. As an actor, he was directed by such film noir veterans as Nicholas Ray and Henry Hathaway. And maybe his sensibility is attuned to this kind of material, to the notion that an ordinary guy can stumble into some pretty strange stuff. The movie has been compared in some quarters with the work of David Lynch, but it's less self-hating and more stylistically exuberant.

The movie is all style and tone, and a lot of the tone is set by the performance of Virginia Madsen as Dolly Harshaw, the boss' wife. It's the kind of work that used to be done by Lana Turner or Barbara Stanwyck—the tough woman with the healthy sexual interest, who sizes a guy up and makes sure he knows what she likes in a man.

Jennifer Connelly, as the innocent bookkeeper down at the office, is perfectly cast as her opposite. She's got the Teresa Wright role, the good girl who has been bruised by an uncaring world. Hopper regards both women with the visual imagination of a cheesecake photographer, which is kind of refreshing. Male superstars have come to dominate action movies so thoroughly that it's rare to find a movie with the time and inclination to linger on beautiful women.

The plot is silly, as such plots always are. It stars Don Johnson as Harry Madox, the stranger from out of town, and he figures out a way to steal money from the bank, and he also finds himself embroiled in violence when the creep in the shack outside of town starts messing with the young girl. And of course the boss' wife also has a connection to the creep, and the key to everything is in the shameful secrets of the past.

A film this simple can best be appreciated by a fairly sophisticated viewer, I think. Your average workaday moviegoer will relate to it on Level One and think it contains clichés and stereotypes.

Only movie lovers who have marinated their imaginations in the great B movies from RKO and Republic will recognize "The Hot Spot" as a superior work in an old tradition—as a manipulation of story elements as mannered and deliberate, in its way, as variations on a theme for the piano.

Issues for Investigation and Discussion

1. How do the reviewers back up their claims about their subject matter—that is, what warrants and backing does each writer supply? What from their backgrounds do the writers bring to the criticism that helps us better understand the subject matter? Where do Yan and Ebert use plot summary to back up their claims—or to allow themselves to comment on the themes of the movie?

2. All three reviewers state their main point at the end of their reviews. Why? What are those points? Why do they delay making their recommendations

until the end? Could they have made those same recommendations at the beginning of the review?

3. Yan fills her paper with oppositions—between her expectations about the movie and what she actually saw, between Saltzman's expectations about China and what he experienced, between her Chinese culture and American perceptions of the culture. How do those oppositions contribute to her point?

4. Why does Virginia Ray discuss more than one experience in ordering from Mulberry St., N.Y.-N.Y.?

5. The reviewers discuss some terms and ideas that are probably unfamiliar to their readers. How do the reviewers handle this problem? Cite examples.

6. Ray's review is notable for its natural and authentic voice. Point out several instances where her voice and sense of humor emerge.

7. Ebert is a professional critic, yet he writes the first paragraph of his review in slangy, informal language. Why? And in the second paragraph, Ebert admits his bias toward the type of movie he reviews. Why?

8. Do any of the reviewers endorse their subject matter without qualification or misgivings? How do their recommendations affect your evaluations of the subject matter?

9. As a way of summarizing your ideas in response to these questions, or to any other matters you observe in the criticisms, turn to your journal and list six or more common traits of effective criticisms (or create a list with several classmates). Let this list guide you as you compose and revise your own report later.

EMPLOYING THE JOURNEY ORGANIZATION

Only rarely does a review fully endorse or condemn its subject. Most reviews arrive at a more balanced opinion: that a work's strengths outweigh its weaknesses or vice versa. You can't paint a picture by throwing a bucket of paint against a wall, but must attend to colors and forms, lines and shading. Each brush stroke, each hue, adds to the breadth of its message. Your readers will ultimately decide for themselves on the worth of a work, so your job is to help them decide.

Because a balanced judgment requires a complexity of responses to the subject, you may choose to explore those responses in what Ken Macrorie calls the *journey organization*. Unlike the thesis-mapping-signposting structure you've employed in earlier writing tasks, the journey organization takes readers on an intellectual excursion through your reactions (not always in a straight line) until they arrive at some final judgment of the work. The journey consists of a series of claims and their support—sometimes plot summary, sometimes plot analysis, but never any more of either than is needed—with transitions that establish connections between the claims along the way. Many journeys also take short visits to the writer's personal experiences that illuminate readers'

understanding of the subject matter. Thus, a typical journey review might take
a form like this:

> background and initial
> feelings toward the
> subject matter (backed by
> personal experiences)

> first response to work
>   reason for response
>   backing: short summary
>   of scene

> second response
>   reason (comparison to another
>   work or personal experience)
>   backing: short summary of scenes
>   or themes from works compared

> third response — a change in viewpoint
>   reason
>   backing: summary and interpretation
>   of scene

> fourth response — a shift back in the direction
> to earlier responses
>   reason: reconsideration of views toward the
>   subject matter
>   backing: personal experiences and examples
>   from the work

> final response: a balanced judgment
>   reason: further interpretation of reactions toward
>   the work
>   backing: short summary of views and main
>   ideas/themes in the work

The good critic is he who narrates the adventures of [his or her] soul among masterpieces.

—*Anatole France*

Invention Activity: Choosing Subjects for Criticism

(Alternatively or additionally, you may follow the procedures of this and subsequent composing/revising activities to compose your argument in the Writing in a Social Context section that begins on p. 162.)

In your journal or computer file, contemplate subjects for a critical review that you feel comfortable responding to because of interest, training, or experience. (Don't, for example, choose to discuss a performance of classical music if you listen mostly to popular music.) Assume you will be writing the review for a newspaper or magazine and that your audience will share some interest in but not extensive knowledge of the subject matter or genre (that is, the type of work you'll be criticizing).

- Begin by listing one or more specific works of art, pieces of writing, public performances, or public entertainments (a play, movie, painting or sculpture, art exhibit, novel, modern poem, concert, musical recording, music video, television show, restaurant, amusement park or amusement park ride, or sporting event) that you've already encountered or plan on encountering.

- Or, if no specific subjects occur to you, brainstorm for a moment about the general types of entertainment that appeal to you (popular music, movies, Stephen King novels, or the Romantic Poets). Then consider specific candidates for criticism.

- Share your list with several classmates so they may comment on the topics they find most interesting, and narrow your choices to one or two.

- Then begin making notes in your journal about your knowledge about the subject. Use free writing, brainstorming, clustering, or whatever invention devices will facilitate your examination. Consider your background in the field (for example, your knowledge about and attitudes toward movies of this type—or its actors) and actual personal experiences that relate to the theme of the work. Would any of this information prove useful in the review? Return to the journal or file if additional ideas occur to you later.

- Also begin some preliminary analysis of your audience. What are they likely to know or not know about your topic? What terms might you need to define or explain? You'll consult both sets of notes later when composing the review.

Invention Activity: Recording Your Responses to the Subject

Either during or after attending, viewing, hearing, or reading the subject you intend to review, explore your reactions to the subject. Using a double-entry format in your journal or computer file, examine these issues:

- What did you think or feel first, and what in the work prompted that response?
- Does any experience or knowledge from your personal life influence this reaction?
- How did you react next, then next, and so on until your reached your final reaction?

Use one side of the journal to summarize each part of the work that elicited your reaction; and use the other side to record that reaction. (The simplest way to organize your reactions is to respond chronologically to each part as it occurred.) Don't settle for short, simplistic statements like "I loved it" or "It was dumb." Explain your responses in detail:

> I enjoyed the wise-cracking exchanges between Gibson and Glover, but more than that, I appreciated the obvious affection and respect between the two. Here for once is a cops-and-bad guys movie in which police officers display a human, vulnerable side.

> While the shoot-em-up ending was exciting, I thought it was a cop-out. The film raises some complex moral and societal issues, yet chooses to resolve them through the clichéd chase scenes and violence we see in nine out of ten Hollywood productions.

Return to the journal as additional ideas occur to you. Record your changing viewpoints, for they can provide rich and complex insights into the subject of your review. Consider, too, what information from your earlier journal entries might clarify or provide additional insights into the work you're reviewing.

Establishing Your Credentials or Acknowledging Your Biases

> *Be sure of yourself and your own reach to know,*
> *How far your genius, taste, and learning go;*
> *Launch not beyond your depth, but be discreet,*
> *And mark the point where sense and dullness meet.*
>
> —*Alexander Pope*, An Essay on Criticism

As readers assess your assessments, they'll probably want to learn a bit about your background and preferences. A well-known professional critic like Roger Ebert needn't establish his credentials, but he isn't afraid to admit his biases. "I feel at home in movies like 'The Hot Spot', he confesses, admitting his fondness for the *film noir* genre.

You're probably not an expect and needn't pretend to be, but you can extract information from your journal notes to indicate what you know or feel about the subject. Here, for example, are the final-draft opening paragraphs of a review in which a student first summarizes his background and tastes in art before starting his critical journey. His ambivalence toward contemporary art helps him to construct the problem he'll explore in the review: Was this student exhibit worth seeing?

> On April 11, I went to the opening of the Masters of Fine Arts Thesis Exhibition by the School of the Art Institute. I've been drawing and painting since childhood, and my most recent interest has been photography, so I jumped at the chance to view works done by students graduating at the school.
>   I like the works of Van Gogh, Cezanne, the masters of the Renaissance, and even some Surrealist art, yet I've had mixed feelings about contemporary art. But the works at the Masters Show cover a variety of disciplines, from painting to holography, so I knew that it would be, at the least, interesting.

In this next example (also from the final draft of a review) a student discusses his tastes in movies, which leads him to begin to answer the problem he constructs in his review: Will "Missing in Action 3" equal the achievements of the action movies he loved as a child?

"MISSING IN ACTION 3": A RESCUE THAT FAILS

Before 1975, all movie theaters in Vietnam showed only two kinds of films: ones made in the United States and others in Hong Kong. I disliked the latter and was a buff for the former. However, I experienced a hiatus of twelve years in which I could see none except films made in Eastern-bloc countries, the majority of which were from the Soviet Union and East Germany. I found them very dull.

Our fast-changing society makes twelve years a long interval, especially when someone wants to follow the trends of Hollywood, where box-office success is the *raison d'être* of virtually every production. Besides the techniques, even the ethics and the artistic performances are tainted by this primary concern. If one used to admire the action films of Robert Taylor and John Wayne, how would he find those starring Chuck Norris or Sylvester Stallone? My curiosity has been satisfied since I've come to America, but some of the movies I've seen have been shockingly irresponsible in their attempts to make money. "Missing in Action 3" is one of them.

—Phu V. Ngo

As you look over your journal notes, consider whether a brief discussion of your background and tastes would help your readers understand and evaluate your observations on the subject. But include these comments only if and where they're relevant. Virginia Ray mentions only in passing that she's a "delivered-food junkie," and her comfort with and lucid explanations of the dishes she orders implicitly make us trust her. A review composed in paint-by-the-numbers fashion—that is, following a formula without thought as to why—is as simplistic as the bucket of paint thrown against a wall.

Proceeding with the Journey

Once the journey begins, you can assume the role of tour guide for your readers, at each stop pointing out how your responses toward the work changed, were reinforced, or took a slightly different direction. And be honest. Your candid admission that you don't understand something will probably increase your audience's trust in your judgments—and lead them to suspect that the problem lies in the work, not in you.

As you compose and revise your review, try to back up each reaction with some reference to the work—its theme, a scene, a character, or plot. But make sure you maintain control of the materials; don't let them control you. If you find yourself trapped in a long plot summary, stop and consider each detail, and cross out any that don't directly support your claim.

The third paragraph of Phu Ngo's review of "Missing in Action 3" briefly summarizes the plot, but only so that readers may understand his criticisms that immediately follow:

In 1985, James Braddock (Chuck Norris) comes back alone into Vietnam to rescue his wife he had thought dead in the chaos of Saigon, 1975. In spite of volleys of mortar shells and bullets sprayed at him, Braddock, badly wounded but still alive, would get out and return to the USA as a hero who brought out with him his own son and dozens of Amerasian teen-agers.

In the body of the review, Ngo subordinates all other details of plot to discussions of the movie's themes and technical faults. Notice the oppositions between his insights and the events portrayed in the movie, all of which lead up to his main point (in italics). Notice the references to Vietnamese culture and even architecture that arise from Ngo's personal experiences. And notice the first sentence of each paragraph, which serves as a signpost marking his arrival at a new destination on his intellectual journey and establishing its logical connection to the last stop.

Braddock's scheme might be an adventure to a naïve American audience, but it is absolutely suicide to any Vietnamese. A foreigner would be spotted as soon as he parachutes from an airplane and drives a jet motor boat on small rivers in the Vietnamese countryside as Braddock does. It is too simple-minded for movie-makers as well as movie-goers to think that kind of plan would work. Furthermore, any Vietnamese will easily detect the technical flaws in the movie. The United States Embassy looks quite different from the real one in Saigon, and I cannot understand why the Vietnamese in the film spoke their native language in an unnatural way that only foreigners could speak. Even in a fanciful feature film, some truths should be respected.

The most obvious distortion is the film's treatment of the Vietcong. It is a fact that they are brutal, sometimes inhuman, but this brutality is expressed in such a distorted and childish way that it would make any McCarthyites blush. Because of the color of their hair, their skin, or their eyes, the Amerasians have always had hard times integrating themselves into the society, no matter what regime is governing the country. But the Communists have never rounded them up behind barbed wire as they do in this film. What would the Communists gain from such a policy?

Braddock's rescue of the children is equally absurd. It is certainly not a heroic act to lead dozens of teen-agers on a ninety-mile march through the tropical jungle without any preparations. Braddock quips, "I don't step on others' toes, I step on others' necks," but the tragedy is that in this case they are not only the necks of the enemy but also of the naïve children. *Ultimately, it seems to me that the plot of this movie is a parody of the American involvement in Vietnam. With impeccable goodwill, innocence, and technological superiority, the Americans just banged in, bogged down, and did not know how to bail out.*

The last paragraph of the journey signals Ngo's arrival at his destination. It summarizes his responses and ends with a punch:

People in America might be frustrated by their failure in the Vietnam War or mortified by their neglect toward the Amerasians, but they cannot make up for their frustration in such a film as "Missing in Action 3." If as Ken Macrorie says, "Good plays and good movies help people understand their lives better as well as provide them with entertainment," "Missing in Action 3" is certainly not a good one.

Notice the resources Ngo has tapped throughout his critical journey: his personal experiences with and tastes in movies; his awareness of Vietnamese customs, practices, language, and geography; short plot summaries; interpretation of scenes and themes; and comparisons to other movies and actual life in Vietnam. Ngo's perspective is unique, of course, but you don't have to come from another culture to compose an effective criticism. Simply draw upon your own resources, chronicle your reactions, and back them up.

Composing Activity: Writing a Draft of Your Review

Look over the double entry materials you recorded in your journal, and compose a first draft of your review in which you journey through your reactions to the subject. Back up each claim and, when necessary, explain what warrants this backing. You may state a claim first and then follow it by warrant and evidence:

I stopped laughing later in the movie [warrant] because the violence became excessive. [backing/evidence] In one especially gruesome sequence, four people are either decapitated or virtually disemboweled—in slow motion, no less.)

Or you may move from claim to backing and further claim:

The violence began to escalate after the first forty-five minutes. [backing/evidence] In one slow-motion sequence, for example, four people are either decapitated or virtually disemboweled. [claim] My initial enjoyment of the movie was beginning to turn to revulsion.

At some point in the composing process—whether prior to or after writing the body of your review—turn your attention to the introduction. What problem—stated or implied—should the beginning paragraph(s) construct for your readers? Should you establish your credentials or state your biases, and if so, which ones and where? (You may find the introduction easier to write after you compose the body.) And in your final paragraph, try to bring your journey to its destination by resolving the issues you've raised throughout the review. Most often, that means stating whether the subject of the review is worth your readers' time and money. As always, don't strive for perfection in your first draft; assume you'll revise the paper (especially its beginning and ending) several times.

While composing or revising the paper (or both), also direct your attention to the signposts at the beginning of each paragraph. Do they establish the point of the paragraph and show the movement from point to point? These matters generally require multiple revisions.

Collaborative Activity: Eliciting Responses to Your Review (25 minutes of class time)

If possible, read your work aloud to several classmates, record their responses on the following Postdraft Analysis questions, and respond to the responses later. Make additional notes, and consider what changes to make as you revise. Then write another draft of the paper.

Postdraft Analysis
(To be completed by the writer or peer reader)

1. Locate the phrases or sentences at the beginning of the review that establish the writer's credentials as well as construct (or imply) the problem for the intended audience. Are both matters clearly established? If not, how might the first paragraph be revised?

2. Look at each major claim. Is it sufficiently backed by relevant facts, examples, or incidents? Is some backing irrelevant? Is some excessive? Indicate in bracketed labels where backing could be expanded or cut.

3. Locate the connections (warrants) between each claim and backing. Are the warrants clear? Are additional warrants needed? Identify with bracketed labels where warrants might be added or expanded.

4. If the review makes four claims, could it manage with three—or, does it need a fifth? What could be cut or added?

5. Does the writer summarize any personal experiences to support his or her observations and responses? If not, consider whether any—and which ones—would be helpful.

6. Look for signposts indicating each stop on the journey. Do they show the direction of the journey and establish clear transitions from one stop to the next? Identify with bracketed labels where signposts might be strengthened.

7. Does the journey arrive at its destination? Is the arrival a logical consequence of the steps leading up to it? If not, identify with bracketed labels what should be changed.

8. Is the language clear, direct, and natural? Look carefully at the tenses of the verbs. Are the tenses consistent? You should discuss your reactions to the work in the past tense—they occurred in the past—but discuss the work itself in the present tense (unless it was a live performance, which also occurred in the past). Maintaining consistency in tense is difficult for even the most experienced reviewers. Bracket where tightening, rewording, or tense changes are necessary.

9. Do any other problems need to be addressed? If so, in what way?

Concluding Activity: Revising and Editing Your Argument

Assemble all your notes and then revise your review, clarifying the transitions between stops along the journey, tightening the sentences, sharpening the details, and editing carefully for consistency of tense and matters of mechanics, grammar, and spelling.

WRITING IN A SOCIAL CONTEXT: ROGER AND GENE

Like the activities at the ends of Chapters 8 through 10, the following activity simulates a real situation in which you and your classmates can gain first-hand experience, devise arguments, debate the issues, and then communicate your ideas in writing. See Chapter 8 for instructions on conducting the activity.

The Context

A local public radio station is auditioning reviewers for a new program entitled "Focus on the Arts," which will cover the major performing and nonperforming arts. Modeled on the popular movie review shows on television, the weekly hour-long program will aid viewers in choosing things to see, read, or hear. The format will feature separate five-minute segments in which pairs of critics discuss and debate their reactions to the same movie, book, play, television show, recorded performance, restaurant, or even a music video. But because the show is on radio, the critics must back up their claims with oral summaries, paraphrases, or quotes from the works they review—not with movie clips or other visual aids.

The critics will also be expected to write longer and more structured versions of their recommendations in a weekly companion magazine, entitled *A Consumer's Guide to the Arts*.

Several auditions will take place simultaneously in different parts of the same studio (or in different studios), in which various assistant producers will observe and evaluate participants before recommending to the producer which ones to hire.

The Participants

Prospective Reviewers.   You would like to become a regular critic on the show, specializing in some field (or fields) in the arts. Prior to the audition, you'll meet with the other prospective reviewers to choose a partner and a work you'll discuss and debate. Both of you will return to the studio to give your performance at an agreed-upon later time.

You'll prepare for the audition by making notes of your reactions to the work, of the backing for your reactions, and of your judgments on the worth of the work. Then during the audition, you'll present and debate your ideas. You needn't disagree with your partner on each point, but you should be ready to expand upon, support, and defend your claims.

Assistant Producers.   You are interested in finding qualified reviewers for the program, people who can articulate their ideas and back them up. You'll observe at least two but no more than three pairs of reviewers, read their written commentaries later, and then recommend to the producer the ones who should be hired.

Composing Activity: Writing Your Argument

Now compose your argument. If you are a prospective reviewer, write an expanded and more formal review of the work you discussed, employing a journey organization and taking care to back up your claims. You should concentrate on your own ideas and needn't debate your partner's argument. You will be addressing a two-fold audience: potential readers of the magazine, and the assistant producers who will evaluate your review on its effectiveness in making its case with these readers.

If you are an assistant producer, recommend to the producer the participants who should be hired. (You needn't—and shouldn't—find fault with or even discuss the less successful performances.) Base your recommendations on the depth and clarity of the participants' spoken and written remarks, and back up your decisions with evidence (summaries, paraphrases, and quotations) from their presentations. Recommend no more than two reviewers, who need not be from the same pairings.

Chapter 12

Defending a Position

The body travels more easily than the mind, and until we have limbered up our imagination we continue to think as if we had stayed home. We have not really budged a step until we take up residence in someone else's point of view.

—*John Erskine*

The best generals respect their adversaries. And in the battle among conflicting viewpoints on any major issue, the best writers respect the counterarguments of their readers. Whether as a student, a parent, a taxpayer, an employee, or a leader, you'll find yourself composing position papers in which you state and defend your position on important issues. You'd do well, therefore, to heed the advice of Aristotle: that you learn to anticipate and refute opposing views, and let those views challenge the validity of your ideas. You should tell readers why they're wrong, but also concede a point if they're right. Your honesty will gain their respect, and they'll more likely accept your point of view.

Which brings us back to Stephen E. Toulmin's analysis of arguments. You'll recall that in Chapter 8 we examined four parts of Toulmin's model: the claim, its support, its warrants, and its qualifiers. Now we'll turn to the final part of the model: the rebuttal, or response to counterarguments.

LOOKING AT ARGUMENTS

The writers of the following two arguments rebut the counterarguments of their audience with varying degrees of rigor. In the first, which appeared in *Essence* magazine in June 1986, De'Lois Jacobs challenges the contentions of an ex-lover and the "defensive arguments" of other African Americans. Her tone is insistent, her argument impassioned, so she acknowledges but concedes only the most minor points in what she regards as untenable counterarguments:

IN OUR OWN IMAGE

Recently one of my greatest concerns and fears was realized when my younger sister told me about a story she had read in a popular Black publication: A teenager committed suicide because his mother would not allow him to have cosmetic surgery on his nose in imitation of his idol, Michael Jackson. This story is more than just sad; it is an outrage. What is it about this society that gets us so completely involved in the material and physical world? Why is it that our Black public figures, particularly in entertainment, tend to be turning more and more to this way of presenting themselves? What are these false images they worship and aspire to look like?

When I look in a mirror, I can clearly see where I come from—the influences of my father's genes and my mother and grandmother in me. It gives me a feeling of warmth, pride and reassurance to be able to see my roots every single day of my life. There is nothing there that needs "fixing."

Yet I've had at least one lover (now "ex") tell me that my nose "spoils" my looks. This was a man who was constantly talking about Black unity, solidarity, beauty and pride. Well, I asked him whether it would please him to see me with a straight or aquiline nose, or maybe one like a popular white model's. This response not only surprised him, but it also shut him up on the subject forever when he realized the absurdity of his remark.

Here in America we are increasingly buying and selling goods and services based on "face value." We are inundated with images that beckon us through advertising, shape attitudes through film and television, and influence thinking through the printed, recorded and spoken word. Before we lay down our hard-earned cash and our principles, let's take a close look at who is selling us this bill of goods and why. As the ads have changed from extolling the wonders of Afro-hairstyle products to those of "curl" activators, so has our idea of ourselves and what we look like.

Now, I have heard many defensive arguments in justification of the things we do to our hair and skin color. Why are some of us so embarrassed by our natural physical traits? I like to look into other Black faces and see the tribes from which we have descended. Lineage is something to be aware of, and pride in it is something to pass on to our young, from generation to generation. I will not renounce that, ever. And here is my question: When we try to change our looks so drastically, what messages are we conveying to our young? Think about it—think long and strong. Think about that young teenager, and then let your conscience be your guide.

This innate insecurity that drives us to change our images must come to an end. Surely we must realize that such changes will not make our most popular and revered singers sing any better, our musicians perform any more brilliantly, or when you take a really close look, appear any more attractive. For instance, although I like Michael Jackson's music, as I always have, I must admit I now feel a remoteness when I look at him, since there is not much there that I can relate to and admire anymore. I do not wish to chastise any particular entertainers, but I am curious about the reasons behind their decisions regarding their looks. Do they even know?

It is sad that our children's heroes seem to want to look like images from which we Black people are the farthest removed. Straighten your nose, then your lips are too full; fix that, then your hips are too wide; tuck those, then your hair is too kinky; relax that, then your hair is too short, wonderweave that, then your skin is too dark; and on and on it goes.

Although the 20-inch Afro is a thing of the past, the feeling of Black pride that accompanied it was fortifying. Let us not lose that feeling. The once often-heard phrases from the sixties—"I'm Black and I'm proud" and "Black is beautiful"—are sorely missed. I thought we didn't need to proclaim them so loudly in the eighties because, finally, we truly believed them. Do we? Look at the conflicting signals our young people get every day about their self-images. We who are parents and grandparents, aunts and uncles, godparents and older siblings have a responsibility to our young. Let us take the time to examine and explain to them those things that have real value and those that do not, so that they can make sounder judgments and better choices in conducting their own lives. Let us help them develop strong self-esteem by setting examples they can follow that are in our own images.

Throughout this next argument, which appeared in the "My Turn" section of *Newsweek* on January 10, 1994, Ken Baker attempts to anticipate and then respond to counterarguments.

THE INVISIBLE MAINSTREAM

The other day I saw myself on TV. Well, not exactly me, but rather who I am thought to be. Has this ever happened to you? That is, seeing someone who claims to be what you claim to be. Did you feel the person spoke for you? Did you say to yourself: "Right on"? That seldom happens to me. Instead, I get a lonely feeling.

Usually I cringe in private while someone vents against gays, when protesters obnoxiously disrupt abortion clinics or when a slick-tongued TV preacher weaves his web. What do others see? Do they see me? You see, I am an evangelical Christian.

Why do I bother explaining what it's like to be an evangelical when people's minds are already made up? Does anyone care? Perhaps not, but I do. I want someone else to know what I feel, someone who would, most likely, not even realize that there are varying points of view in our own community. I'm not asking you to "be like me." I'm just asking for understanding.

Oh no, another voice from the wilderness whining for "special-interest group" status. I know, I know, what nerve I have to imply such a need when "I" have oppressed and ignored so many with "my" high-minded bigotry. "I" have had my day (centuries?) in the sun, and "my" mastery has finally found its end. You're right! . . . to a point.

True to my baby-boomer roots, I abhor labels. They never really stick just right. And besides, everyone reads them the way they want to anyway. Labels are constantly being reworked, especially in the current climate of political correctness. If you think about it, you probably have a gripe about something someone said who supposedly speaks for you.

Does Jerry Falwell speak for me? How about Jimmy Swaggart, Phyllis Schlafly or Randall Terry? Supposedly they represent who I am and what I believe. Yet public figures often fail to explain how their "constituency" might feel. Usually they express how they feel. The rest of us form a speechless throng. Why don't they ask me?

As a result, I often feel misunderstood and caricatured. Well, maybe not me so much as "us." It seems that evangelical Christians are one of the few groups in America that can be widely maligned with impunity. I know why: the stereotypical evangelical is an old-fashioned and passé Bible thumper. Absolutes are out, relativism is in; conservative is out, liberal is in; intolerance is out, tolerance is in.

Tolerance? In my dreams! Acceptance? Now I've heard everything. The usual reaction at the mention of anything Christian is a collective dizzy spell from all the rolling eyes. Whatever I say here will probably not change your perception of "our" image. But let me speak about individuals, not categories.

Issues are important, but behind each cause there are people who have hopes, fears, and concerns. Far too often we hide behind these shields, replacing our identities. Can we even relate to one another without them? When we let down our guards there is potential. So what if we don't agree? Relationships are more important. Passion about these issues causes more pain than progress. It blinds us to people. If you were to talk to me you might make a friend. We may disagree, but I will listen and I will care. Then, we could give each other some room to believe differently with dignity.

Isn't this the bottom line, getting beyond labels and stereotypes and treating everyone with worth and dignity? If my fellow Christians abuse you, shun you or belittle you, we are wrong. I'm sorry. Visible evangelicals are not the only kind. There are millions of others who act with compassion and integrity far from the headlines.

Most evangelicals believe that abortion is morally wrong (certainly this is not news to you); probably the majority believe the clinic-blocking tactics of Operation Rescue are also wrong. Young women with an unplanned pregnancy are at a crisis point in their lives. They need compassion and support regardless of their ultimate choice. We must never forget that we are not in their shoes, walking their path.

When I see someone carrying a placard saying, PRAISE GOD FOR AIDS! my heart breaks. What twist of theology justifies any claim to rejoice at the suffering of another person? I've held the hand of a friend, ravaged and near death from AIDS. I have wept with his gathered family. I've worked in West Africa, where every family is subject to the menace of AIDS. There is no joy in another's pain.

My anger boils forth at the greed that fuels the "I'll tell you what you want to hear" rhetoric of some TV preachers whose "ministries" feed on the guilt of trusting souls who part with their earnings in a grasp of hope. But what hope can they expect other than the certainty of another solicitation?

Like any group that feels misrepresented, I am tempted to point my finger to assess blame. The media are always an easy target. But the media are damned if they do, damned if they don't: they're either paying too much attention to us or too little. Perhaps the final responsibility lies with most of us evangelicals who are unwilling to speak out. It isn't due to lack of desire but to lack of a forum.

Then again, maybe I should give people more credit. Maybe I haven't the need to say anything. Maybe you already discern between the fringe radicals and the mainstream. My wife, Gwen, tells of an airplane conversation with a Fortune 500 executive who saw a big difference between publicity-grabbing evangelical extremists and unsung, caring people who make a lasting difference in people's lives. In the end, this is where true understanding succeeds: one life at a time.

Issues for Investigation and Discussion

1. Who are the audiences for each of the arguments? What problems do the writers construct for them?

2. What is Jacobs's central point or thesis? What major points support it? Identify the sentences that introduce those points.

3. How does Jacobs rebut her ex-boyfriend's criticism and the "defensive arguments" of some blacks?

4. By writing in the first-person plural *(we/us)*, Jacobs includes herself among those whose mistaken viewpoints she wishes to correct. How might readers react to an argument in the second-person, with Jacobs addressing them as *you?*

5. Baker frequently addresses his audience in the second-person *you* or the first-person-plural *we*. Baker also asks questions of his audience several times. Why?

6. Immediately after Baker states the goal of his argument, he admits that his audience has a right to be annoyed at his whining "for special-interest group status." Why does he make this concession?

7. Where else does Baker anticipate the objections to or arguments against his claims? How does he deal with each?

8. How does Baker distinguish himself from other evangelical Christians? How does he attempt to establish a commonalty with his readers?

9. Based on your answers to these questions and any other matters you observe, turn to your journal or computer file and list six or more common traits of arguments that effectively respond to counterarguments (or create a list with several classmates). Let this list guide you as you revise your own argument later.

RESPONDING TO COUNTERARGUMENTS

[He was] watching the company, with six or seven senses not available to ordinary men, judging character, motive, and subconscious impulse, perceiving what each was thinking and even what each was going to say next, and compounding with telepathic instinct the argument or appeal best suited for the vanity, weakness, or self-interest of his immediate auditor.

—*John Maynard Keynes about Lloyd George*

The larger and more important the issue, the more varied and strongly held the viewpoints of readers. Thus, anticipating and responding to your readers' objections or questions requires careful thought during both invention and revision. The purpose of an argument is to alter the attitudes or behavior of your audience. But few people will change their minds or actions unless their objections are answered and their doubts dispelled. Effective rebuttals must therefore employ a variety of approaches (and voices)—diplomacy, flattery, scolding, analogy, clear logic, and presentation of facts—based on the needs and motivations of your audience.

Readers must understand that you understand their concerns, so a typical rebuttal makes clear what it is rebutting. You may incorporate the counterargument in your response, as does Jacobs when she is denying the implicit charge that she means to attack black entertainers personally:

> . . . *Although I like Michael Jackson's music, as I always have,* I must admit I now feel a remoteness when I look at him, since there is not much there that I can relate to and admire anymore. *I do not wish to chastise any particular entertainers,* but I am curious about the reasons behind their decisions regarding their looks.

Baker likewise anticipates and rebuts an implicit counter-charge, that he's asking for the compassion and understanding he and fellow evangelicals have always denied other people:

> Oh, no, *another voice from the wilderness whining for special-interest group status.* I know, I know, *what nerve I have* to imply such a need when "I" have oppressed and ignored so may with "my" high-minded bigotry. "I" have had my day (centuries?) in the sun, and "my" mastery has finally found its end. *You're right!. . . to a point.*

Collaborative Activity: Practicing Identification and Response to Counterarguments (25 minutes of class time)

Perhaps while reading the essays of Jacobs and Baker, you thought of one or more counterarguments they don't anticipate. With a small group of classmates, list those counterarguments or brainstorm about others until your group arrives at a list of the two or three strongest. Then discuss the reasoning and evidence Jacobs and Baker might use to rebut these counterarguments, and locate the places in their essays where the rebuttals might be introduced. Make notes of these discussions in your journal, and compose these rebuttals away from the group later on. Be sure to summarize or clearly imply each counterargument while responding to it.

Directly Stating and Refuting Counterarguments

Sometimes your readers hold such strongly opposing viewpoints that you must acknowledge and confront their counterarguments directly. Martin

Luther King, Jr., for example, employs such a strategy throughout his "Letter from Birmingham Jail," one of the most powerful arguments ever written, which he composed after his arrest for protesting segregation in that city.

As King sits in his jail cell for protesting an unjust law, fully aware of the criticism his fellow clergy have leveled against him, he decides that he must meet those charges head-on. He cannot display anger or engage in name-calling, however, partly because such actions violate his principles, but more importantly because he wishes to enlist his colleagues in support of his crusade. King takes the high moral ground, addressing his audience with respect while increasing the emotional intensity of his responses. Moreover, King doesn't conceal his purpose; he states it directly at the beginning of his letter:

April 16, 1963
My Dear Fellow Clergymen:
    While confined here in the Birmingham city jail, I came across your recent statement calling my present activities "unwise and untimely." Seldom do I pause to answer criticism of my work and ideas. . . . But since I feel that you are men of genuine good will and that your criticisms are sincerely set forth, I want to try to answer your statement in what I hope will be patient and reasonable terms.

King next systematically articulates and rebuts each criticism his colleagues have raised or accepted. He responds to their first objection by reviewing the facts they may not know or fully understand:

    I think I should indicate why I am here in Birmingham, since you have been influenced by the view which argues against "outsiders coming in." I have the honor of serving as president of the Southern Christian Leadership Conference, an organization operating in every southern state. . . . We have some eighty-five affiliated organizations across the South, and one of them is the Alabama Christian Movement for Human Rights. . . . Several months ago the affiliate here in Birmingham asked us to be on call to engage in a nonviolent direct-action program if such were deemed necessary. We readily consented, and when the hour came we lived up to our promise. So I, along with several members of my staff, am here because I was invited here. I am here because I have organizational ties here.

Then King moves on to a stronger response: an appeal to the moral sense of his colleagues. He has done not only what is ethically right, but, he implies, what they should be doing as well:

    But more basically, I am in Birmingham because injustice is here. Just as the prophets of the eighth century B.C. left their villages and carried their "thus saith the Lord" far beyond the boundaries of their home towns, and just as Paul left his village of Tarsus and carried the gospel of Jesus Christ to the far corners of the Greco-Roman world, so I am compelled to carry the gospel of freedom beyond my own home town. . . .

Moreover, I am cognizant of the interrelatedness of all communities and states. . . . Injustice anywhere is a threat to justice everywhere. . . . Whatever affects one directly, affects all indirectly. Never again can we afford to live with the narrow, provincial "outside agitator" idea.

To his audience's second complaint, King responds with both flattery and a reprimand. His colleagues, he maintains, are too wise not to recognize the deeper issues beneath the superficialities, but so far they haven't seen them:

You deplore the demonstrations taking place in Birmingham. But your statement, I am sorry to say, fails to express a similar concern for the conditions that brought about the demonstrations. I am sure that none of you would want to rest content with the superficial kind of social analysis that deals merely with effects and does not grapple with underlying causes. It is unfortunate that demonstrations are taking place in Birmingham, but it is even more unfortunate that the city's white power structure left the Negro community with no alternative.

King doesn't deny his audience's third complaint—that he has created "tension"—for, he asserts, that tension is intentional and will foster the negotiations his colleagues so strongly desire:

I must confess that I am not afraid of the word "tension." I have earnestly opposed violent tension, but there is a type of constructive, nonviolent tension which is necessary for growth. Just as Socrates felt that it was necessary to create a tension in the mind so that individuals could rise from the bondage of myths and half-truths to the unfettered realm of creative analysis and objective appraisal, so must we see the need for nonviolent gadflies to create the kind of tension in society that will help men rise from the dark depths of prejudice and racism to the majestic heights of understanding and brotherhood.

The purpose of our direct-action program is to create a situation so crisis-packed that it will inevitably open the door to negotiation. I therefore concur with you in your call for negotiation. . . .

King answers their final criticism (which he quotes directly) by summarizing and analyzing the events that have led to his actions, a summary that grows to an impassioned dramatic climax:

One of the basic points in your statement is that the action that I and my associates have taken in Birmingham is untimely. Some have asked: "Why didn't you give the new city administration time to act?" The only answer that I can give to this query is that the new Birmingham administration must be prodded about as much as the outgoing one, before it will act. . . . I have hope that [Mayor] Boutwell will be reasonable enough to see the futility of massive resistance to desegregation. But he will not see this without pressure from devotees of civil rights. My friends, I must say to you that we have not made a single gain in civil rights without determined legal and nonviolent pressure. . . .

We know through painful experience that freedom is never voluntarily given by the oppressor; it must be demanded by the oppressed. Frankly, I have yet to engage in a direct-action campaign that was "well timed" in the view of those who have not suffered unduly from the disease of segregation. For years now I have heard the word "Wait!" It rings in the ear of every Negro with piercing familiarity. This "Wait" has almost always meant "Never." We must come to see, with one of our distinguished jurists, that "justice too long delayed is justice denied."

We have waited for more than 340 years for our constitutional and God-given rights. The nations of Asia and Africa are moving with jetlike speed toward gaining political independence, but we still creep at horse-and-buggy pace toward gaining a cup of coffee at a lunch counter. . . . But when you have seen vicious mobs lynch your mothers and fathers at will and drown your sisters and brothers at whim; when you have seen hate-filled policemen curse, kick and even kill your black brothers and sisters; when you see the vast majority of your twenty million Negro brothers smothering in an airtight cage of poverty in the midst of an affluent society; when you suddenly find your tongue twisted and your speech stammering as you seek to explain to your six-year-old daughter why she can't go to the public amusement park that has just been advertised on television, and see tears welling up in her eyes when she is told that Funtown is closed to colored children, and see ominous clouds of inferiority beginning to form in her little mental sky, and see her beginning to distort her personality by developing an unconscious bitterness toward white people; when you have to concoct an answer for a five-year-old son who is asking: "Daddy, why do white people treat colored people so mean?"; when you take a cross-country drive and find it necessary to sleep night after night in the uncomfortable corners of your automobile because no motel will accept you; when you are humiliated day in and day out by nagging signs reading "white" and "colored"; when your first name becomes "nigger," your middle name becomes "boy" (however old you are) and your last name becomes "John," and your wife and mother are never given the respected title "Mrs."; when you are harried by day and haunted by night by the fact that you are a Negro, living constantly at tiptoe stance, never quite knowing what to expect next, and are plagued with inner fears and outer resentments; when you are forever fighting a degenerating sense of "no-bodiness"—then you will understand why we find it difficult to wait. There comes a time when the cup of endurance runs over, and men are no longer willing to be plunged into the abyss of despair. I hope, sirs, you can understand our legitimate and unavoidable impatience.

King's "Letter from Birmingham Jail" is a virtuoso performance in rebutting counterarguments, a performance that employs appeals to reason, appeals to justice, appeals to morality, and appeals to basic human decency. King interprets, reinterprets, and analyzes facts; makes comparisons; and conveys through specific instances the debilitating and humiliating consequences of racism and segregation on his people and himself. We'll look at the letter further in Chapter 14 when we discuss extended definitions, for King's letter also exemplifies the best uses of definition in support of an argument.

The perversion of the mind is only possible when those who should be heard in its defense are silent.

—Archibald MacLeish

Collaborative Activity: Analyzing King's Voice and Tone (15 minutes of class time)

"Letter from Birmingham Jail" has long been noted for its brilliance, not only in the quality of its arguments, but in its masterful control over voice and tone at each point. Describe King's voice and tone in each paragraph, and discuss how they buttress his arguments.

While no one expects you to match the power and eloquence of Martin Luther King, Jr., —few if any professional writers could—you can learn from his behavior in considering how to rebut counterarguments. Consider your audience's objections and respond to them. Consider your audience's motivations and appeal to them. In fact, consider all of the following issues:

- What questions does your audience have? Answer those questions.
- What does your audience know? Reinforce and appeal to that knowledge.
- What doesn't your audience know? Provide that information or explanation.
- What does your audience misunderstand? Analyze and clarify the issues.
- Whom does your audience respect? Cite that person's viewpoints.
- What valid objections does your audience raise? Concede those points but shape them to support your argument.
- What tone(s) should you employ in your argument: angry, calm, insistent, sarcastic, humorous? What voice(s) should you employ: conversational, chatty, clever, formal? How should you address your audience: as *we, you,* or not at all?

I always start out with a position I later discover to be too simple. That's the nature of things—what physicists call complementarity. What's interesting is that my ideas prove too simple in ways I never could have anticipated. In everything I've written I've come to the realization that I was missing something, telling myself lies.

—John Gardner

Collaborative Activity: Identifying Counterarguments to Your Own Essay (25 minutes of class time)

(Alternatively or additionally, you may skip this activity and follow the guidelines of the remaining composing/revising activities in the chapter to compose

an argument based on your role in the Writing in a Social Context section that begins on p. 176.)

In small groups, take turns reading aloud and responding to an argument each person has written earlier in the term. As you listen to another group member's paper, assume the role of a demanding critic. Make notes of ways to challenge each of the author's claims, asking "But what about. . . ?" "Who says so?" and "How do I know that's true?" Then state your challenges after the author finishes reading. No author should attempt to defend himself or herself, but should simply record the objections in his or her journal and then, away from the group, return to the journal or computer file to brainstorm ways of rebutting the counterarguments. Continue this reading and responding process with the group until all members have read and heard responses to their work.

If working with the group isn't possible, assume the role of your most hostile critic and read through your paper yourself, challenging and responding to your claims.

Invention Activity: Planning Rebuttals to Counterarguments

Continue to consider the counterarguments to your paper and how you might respond to them. As new ideas occur to you, add them to your journal or computer file notes and then, using the following set of questions as a guide, plan a new version of your paper in which you rebut the counterarguments. Don't be surprised if this new version is entirely different from the original. The first attempt possesses an internal logic that may be ill-suited to your additions or changes.

Planning and Revising Questions

1. What is your goal in making your argument? That is, what do you expect your readers to do with its information?

2. Who is your audience? What do they know about the subject? What is their attitude toward your position?

3. How have you constructed the problem for your audience? In light of the counterarguments you've considered, should you construct the problem differently? If so, how?

4. What are the most important counterarguments your readers might raise? How should you respond to each?

5. How should you address the counterarguments—by implying them in your responses or by stating and then responding to each directly?

6. Where should your responses appear—at the beginning of the paper, after each major point, or in the final stages of the argument? (You may wish to indicate where in bracketed notes on the original paper.)

7. In responding to the counterarguments, should you change the voice and tone you employed in the previous draft of the essay? If so, where? Should you address your audience in the second person or first-person plural?

Composing Activity: Writing and Revising Your Argument

Now compose and revise the argument. Before completing the final draft, you may wish to discuss it with a group of several classmates according to the guidelines of the following Postdraft Analysis questions (some of which return to issues you've addressed in composing the original version of the paper).

Postdraft Analysis
(To be completed by the writer or peer reader)

1. Locate the sentence or sentences that construct the problem for the intended audience. Is the problem constructed effectively? If not, how might the first paragraph be revised? After reading the first paragraph, pause and let your listeners raise counterarguments they'd expect to be addressed. List their responses and then see if the essay addresses them.

2. Examine the backing for each major claim. Are relevant facts, examples, or incidents provided? Is some backing irrelevant? Is some excessive? Indicate in bracketed labels where backing could be expanded or cut.

3. Locate the connections (warrants) between each claim and backing. Are these warrants clear and sufficient? If not, identify with bracketed labels where warrants might be revised, added, or expanded.

4. Locate the argument's rebuttals of counterarguments. Are these rebuttals appropriate in their logic, backing, tone, and voice? If not, indicate in brackets where they might be changed.

5. Examine the transitions introducing and following the rebuttals. Are they graceful and logical? If not, how should they be modified? (Are transitions needed, or should the rebuttals be shifted to other locations?) Indicate these changes in bracketed notes in the margins of the paper.

6. What other changes would increase the effectiveness of the argument?

Concluding Activity: Revising and Editing Your Argument

Assemble all your notes and then revise your argument, rearranging materials, supplying or strengthening transitions, tightening the sentences, sharpening the details, and editing carefully for consistency of tense and matters of mechanics, grammar, and spelling.

WRITING IN A SOCIAL CONTEXT: POLITICALLY CORRECT SPEECH?

The following activity simulates a real situation in which you and your classmates can gain first-hand experience, devise arguments, debate the issues, and then communicate your ideas in writing. Read the material provided before coming to class, choose one of four roles to play, and then present your case in an open meeting. The entire activity should require no more than forty-five to seventy-five minutes, divided as follows:

- five minutes for choosing roles
- ten to fifteen minutes for determining strategy
- twenty to forty minutes to present arguments
- ten to fifteen minutes for rebuttal

After choosing or being assigned to a group representing one of the four roles, you and the other group members will meet to discuss your claims, backing, reasoning, and refutations of counterarguments, based on the materials provided and any stories (real or imagined) you devise. Then your instructor will convene the whole class, first allowing each group five to ten minutes to make its case, followed by perhaps ten minutes of give-and-take among the groups. Finally, again within your role, you will compose a written argument addressed to a specified audience.

Alternatively, you may simply read through the materials and discuss them in class before composing an argument within one of the four roles.

The Context

After several incidents in which hate groups have scrawled graffiti, painted slogans, and orchestrated verbal attacks on homosexuals, minority groups, and others, Fairfax University is considering a code of conduct banning any bigoted action or speech. While many faculty and students sympathize with the intent of the code, the debate over the issue has begun to polarize the campus. On the one side are those who feel that attacks on any person's racial or ethnic heritage, religious beliefs, and sex or sexual orientation have no place in a university. They contend that a university should foster an atmosphere of collegiality that respects all points of view; thus, slurs or insults against any group should not be condoned or tolerated.

On the other side are those who feel that, distasteful as hate speech and action may be, the laws and customs of America (and, by extension, the university) protect the expression of such hatred. They also feel that the advocates of "politically correct" speech and action are so extreme in their beliefs that the code of conduct could lead to all sorts of abuses against people who commit only the most minor transgressions.

The Chancellor of Fairfax University has appointed a committee of deans, faculty, and students to discuss and debate the issue and has encouraged all involved to compose their arguments for a publication to be distributed to the entire campus. Submissions may include reports of personal encounters with hate speech and action, reports on the experiences of other colleges and universities concerning the issue, arguments in support of or in opposition to the code, and even attempts at drafting the code itself. Prior to writing their arguments, however, the participants have been asked to present their viewpoints in an open forum.

The Participants

Supporters of the Code.   You strongly support the code of conduct, either because, as feminists or members of minority groups, you have encountered hate speech and action directed against you and your peers, or because you believe a university should create an environment in which diversity is both tolerated and encouraged. Other colleges and universities have established such codes, and you believe that Fairfax can benefit from their experiences.

Opponents of the Code.   You oppose such a code of conduct because in your view it infringes on the rights of free speech and assembly and smacks of neofascism. While you do not condone hate speech or action, you believe the Constitution protects such activities. Furthermore, you believe that a university must permit such activities, for the purpose of a university is provide a forum for all voices on all issues.

Teachers in the Law School.   You support or oppose the issue on legal grounds: with some contending that such a code is unconstitutional; and others contending that the Constitution protects citizens against attacks on their religions, beliefs, and life-styles.

The Dean and Assistant Deans.   While you differ among yourselves in attitudes toward the code of conduct, your primary concern is to settle the issue peaceably. Thus, you are searching for a compromise solution, a code that is both moderate and fair.

The Facts

1. A sophomore student of Chinese extraction at a state-run Eastern university was banned from campus dormitories and cafeterias for a year because she had violated the student-behavior code that prohibited "posting or advertising publicly offensive, indecent or abusive matter concerning persons . . . and making personal slurs or epithets based on race, sex, ethnic origin, disability, religion or sexual orientation." The reason for her punishment was a sign she allegedly had put on her door as a joke, specifying that

the following people will be "shot on sight": "preppies," "bimbos," "men without chest hair," and "homos." Gay students and faculty complained about the sign (but no one else—such as men without chest hair—protested). After threatening a federal lawsuit, she was allowed to move back onto campus, and the Code of Student Conduct was revised to conform to the First Amendment to the Constitution.

2.   At the same university, a proclamation was issued banning "inappropriately directed laughter" and "conspicuous exclusion of students from conversations."

3.   The National Association of Scholars in Princeton, New Jersey, which is "committed to rational discourse as the foundation of academic life," opposes politically correct (PC) speech. While receiving most of its funding from conservative foundations, its membership of 1,400 as of December 1990, included a number of prominent liberal academics.

4.   The head of the English Department at Duke University called the NAS members "racist, sexist and homophobic." A member of the NAS compared this response to "calling someone a communist in the McCarthy years."

5.   At a law school in New York, students were about to force the cancellation of an assignment to debate the custody rights of a lesbian mother. One of the students involved in a campaign wrote that "Written arguments [against the mother's side] are hurtful to a group of people and thus hurtful to all of us." A law professor responded, "The declaration that any legal issue is not an open question in law school is a declaration of war upon everything that a law school is." The assignment was later reinstated.

6.   The First Amendment to the Constitution reads, "Congress shall make no law respecting an establishment of religion, or prohibiting the free exercise thereof; or abridging freedom of speech, or of the press; or the right of people peaceably to assemble, and to petition the Government for a redress of grievances." The Fourteenth Amendment extends those prohibitions to the states, reading in part: "No State shall make or enforce any law which shall abridge the privileges or immunities of citizens of the United States; nor shall any State deprive any person of life, liberty, or property, without due process of law; nor deny to any person within its jurisdiction the equal protection of the law."

7.   One interpretation of the First Amendment is that it protects the right to disparage anyone from any group. The courts have consistently ruled unconstitutional any restrictions of speech that are not dangerous, libelous, or slanderous.

8.   A well-known sociologist says, "You have to let students say the most outrageous and stupid things. To get people to think and talk, to question their own ideas, you don't regulate free speech."

9. The PC position is that hostility toward minorities restricts their right to an equal education. "Sure you have the right to speech, " says an associate dean at an Ivy League college for women. "But I want to know: what is it going to do to our community? Is it going to damage us?"

10. At another prominent Ivy League college for women, a handout from the Office of Student Affairs lists ten different kinds of oppression that stem from making judgments about people such as:

"ageism—oppression of the young and old by young adults and the middle aged";

"heterosexism—oppression of those of sexual orientations other than heterosexual . . . this can take place by not acknowledging their existence";

"lookism—construction of a standard for beauty/attractiveness";

"ableism—oppression of the differently abled, by the temporarily able."

("differently abled are just that, not less or inferior in any way.")

11. Additional PC terminology: "non-traditional-aged"(instead of old) and "people of color" (but not colored people).

12. Meg Greenfield, a columnist for *Newsweek*, writes: ". . . it is a loss when people mute their own more provocative ideas in order to stay within the limits of well-received argument."

13. Nadine Strossen, a professor of law at New York Law School and president of the American Civil Liberties Union, writes that opponents to PC speech often engage in the "unfair singling out of extreme interpretations and applications of policies that may be fundamentally sound." These attacks have created a backlash, she maintains, that has led to "unfairly dismissing the legitimate aspects of the PC critique along with its excesses." She contends that PC's recommended word choice is a matter of common courtesy—referring to people by the names they prefer—and more importantly of conveying respect for groups "that have been the target of bias." While she opposes hate-speech codes as unconstitutional, she does say that "harassing, intimidating, or assaultive conduct" cannot be protected, even if it partly consists of words.

14. At a New York university, the African-American chair of the Black Studies Department was removed from his position (but allowed to continue teaching) after he said that a number of Jews and Italian-Americans in Hollywood had conspired to disparage blacks in movies.

15. A small liberal arts college in Ohio has instituted a policy on Sexual Violence and Safety, which includes these provisions:

"All sexual contact and conduct between two people must be consensual;

"Consent must be obtained verbally before there is any sexual contact or conduct;

"If the level of sexual intimacy increases an interaction (i.e., if two people move from kissing while fully clothed—which is one level—to undressing for physical contact, which is another level), the people involved need to express their clear verbal consent before moving to that new level;

"If one person wants to *initiate* moving to a higher level of sexual intimacy in an interaction, *that person is responsible for getting the verbal consent of the other person(s) involved before moving to that level;*

"If you have had a particular level of sexual intimacy before with someone, you must still ask each and every time;

". . . Asking 'Do you want to have sex with me?' is not enough. The request must be specific to each act."

The policy also defines "Insistent and/or Persistent Sexual Harassment" as "any insistent and/or persistent emotional, verbal or mental intimidation or abuse found to be sexually threatening or offensive," which includes "but is not limited to, unwelcome and irrelevant comments, references, gestures or other forms of personal attention which are inappropriate and which may be perceived as persistent sexual overtones or denigration."

Composing Activity: Writing a Submission for Publication

Within the role you have assumed, compose an argument representing your (or your group's) point of view, supporting your claims, and refuting the most important counterarguments of your opponents. Revise the argument according to the guidelines of the Postdraft Analysis questions shown earlier in the chapter.

Follow-Up Activity: Exploring the Issue at Your College

You may wish to investigate your own college's policies concerning bigoted speech and action, and then compose either a report on what is being done or an argument for what should be done. Assume that your audience will be the entire college community—students, professors, staff, and administration.

1. Discuss with your class the best potential sources of information and opinion. Does a published code exist? If so, where can you find it? Who was involved in formulating the code, and what procedures did they follow? Who might be interviewed to provide background or opinion on the issue?

   If no code exists, identify several people within the college community who might be interviewed concerning their views on the issue. Seek a variety of viewpoints.

2. To avoid duplication of effort, form several small committees to conduct interviews or do research and then report their findings both orally and in writing to the class as a whole.

3. Then discuss the most appropriate medium for publishing your report(s) or argument(s), and compose the work(s) either individually or collaboratively. (You may wish to examine and discuss all the works to determine which are best suited for publication.)

4. Alternatively, you may wish to compose a model code of conduct and submit it for publication.

Chapter 13

Arguing Through Comparisons and Contrasts

In many ways writing is the act of saying I, *of imposing oneself upon other people, of saying* listen to me, see it my way, change your mind.

—Joan Didion

You've seen repeatedly that effective writing demands oppositions, a tension between thesis and antithesis that leads to synthesis. Whether in narratives, critical journeys through your reactions to a performance or work of art, or conscious attempts to rebut counterarguments, you've allowed opposing ideas to clash, evolve, or be resolved. Implicit in the clash and resolution of ideas are comparisons and contrasts—comparisons to reveal similarities, contrasts to disclose differences—which we'll explore explicitly in this chapter.

Comparisons and contrasts serve a variety of functions. For example, you can explain an unfamiliar process by comparing it through *analogy* to a familiar one: an atomic chain reaction is like a ping-pong ball thrown into a box of balls, with one ball striking two, and two striking four and so on—except that in the chain reaction subatomic particles collide. You can create humor by comparing dissimilar ideas, objects, or behaviors. (You'll see an example of that shortly.) Or you can argue for the superiority of one idea, object, or behavior over another by drawing contrasts between or among them: "Buy Foamy Toothpaste," an advertisement might proclaim. "Clinical tests show it outcleans the competition two to one!"

LOOKING AT ARGUMENTS

Comparisons and contrasts figure prominently in the following two essays. In the first, Russell Baker, a syndicated columnist with the *New York Times*, aims to entertain but also makes a semi-serious point.

THE TWO ISMO'S

American city life is now torn by two violently opposed doctrines of social conduct. One is machismo. Its adherents pride themselves on being "machos." The opposing dogma is quichismo (pronounced "key shizmo"), and its practitioners call themselves quiche-o's (pronounced "key shows").

A good study of a quichismo victory over machismo in an urban war zone can be found in Philip Lopate's "Quiche Blitz on Columbus Avenue," included in his recent book, "Bachelorhood." Curiously, however, Mr. Lopate refers to the quichismo doctrine by its French name, *quichisme.*

In doing so he unwittingly reveals that he is himself a quiche-o of the highest order, for no macho would dream of using a French word when discussing philosophy, and even the average quiche-o would avoid a word as difficult to pronounce as *quichisme* for fear of getting it wrong and being sneered at as unquiche-o.

For practitioners of quichismo there is no defense against being sneered at, and they live in dread of it. The machismo adherent, on the other hand, positively enjoys being sneered at since it entitles him to punch the sneerer in the nose, a ritual act ceremonially confirming that he is truly macho.

When a quiche-o is sneered at, his only recourse is to jog until he achieves a higher sense of total fulfillment. This is one reason behind the machismo slogan, "Machos have more fun."

Maybe so, quiche-o's say, but machos don't have French dry cleaning or white bucks. Machos prefer no dry cleaning at all though they sometimes get their clothes pressed if they've slept in them all week and want to impress females during the weekend.

Machos impress females by taking them to bars after opening the top four buttons on their shirts to show off the hair on their chests. Quiche-o women impress males by inviting them to dinner and serving salad from the carry-out gourmet shop, followed by a kiwi fruit. There are no macho women. If there were they would serve pigs' feet and beer because machos believe that real people don't eat salad, kiwi fruit or anything else that comes from gourmet shops.

Quiche-o people buy Swedish toothpaste at gourmet drugstores, Italian loafers at gourmet shoe shops, newspapers at gourmet newsstands and dogs at gourmet pet centers. Afterwards they have them wormed by gourmet veterinarians. They also go to the islands for a month or two, especially Bermuda, St. Bart's, Barbados and Trinidad. Machos also go to the islands—Coney and Long—usually for a Sunday afternoon. To primp for these vacations, machos first go to the barber.

No quiche-o has set foot in a barber shop for the last 20 years. He goes to a gourmet hairdresser for a styling, then, before jetting off to the islands, goes to the gourmet luggage shop for suitcases covered with the initials of gourmet designers. The macho packs a change of underwear and a drip-dry shirt in a zippered plastic briefcase his uncle brought back from a 1977 convention of T-shirt salesmen.

Quiche-o's are always redecorating. Machos are always repainting the room that has the TV set in it. When a macho's couch and chairs are finally ruined he goes to a department store and buys "a suit of furniture." Quiche-o furniture is never ruined, but it goes out of style every two years, and when it does the quiche-o goes to an environmental systems boutique and buys a new environment.

No quiche-o would ever take a walk in his undershirt unless it had something amusing printed on it, like *"Ou sont les neiges d'antan?"* No macho would ever appear on the beach in a male bikini. No quiche-o would ever wear black U.S. Keds with white soles and laces. No macho would ever walk into a hardware store and ask for a wok spatula.

Machos don't see anything funny about New Jersey. Quiche-o's never laugh at people who drive Volvos, people who pay $5.50 for a hamburger, or quiche jokes, unless they're told by another quiche-o. Quiche-o's like a lot of butcher block and stainless steel. Machos like a lot of children.

Machos never bake carrot cake and don't go out with women who do. Quiche-o's are proud of their cholesterol levels and never belch in public and never go out with women who do since they recognize them instantly as unquiche-o and unlikely ever to serve them a salad dinner followed with a kiwi fruit.

In the essay that follows, Lewis Thomas contrasts two interpretations of the antisocial behavior of primitive people: an anthropologist's and his own. He then draws an extended analogy to argue his main point. Think about that point as you read his essay, and think about how he structures his comparisons as well.

THE IKS

The small tribe of Iks, formerly nomadic hunters and gatherers in the mountain valleys of northern Uganda, have become celebrities, literary symbols for the ultimate fate of disheartened, heartless mankind at large. Two disastrously conclusive things happened to them: the government decided to have a national park, so they were compelled by law to give up hunting in the valleys and become farmers on poor hillside soil, and then they were visited for two years by an anthropologist who detested them and wrote a book about them.

The message of the book is that the Iks have transformed themselves into an irreversibly disagreeable collection of unattached, brutish creatures, totally selfish and loveless, in response to the dismantling of their traditional culture. Moreover, this is what the rest of us are like in our inner selves, and we will all turn into Iks when the structure of our society comes all unhinged.

The argument rests, of course, on certain assumptions about the core of human beings, and is necessarily speculative. You have to agree in advance that man is fundamentally a bad lot, out for himself alone, displaying such graces as affection and compassion only as learned habits. If you take this view, the story of the Iks can be used to confirm it. These people seem to be living together, clustered in small, dense villages, but they are really solitary, unrelated individuals with no evident use for each other. They talk, but only to make ill-tempered demands and cold refusals. They share nothing. They never sing. They turn the children out to forage as soon as they can walk, and desert the elders to starve whenever they can, and the foraging children snatch food from the mouths of the helpless elders. It is a mean society.

They breed without love or even casual regard. They defecate on each other's doorsteps. They watch their neighbors for signs of misfortune, and only then do they laugh. In the book they do a lot of laughing, having so much bad luck. Several times they even laughed at the anthropologist, who found this especially repellent (one senses, between the lines, that the scholar is not himself the world's luckiest man). Worse, they took him into the family, snatched his food, defecated on his doorstep, and hooted dislike at him. They gave him two bad years.

It is a depressing book. If, as he suggests, there is only Ikness at the center of each of us, our sole hope for hanging onto the name of humanity will be in endlessly mending the structure of our society, and it is changing so quickly and completely that we may never find the threads in time. Meanwhile, left to ourselves alone, solitary, we will become the same joyless, zestless, untouching lone animals.

But this may be too narrow a view. For one thing, the Iks are extraordinary. They are absolutely astonishing, in fact. The anthropologist has never seen people like them anywhere, nor have I. You'd think, if they were simply examples of the common essence of mankind, they'd seem more recognizable. Instead, they are bizarre, anomalous. I have known my share of peculiar, difficult, nervous, grabby people, but I've never encountered any genuinely, consistently detestable human beings in all my life. The Iks sound more like abnormalities, maladies.

I cannot accept it. I do not believe that the Iks are representative of isolated, revealed man, unobscured by social habits. I believe their behavior is something extra, something laid on. This unremitting, compulsive repellence is a kind of complicated ritual. They must have learned to act this way; they copied it, somehow.

I have a theory, then. The Iks have gone crazy.

The solitary Ik, isolated in the ruins of an exploded culture, has built a new defense for himself. If you live in an unworkable society you can make up one of your own, and this is what the Iks have done. Each Ik has become a group, a one-man tribe on its own, a constituency.

Now everything falls into place. This is why they do seem, after all, vaguely familiar to all of us. We've seen them before. This is precisely the way groups of one size or another, ranging from committees to nations, behave. It is, of course, this aspect of humanity that has lagged behind the rest of evolution, and this is why the Ik seems so primitive. In his absolute selfishness, his incapacity to give anything away, no matter what, he is a successful committee. When he stands at the door of his hut, shouting insults at his neighbors in a loud harangue, he is a city addressing another city.

Cities have all the Ik characteristics. They defecate on doorsteps, in rivers and lakes, their own or anyone else's. They leave rubbish. They detest all neighboring cities, give nothing away. They even build institutions for deserting elders out of sight.

Nations are the most Iklike of all. No wonder the Iks seem familiar. For total greed, rapacity, heartlessness, and irresponsibility there is nothing to match a nation. Nations, by law, are solitary, self-centered, withdrawn into themselves. There is no such thing as affection between nations, and certainly no nation ever loved another. They bawl insults from their doorsteps, defecate into whole oceans, snatch all the food, survive by detestation, take joy in the bad luck of others, celebrate the death of others, live for the death of others.

That's it, and I shall stop worrying about the book. It does not signify that man is a sparse, inhuman thing at his center. He's all right. It only says what we've always known and never had enough time to worry about, that we haven't yet learned how to stay human when assembled in masses. The Ik, in his despair, is acting out this failure, and perhaps we should pay closer attention. Nations have themselves become too frightening to think about, but we might learn some things by watching these people.

Issues for Investigation and Discussion

1. Who are the audiences for each writer's arguments? What purpose does each writer attempt to accomplish?

2. What problems does each writer construct for his readers, and where does he construct the problem?

3. In "The Two Ismo's," Russell Baker implies but doesn't explicitly state his point. What is that point? (You may not be able to summarize it in a single sentence.)

4. Baker contrasts the "machos" to the "quiche-o's" throughout. Does he favor one group over the other? Does he criticize both groups? Support your claims with examples.

5. Baker gets a lot of mileage out of the word "gourmet." Why does he use it repeatedly?

6. Examine the organization of Baker's argument. How does he structure the contrasts between machos and quiche-o's? How would your reaction to his argument change if he had discussed all the traits of one group before moving on to discuss the second group?

7. In "The Iks," what is Lewis Thomas comparing? How is the organization of his essay similar to or different from Baker's?

8. Lewis sharply contrasts his interpretation of the Iks' behavior with the interpretation of an anthropologist who "despises" the Iks. How do the interpretations differ?

9. Why does Thomas make his point toward the end of his argument? What is that point?

10. What words and phrases in both essays signal comparisons and contrasts? How else do the writers signal them?

11. Based on your answers to these questions and any other matters you observe, turn to your journal or computer file and list a half-dozen or more common traits of arguments based on comparisons and contrasts (or create a list with several classmates). Let this list guide you as you compose and revise your own argument later.

GENERATING COMPARISONS OR CONTRASTS

Success in solving the problem depends on choosing the right aspect, on attacking the fortress from its accessible side.

—*George Polya*

Most comparisons or contrasts are organized in one of two ways: in point-to-point or a whole-to-whole organization. In point-to-point, you discuss a single similarity or difference between your subjects, then another and another until you've covered them all. This approach works best with subjects familiar to your readers. For example, because we already recognize macho and quiche-o behaviors (although certainly not the name of the latter group), Russell Baker can move back and forth between them to draw humorous contrasts. The whole-to-whole approach works best when an overview helps readers understand unfamiliar subjects. So, for example, Lewis Thomas first describes all the behavioral traits of the Iks before drawing any comparisons. Often, however, you may need to experiment to find which organization best suits your purposes.

A useful practice during the invention stage is to list the points of comparisons and/or contrasts on a grid. The grid not only helps structure your ideas, but forces you to see comparisons you might otherwise have overlooked. Suppose, for example, that you wished to argue for the superiority of one car over its competitors. Your grid, in part, might look like this:

	The Cheetah LE	**The Supervia RX**	**The Luxant**
Style	2-door convertible	2-door hardtop	4-door with sunroof
Wheel base	120 inches	118 inches	124 inches
Seating capacity	2 passengers	2 adults and possibly 2 children	4 adults
Engine	V-4, 220 horsepower	V-6, 260 horsepower	V-8, 300 horsepower
Repair history	average	above average	below average
Standard Equipment	dual airbags	driver's side airbag	dual airbags
	air conditioning	air conditioning	air conditioning
	stereo cassette radio	stereo cassette 6-speaker radio	radio, cassette, and compact disc player

	The Cheetah LE	The Supervia RX	The Luxant (continued)
	cloth interior	cloth interior	leather interior
	manual windows	power windows	power windows
			power windows and remote-control door locks
		anti-lock brakes	anti-lock brakes
Cost	$18,000	$21,000	$34,000

You can read across the rows of the completed grid to make a point-to-point comparison, or down each column to make a whole-to-whole comparison. You'll probably also rearrange the items in the grid to suit your purposes, listing similarities first and then differences (or vice versa), or moving from most important comparisons to the least (or vice versa).

Since an effective argument must acknowledge and rebut the counterarguments of your readers, don't oversimplify the comparisons, claiming, for example, that the Luxant is better in every way. (It's a lot more expensive than its competitors—which may not be an advantage.) You might argue instead, that, on balance, the Luxant is the fastest and most comfortable car for people who can afford it.

One other piece of advice. Laying out the data on a grid and deciding on an organization are only preliminary steps. What looks good in theory often doesn't work out in practice. Don't be surprised, therefore, if your argument takes on a different shape as it evolves during the composing process. Effective arguments follow their own internal logic and shouldn't be forced into a paint-by-numbers format. Planning helps, but it shouldn't inhibit discovery and change.

COMPOSING AN ARGUMENT

Use the information in the Writing in a Social Context activity below to compose an argument employing comparisons or contrasts. Alternatively or additionally, you may follow composing and revising procedures similar to those discussed in this activity to compose an argument based on your role in the second Writing in a Social Context section that begins on p. 193.

WRITING IN A SOCIAL CONTEXT: THE END OF HIGH SCHOOL ATHLETICS?

The following material simulates a real situation in which you and your classmates can gain first-hand experience, devise arguments, debate the issues, and then communicate your ideas in writing. You'll read the material provided before coming to class, choose one of four roles to play, and then present your case in an open meeting. The entire activity should require no more than forty-five to seventy-five minutes, divided as follows:

- five minutes for choosing roles
- ten to fifteen minutes for determining strategy
- twenty to forty minutes to present arguments
- ten to fifteen minutes for rebuttal

After choosing or being assigned to a group representing one of the four roles, you and the other group members will meet to discuss the claims, backing, and reasoning you'll present, based on the materials provided and any stories (real or imagined) you devise. Then your instructor will convene the whole class, first allowing each group five to ten minutes to make its case, followed by ten minutes or so of give-and-take among the groups. Finally, again within your role, you will compose a written argument addressed to a specified audience. Alternatively, you may simply read through the materials and discuss them in class before composing an argument within one of the four roles.

The Context

Conrad Consolidated High School, serving three thousand students from five small towns in a southern state, is attempting to deal with a financial emergency. The operating budget for the coming school year faces a deficit of $1 million. The money cannot be raised through taxes. Voters have already rejected two separate referenda to increase property taxes, and the state legislature will not increase its allocation to the public schools. After long debate over what programs to cut, the School Board has recommended that it save $300,000 by canceling all varsity athletics, including boys' baseball, football, basketball, soccer, tennis, golf, and track; and girls' softball, basketball, volleyball, field hockey, tennis, golf, and track.

These programs are long-established, and matches between Conrad and surrounding high schools draw large admission-paying crowds. Friday night football and basketball games are local institutions, and many students in the sports programs have gone to college on athletic scholarships. In fact, current senior- and junior-year players would lose the opportunity to be scouted by college coaches and recruiters if the programs were eliminated.

After protests from the athletes, parents, and local merchants and civic organizations in the five towns, the School Board has postponed a final decision and has scheduled a meeting so that all interested parties may debate the issue, and following the meeting, submit their arguments and proposals to the Board in writing. Each group will doubtless compare the costs and benefits—both financial and nonfinancial—in eliminating the athletic or any other programs.

The Participants

Parents and Community Groups Opposing the Cuts. While conceding that the money to erase the deficit is not available, you feel that varsity athletics are too important to be eliminated. The program brings pride and cohesiveness to the community, keeps high school students out of trouble, and affords a number of young people the opportunity to attend college on scholarship. You will argue that varsity athletics should be retained and suggest that other programs be cut, comparing and contrasting their costs and benefits to the students and the larger community.

Parents Supporting the Cuts.   While acknowledging the popularity of varsity sports, you feel that Conrad High School can ill afford to continue them in difficult economic times. Furthermore, you believe the post-game celebrations and parties lead to excessive drinking and vandalism that might otherwise not occur. You would rather the school continue other programs that serve all students, not just the elite few who participate in varsity sports. In making your argument, you will compare and contrast their costs and benefits to the students and the larger community.

Coaches and Teachers Opposing the Cuts.   As faculty members at Conrad High, you cannot countenance discarding a successful program that has taken many years to build. You see too much waste and unnecessary spending in the school in areas outside of the athletic program and will argue that the Board should make cuts in these areas, comparing and contrasting their costs and benefits to the students and the larger community.

Teachers and Administrators Supporting the Cuts.   Not only do you support the judicious action of the School Board, but you strongly wish to protect programs that would be decimated if the athletic program were allowed to continue. You will argue that these programs should not be sacrificed to maintain varsity sports, and you will also compare and contrast their costs and benefits to the students and the larger community.

The Facts

1. Conrad High's fiscal year budget is $18.1 million.
2. Conrad employs 150 teachers and 25 counselors, whose average salary is $40,000, the third highest in the state.
3. The seventeen administrators—including the district superintendent, the principal, four assistant principals, and deans—are paid a total of $1.25 million in salaries.
4. The ten coaches of varsity sports are certified to teach academic subjects, so none would lose his or her job.
5. The total budget is as follows:

building maintenance:	$1,000,000
utilities	$750,000
books and supplies	$750,000
food and beverages	$1,250,000
building security	$500,000
equipment	$500,000
transportation	$400,000
insurance and pensions	$3,000,000
varsity sports	$300,000
student activities	$400,000
secretarial services	$200,000
printing and mailing	$200,000
travel and conference fees	$100,000

Invention Activity: Planning Your Argument

Within your specified role, begin the process of composing a letter to the School Board, arguing for the continuation or abolition of the athletics program, comparing your position to those of the other participants in the controversy. Support your claims with pertinent facts, statistics, or short stories. At various stages in the invention and composing process, you may wish to discuss your plans and drafts with students who share your role.

The following questions should help you devise a persuasive strategy. If you wish, write a first draft and then answer the questions. And use whatever additional activities (free writing, brainstorming, clustering, and looping) you might find helpful in exploring and scrutinizing your ideas.

Planning or Revising Questions

1. How should you construct the problem for your audience?
2. What points should you emphasize in your argument? What backing should you provide for each claim?
3. Prepare a grid that lists the points of comparison and contrast between your position and the opposing one.
4. Would a whole-to-whole or point-to-point organization best achieve your objectives?

5. What counterarguments should you refute? Where?

6. Rearrange the points of comparison in an order that best achieves your objectives.

Composing Activity: Writing a First Draft

Now compose a draft of your argument. Construct the problem at the beginning, establishing points of comparison (both similarities and differences) to support your claims and arriving at a logical conclusion. Include transitions that signal comparisons (*similarly, too, also, like, the same, likewise, and, on the one hand*) or contrasts (*but, however, on the other hand, by contrast, unlike*) as they occur.

Collaborative Activity: Evaluating Your Argument (25 minutes of class time)

Take turns with several classmates reading your early drafts of the arguments. Stop at the end of the first paragraph and periodically throughout the paper so that listeners can predict what will follow. Then test their predictions against what you actually say. Answer the following questions to guide you further in revising.

Postdraft Analysis
(To be completed by the writer or peer reader)

1. Locate the phrases or sentences at the beginning of the argument that construct (or imply) the problem for the intended audience and suggest or state a solution. Are both matters clearly established? If not, how might the first paragraph be revised?

2. Does the paper employ whole-to-whole or part-to-part comparisons? Would another approach work better? If so, how should the materials be rearranged?

3. Find each comparison and/or contrast. Are they all relevant to the argument's point? If not, bracket the ones that could be eliminated. Should additional comparisons or contrasts be included? Indicate where in brackets in the margins of the paper.

4. Underline the first and last sentences of each paragraph and then examine these sentences carefully. Are the connections between ideas unclear in any places—that is, are the ideas related in ways you haven't shown? If so, add in brackets words that explain the relationships. Are additional signposts needed to clarify the organizational structure? If so, indicate where in brackets.

5. Does the argument conclude effectively? If not, how might the conclusion be improved?

Concluding Activity: Revising and Editing Your Argument

Consider the responses to the Postdraft Analysis questions, and then do a final revision of the argument—adding and rearranging material, rewording ideas, clarifying connections between ideas and events, and editing the paper carefully for matters of mechanics, grammar, and spelling.

WRITING IN A SOCIAL CONTEXT: SELLING A COMMUNICATIONS SERVICE

The following material simulates yet another situation in which you can compose an argument utilizing comparisons and contrasts. Follow the same steps outlined and explained in the previous Writing in a Social Context section.

The Context

Next-Day Express, a package- and letter-carrying service with over two hundred trucks in the greater metropolitan area of a large East Coast city, is considering the installation of cellular telephone, modem, and telefax services in all of its trucks. Up to now, the drivers have relied on antiquated intercom communications similar to those found in taxicabs. However, the demands of express delivery require much more sophisticated devices that would allow drivers to notify the dispatch office of their location and progress, and the dispatch office to inform drivers of route changes, high-priority demands, traffic problems, new pick-ups, and last-minute modifications in billing.

Three communications companies are competing for exclusive rights to service, which include not only the broadcast cellular network but also the phones, modems, and fax machines. Representatives will be making presentations to the chief purchasing officers of Next-Day Express, who will examine the oral and written proposals before making their recommendations to the Company Board of Directors. Each of the three companies will base their presentations on the data sheets shown on following pages.

The Participants

Representatives of Each Communications Company. You'll be highlighting the services and equipment your company can offer, emphasizing its advantages over the competition, whether in price of the equipment, price of service, clarity of broadcast, versatility of the equipment or services, reliability, potential to be upgraded, and ease of repair. After your oral presentation, you'll be writing a follow-up letter to the purchasing officers, thanking them for giving you the opportunity to speak and arguing why they should choose your company's services instead of the services of the other two companies. (This argument will incorporate comparisons and contrasts among the three companies.)

Purchasing Officers.   Facing a major and expensive change in your communications system, you want the best service at the best price. The system should be versatile, allowing the greatest mix of services (voice, telefax, and modem communications) and equipment. Ideally, you'd like to minimize the cost of purchasing, operating, and maintaining equipment. But you'll probably have to compare and contrast these costs to arrive at a balance. You're willing to pay a bit more initially if operating and maintenance expenses save money over the long term.

You anticipate that each truck will be making or receiving 120–150 transmissions over its twelve hours of service (from 6 A.M. to 6 P.M.), but that number should increase if, as anticipated, the company's business expands after the installation of the new communications system. You expect that increased efficiencies from the new communications system will eventually raise your profit margin by 10 percent.

After hearing the presentations of the salespeople from the three companies and the opinions of the truck drivers, you'll be writing a memo to your firm's chief executive officer, comparing the services of the three communications companies and recommending which company Next-Day Express should choose.

Drivers of the Trucks.   You know first-hand the demands of the job and can offer valuable input into the choice of both services and hardware. You average ten deliveries per hour and are away from your truck at least 1/3 of the time. You encounter frequent traffic tie-ups, experience route changes, receive requests for emergency pick-ups and deliveries, calculate and print bills for these emergencies, correct billing errors, and collect and record payments for C.O.D. and even non-C.O.D. orders. Furthermore, you must obtain signatures from customers receiving deliveries and notify some senders that the delivery was made.

Thus, not only do you want reliable, fast, static-free transmission, but also the ability to communicate with dispatchers even when you're away from the truck, or to access voice-mail messages when you return to the truck. You want fax capabilities and as many other options as the company can supply: voice mail, call waiting, teleconferencing, modems, computer voice- and handwriting-recognition—although you realize that all these features may be too expensive.

After making your oral recommendations, you'll be writing a memorandum to the purchasing officers in which you compare the services available from the three communications companies and recommend which you'd prefer.

DATA SHEETS

AmeriCom Communications

The largest integrated communications service in the United States, AmeriCom offers the largest network available, reaching every part of the greater metropolitan area. Furthermore, AmeriCom provides the clearest signal through its digitized transmission system. It cannot currently supply computer or modem service, but it does accommodate high-speed fax transmissions and expects to be able to add the other services within the next year.

AmeriCom manufactures the newest mobile phone: the Flexiphone, which can be hand carried and can send and receive telefaxes when plugged into the base module in the truck. The phone weighs only two ounces and retains battery power for ten hours. The base module also serves as a battery charger. The cost per phone is $300, including base module, and the equipment is warranted for one year.

Range of services: 250 square miles

Peak hours: 7 A.M. to 7 P.M.

Pricing: (All prices are per truck)

A. High-volume package (100 five-minute calls $100
       during peak hours)
       Each call after 100 (peak hours) $.25 per minute

B. Unlimited package (during peak hours) $150 per truck

       Non-peak-hour costs $.05 per minute

Optional services: (prices are per truck)

       Call-waiting $10 monthly

       Voice mail $5 monthly

       Three-way teleconferencing $5 monthly, plus cost of calls

       Caller ID $3 monthly

Installation and activation fee (each truck): $35

Repair Costs to Equipment: $45 per hour

Cellular Force Communications

The second-largest but oldest telecommunications service, Cellular Force lacks digital transmission and reception, but covers the greater metropolitan area. It offers telefax transmissions, but at slow speeds. Currently, it cannot supply customers with computers or modems but hopes to once it installs digital capabilities.

Equipment:

1. The Mobilefax Phone, a truck-mounted phone which sends and receives faxes as well as normal transmissions, but which cannot be removed from the truck. No battery recharging is necessary. Cost per phone: $350. Warranted for two years.

2. The hand-held Convenience Phone (weight 4 ounces, battery life 10 hours) available on a second telephone line. Cost per phone: $159. Warranted for one year.

Range of services: 250 square miles

Peak hours: 8 A.M. to 5 P.M.

Pricing: (All prices are daily per truck)

A. Economy package for first line (150 five-minute calls during peak hours)	$125
Each call after 150 (peak hours)	$.15 per minute
B. Unlimited package for first line	$140
Non-peak-hour costs	$.03 per minute
Cost for second line (with either package)	$10 (including 50 minutes of peak-hour time, then $.25 per minute)

Optional services: (prices are per truck)

Call-waiting	$8 monthly
Voice mail	$4 monthly
Three-way teleconferencing	$4 monthly, plus cost of calls
Caller ID	$3 monthly

Installation and activation fee (each truck): $45

Repair Costs to Equipment: $45 per hour

Galaxy Communications

Having started its operations just six months ago, Galaxy offers the lowest-cost service available, although its range is somewhat limited (4 percent of the calls in the metropolitan area might encounter interference). Galaxy uses the Mobilefax phone and/or the Convenience Phone and provides hand-held computers with voice and handwriting recognition for no additional charge. Clients may also rent phones, thus significantly lowering initial costs as well as repair and replacement costs. Galaxy charges the same for peak- and non-peak-hour transmissions.

Costs of phones:

	Mobilefax phone	$350 (if purchased)
		$10 per month (if rented, with free replacement of defective phones)
	Convenience Phone	$179 (if purchased)
		$10 per month (if rented, with free replacement of defective phones)

Range of services: 240 square miles

Pricing: (All prices are daily per truck)

A. Preferred package (140 five-minute calls during peak hours)	$100
Each call after 140	$.05 per minute
B. Calls Unlimited package	$120 per truck

Optional services: (prices are per truck)

Call-waiting	$6 monthly
Voice mail	$3 monthly
Three-way teleconferencing	$3 monthly, plus cost of calls
Caller ID	$2 monthly

Installation and activation fee (each truck): $25

Repair Costs to Equipment: $35 per hour

Composing Activity: Writing an Argument

Compose a letter to the audience specified, comparing the three communications companies to argue why one should be chosen instead of the others. Support your claims with any pertinent facts, statistics, or short stories that support or illustrate your claims. At various stages in the composing and revising process, discuss your paper with members of your group. Follow the procedures (including the use of the Postdraft Analysis questions) introduced in this chapter.

Collaborative Activity: Examining the Coherence of Your Argument (45 minutes of class time)

Read your paper to the other people who've assumed your role, and discuss its effectiveness. You may wish to engage in predicting activities and to examine the first and last sentence of every paragraph for clear linkage between paragraphs (that is, whether you've established a logical and coherent progression of ideas). Be sure to see that the comparisons in your paper are clear and that each contributes to your argument.

Chapter 14

Making Your Case

Human beings do not live in the objective world alone. . . . The fact of the matter is that the "real world" is to a large extent unconsciously built up on the language habits of the group. . . . The worlds in which different societies live are distinct worlds, not merely the same world with different labels attached.

—*Edward Sapir*

Adam's first task was to name every beast and fowl in his environment, and that process of naming hasn't stopped. We define—and to some extent construct—our world through language, so the difference between condemning and praising something often lies in the words we use to describe it. In the minds of many colonists during the Revolutionary War, for example, Washington, Jefferson, and Franklin were traitors to their country—Great Britain*—but in the minds of other colonists (whose country existed only in a declaration, not in actuality, at that time), these men were patriots and heroes. The greater the distance between your mental world and your readers', the more you need to define and explain the assumptions behind important terms in any argument you make.

Furthermore, the meanings of words are often evasive, ambiguous. A term may carry a variety of meanings, be unfamiliar to readers, or be intended by a writer to convey a special significance. So you often must define your terms to achieve the goals of your argument. Consider the roles of definitions in essays you've encountered earlier in this book: Roy C. Selby, Jr.'s translating medical terminology to clarify his description of a surgical procedure; *Consumer Reports'* specifying criteria to evaluate chocolate-chip cookies; Stephen Jay Gould's explaining *mean* and *median* to support his claim about the importance of scientific inquiry; Russell Baker's distinguishing between *macho* and *quiche-o* behaviors to criticize the faddish pretensions of "sophisticated" people. Without these definitions, the arguments would be diminished—rendered unclear at best, unconvincing at worst.

*Among those holding this view was Benjamin Franklin's son, who returned to Britain to live.

Finally, definitions are not mere exercises in manipulating language; they can profoundly affect our lives. Should a person who has killed another be executed, released without punishment, or honored? The answer depends on the definitions of murder, self-defense, and heroism. What are the criteria for each, and how do the actions and circumstances of the killing satisfy those criteria? Lawyers frame their arguments in precisely this way, and, while you may never be a lawyer, you must often support and defend your claims in a similar manner.

Where law ends, tyranny begins.

—*William Pitt, Earl of Chatham*

LOOKING AT ARGUMENTS

The essay that follows was originally delivered as an unpublished speech in Deland, Florida, on December 27, 1965. Professor George Henderson chose to include it in his 1971 book on children in schools outside suburbia. You'll see why as you read on.

WHAT IS POVERTY?

You ask me what is poverty? Listen to me. Here I am, dirty, smelly, and with no "proper" underwear on and with the stench of my rotting teeth near you. I will tell you. Listen to me. Listen without pity. I cannot use your pity. Listen with understanding. Put yourself in my dirty, worn out, ill-fitting shoes, and hear me.

Poverty is getting up every morning from a dirt- and illness-stained mattress. The sheets have long since been used for diapers. Poverty is living in a smell that never leaves. This is a smell of urine, sour milk, and spoiling food sometimes joined with the strong smell of long-cooked onions. Onions are cheap. If you have smelled this smell, you did not know how it came. It is the smell of the outdoor privy. It is the smell of young children who cannot walk the long dark way in the night. It is the smell of the mattresses where years of "accidents" have happened. It is the smell of the milk which has gone sour because the refrigerator long has not worked, and it costs money to get it fixed. It is the smell of rotting garbage. I could bury it, but where is the shovel? Shovels cost money.

Poverty is being tired. I have always been tired. They told me at the hospital when the last baby came that I had chronic anemia caused from poor diet, a bad case of worms, and that I needed a corrective operation. I listened politely— the poor are always polite. The poor always listen. They don't say that there is no money for iron pills, or better food, or worm medicine. The idea of an operation is frightening and costs so much that, if I had dared, I would have laughed. Who takes care of my children? Recovery from an operation takes a long time. I have three children. When I left them with "Granny" the last time I had a job, I came home to find the baby covered with fly specks, and a diaper that had not been changed since I left. When the dried diaper came off, bits of my baby's flesh came with it. My other child was playing with a sharp bit of broken glass, and my oldest was playing alone at the edge of a lake. I made twenty-two dollars a week, and a good nursery school costs twenty dollars a week for my three children. I quit my job.

Poverty is dirt. You say in your clean clothes coming from your clean house, "Anybody can be clean." Let me explain about housekeeping with no money. For breakfast I give my children grits with no oleo or cornbread without eggs and oleo. This does not use up many dishes. What dishes there are, I wash in cold water and with no soap. Even the cheapest soap has to be saved for the baby's diapers. Look at my hands, so cracked and red. Once I saved for two months to buy a jar of Vaseline for my hands and the baby's diaper rash. When I had saved enough, I went to buy it and the price had gone up two cents. The baby and I suffered on. I have to decide every day if I can bear to put my cracked, sore hands into the cold water and strong soap. But you ask, why not hot water? Fuel costs money. If you have a wood fire it costs money. If you burn electricity, it costs money. Hot water is a luxury. I do not have luxuries. I know you will be surprised when I tell you how young I am. I look so much older. My back has been bent over the wash tubs for so long, I cannot remember when I ever did anything else. Every night I wash every stitch my school-age child has on and just hope her clothes will be dry by morning.

Poverty is staying up all night on cold nights to watch the fire, knowing one spark on the newspaper covering the walls means your sleeping children die in flames. In summer poverty is watching gnats and flies devour your baby's tears when he cries. The screens are torn and you pay so little rent you know they will never be fixed. Poverty means insects in your food, in your nose, in your eyes, and crawling over you when you sleep. Poverty is hoping it never rains because diapers won't dry when it rains and soon you are using newspapers. Poverty is seeing your children forever with runny noses. Paper handkerchiefs cost money and all your rags you need for other things. Even more costly are antihistamines. Poverty is cooking without food and cleaning without soap.

Poverty is asking for help. Have you ever had to ask for help, knowing your children will suffer unless you get it? Think about asking for a loan from a relative, if this is the only way you can imagine asking for help. I will tell you how it feels. You find out where the office is that you are supposed to visit. You circle that block four or five times. Thinking of your children, you go in. Everybody is very busy. Finally, someone comes out and you tell her that you need help. That never is the person you need to see. You go see another person, and after spilling the whole shame of your poverty all over the desk between you, you find that this isn't the right office after all—you must repeat the whole process, and it never is any easier at the next place.

You have asked for help, and after all it has a cost. You are again told to wait. You are told why, but you don't really hear because of the red cloud of shame and the rising black cloud of despair.

Poverty is remembering. It is remembering quitting school in junior high because "nice" children had been so cruel about my clothes and my smell. The attendance officer came. My mother told him I was pregnant. I wasn't, but she thought that I could get a job and help out. I had jobs off and on, but never long enough to learn anything. Mostly I remember being married. I was so young then. I am still young. For a time, we had all the things you have. There was a little house in another town, with hot water and everything. Then my husband lost his job. There was unemployment insurance for a while and what few jobs I could get. Soon, all our nice things were repossessed and we moved back here. I was pregnant then. This house didn't look so bad when we first moved in. Every week it gets worse. Nothing is ever fixed. We now had no money. There were a few odd jobs for my husband, but everything went for food then, as it does now. I don't know how we lived through three years and three babies, but we did. I'll tell you something, after the last baby I destroyed my marriage. It had been a good one, but could you keep on bringing children in this dirt? Did you ever think how much it costs for any kind of birth control? I knew my husband was leaving the day he left, but there were no good-byes between us. I hope he has been able to climb out of this mess somewhere. He never could hope with us to drag him down.

That's when I asked for help. When I got it, you know how much it was? It was, and is, seventy-eight dollars a month for the four of us; that is all I ever can get. Now you know why there is no soap, no needles and thread, no hot water, no aspirin, no worm medicine, no hand cream, no shampoo. None of these things forever and ever and ever. So that you can see clearly, I pay twenty dollars a month rent, and most of the rest goes for food. For grits and cornmeal, and rice and milk and beans. I try my best to use only the minimum electricity. If I use more, there is that much less for food.

Poverty is looking into a black future. Your children won't play with my boys. They will turn to other boys who steal to get what they want. I can already see them behind the bars of their prison instead of behind the bars of my poverty. Or they will turn to the freedom of alcohol or drugs, and find themselves enslaved. And my daughter? At best, there is for her a life like mine.

But you say to me, there are schools. Yes, there are schools. My children have no extra books, no magazines, no extra pencils, or crayons, or paper and the most important of all, they do not have health. They have worms, they have infections, they have pink-eye all summer. They do not sleep well on the floor, or with me in my one bed. They do not suffer from hunger, my seventy-eight dollars keeps us alive, but they do suffer from malnutrition. Oh yes, I do remember what I was taught about health in school. It doesn't do much good. In some places there is a surplus commodities program. Not here. The county said it cost too much. There is a school lunch program. But I have two children who will already be damaged by the time they get to school.

But, you say to me, there are health clinics. Yes, there are health clinics and they are in the towns. I live out here eight miles from town. I can walk that far (even if it is sixteen miles both ways), but can my little children? My neighbor will take me when he goes; but he expects to get paid, *one way or another*. I bet you know my neighbor. He is that large man who spends his time at the gas station, the barbershop, and the corner store complaining about the government spending money on the immoral mothers of illegitimate children.

Poverty is an acid that drips on pride until all pride is worn away. Poverty is a chisel that chips on honor until honor is worn away. Some of you say that you would do *something* in my situation, and maybe you would, for the first week or the first month, but for year after year after year?

Even the poor can dream. A dream of a time when there is money. Money for the right kinds of food, for worm medicine, for iron pills, for toothbrushes, for hand cream, for a hammer and nails and a bit of screening, for a shovel, for a bit of paint, for some sheeting, for needles and thread. Money to pay *in money* for a trip to town. And, oh, money for hot water and money for soap. A dream of when asking for help does not eat away the last bit of pride. When the office you visit is as nice as the offices of other governmental agencies, when there are enough workers to help you quickly, when workers do not quit in defeat and despair. When you have to tell your story to only one person, and that person can send you for other help and you don't have to prove your poverty over and over and over again.

I have come out of my despair to tell you this. Remember I did not come from another place or another time. Others like me are all around you. Look at us with an angry heart, anger that will help you help me. Anger that will let you tell of me. The poor are always silent. Can you be silent too?

—Jo Goodwin Parker

Parker's argument is based entirely on her personal experiences. But the next argument, excerpted from "Letter from Birmingham Jail"(you read another part of it in Chapter 12), demands far more sophisticated support for its claims. The writer, Martin Luther King, Jr., addresses a large, diverse, and well-educated audience of clergy throughout the country and even the world. And he is asking that they join him in breaking the law. This is no trivial request, so his reasoning must be impeccable. He must painstakingly define his terms, explain what warrants these definitions, make careful distinctions, and cite respected authorities as backing.

You express a great deal of anxiety over our willingness to break laws. This is certainly a legitimate concern. Since we so diligently urge people to obey the Supreme Court's decision of 1954 outlawing segregation in the public schools, at first glance it may seem rather paradoxical for us consciously to break laws. One may well ask: "How can you advocate breaking some laws and obeying others?" The answer lies in the fact that there are two types of laws: just and unjust. I would be the first to advocate obeying just laws. One has not only a legal but a moral responsibility to obey just laws. Conversely, one has a moral responsibility to disobey unjust laws. I would agree with St. Augustine that "an unjust law is no law at all."

Now, what is the difference between the two? How does one determine whether a law is just or unjust? A just law is a man-made code that squares with the moral law or the law of God. An unjust law is a code that is out of harmony with the moral law. To put it in the terms of St. Thomas Aquinas: An unjust law is a human law that is not rooted in eternal law and natural law. Any law that uplifts human personality is just. Any law that degrades human personality is unjust. All segregation statutes are unjust because segregation distorts the soul and damages the personality. It gives the segregator a false sense of superiority and the segregated a false sense of inferiority. Segregation, to use the terminology of the Jewish philosopher Martin Buber, substitutes an "I–it" relationship for an "I–thou" relationship and ends up relegating persons to the status of things. Hence segregation is not only politically, economically and sociologically unsound, it is morally wrong and sinful. Paul Tillich has said that sin is separation. Is not segregation an existential expression of man's tragic separation, his awful estrangement, his terrible sinfulness? Thus it is that I can urge men to obey the 1954 decision of the Supreme Court, for it is morally right; and I can urge them to disobey segregation ordinances, for they are morally wrong.

Let us consider a more concrete example of just and unjust laws. An unjust law is a code that a numerical or power majority group compels a minority group to obey but does not make binding on itself. This is *difference* made legal. By the same token, a just law is a code that a majority compels a minority to follow and that it is willing to follow itself. This is *sameness* made legal.

Let me give another explanation. A law is unjust if it is inflicted on a minority that, as a result of being denied the right to vote, had no part in enacting or devising the law. Who can say that the legislature of Alabama which set up that state's segregation laws was democratically elected? Throughout Alabama all sorts of devious methods are used to prevent Negroes from becoming registered voters, and there are some counties in which, even though Negroes constitute a majority of the population, not a single Negro is registered. Can any law enacted under such circumstances be considered democratically structured?

Sometimes a law is just on its face and unjust in its application. For instance, I have been arrested on a charge of parading without a permit. Now, there is nothing wrong in having an ordinance which requires a permit for a parade. But such an ordinance becomes unjust when it is used to maintain segregation and to deny citizens the First-Amendment privilege of peaceful assembly and protest.

I hope you are able to see the distinction I am trying to point out. In no sense do I advocate evading or defying the law, as would the rabid segregationist. That would lead to anarchy. One who breaks an unjust law must do so openly, lovingly, and with a willingness to accept the penalty. I submit that an individual who breaks a law that conscience tells him is unjust, and who willingly accepts the penalty of imprisonment in order to arouse the conscience of the community over its injustice, is in reality expressing the highest respect for law.

Issues for Investigation and Discussion

1. What problems does Jo Goodwin Parker construct for her readers? In other words, what is Parker's purpose in defining poverty?

2. In each paragraph, Parker describes a different aspect of poverty. What sentences serve as signposts to introduce these descriptions?

3. Parker frequently addresses her reader in the second-person *you*. Why? Does the reason change at various points in the essay?

4. A casual reading of Parker's argument might suggest that she merely lists and describes different aspects of poverty. But does Parker explain what warrants her claims? Does she anticipate and rebut the objections or questions of her reader? If so, where?

5. What are King's formal definitions of *just laws* and *unjust laws*? Why doesn't Parker include a formal definition of *poverty*?

6. King backs his claims through a series of comparisons and contrasts. Why?

7. King also cites a number of cases that illustrate and test the definitions. Where does he do so and why? Where does he anticipate the objections and questions of his readers? Where does he explain the warrants for his claims? How do these actions further his argument?

8. What similarities and differences between the arguments of the two writers do you observe?

9. Based on your answers to these questions and any other matters you observe, turn to your journal or computer file and list six or more common traits of arguments that employ definitions (or create a list with several classmates). Let this list guide you as you compose and revise your own argument later.

DEFINING TERMS

A definition may require only a few words or many paragraphs, depending on your subject, purpose, and audience. If you're explaining a procedure, as does Roy Selby, Jr., in Chapter 10, you may define terms through short phrases (". . . the brainstem, which conveys nerve impulses between the body and the brain") or simple synonyms. But if your argument demands careful distinctions among ideas, actions, or circumstances, as does Dr. King's, you may need to compose an extended definition comprising most or all of the following parts:

- a formal definition,
- backing through contrasts and borderline cases,
- backing through real or hypothetical examples,
- explanations of what warrants a claim, including responses to counterarguments.

Composing a Formal Definition

A formal definition follows the pattern found in dictionaries: placing the term in a category and explaining its distinguishing characteristics. You may compose and revise the definition yourself or take it from a dictionary, but be sure to acknowledge the source.

Term	Category	Distinguishing Characteristics
Data are	factual information	used as a basis for reasoning, discussion, or calculation. (from *Webster's Collegiate Dictionary*)
"... given a placebo,	a medication	prescribed more for the mental relief of a patient than for its actual effect on the disorder, ... " (from Dr. Roy C. Selby)

Don't strain to compose a "perfect" definition, for the pattern is flexible. You may introduce the elements in any order that fits logically into the context of your discussion, as in this example from Dr. Selby:

> Beneath the bone is a yellow leather-like [distinguishing characteristics] membrane [category], the dura, [term] that surrounds the brain [distinguishing characteristics].

The best approach, therefore, is probably to reexamine your definition throughout the invention, composing, and revising process to ensure that it's complete and accurate.

Backing the Definition Through Contrasts

The contrast control sharpens a television picture's focus by opposing bright with dark dots on the screen. A definition, likewise, is sharper when developed through contrasts between what a term means and doesn't mean.* Thus, as you compose and revise your extended definition, look for such clarifying contrasts. You've already read King's careful distinctions between *just* and *unjust laws*. Here's another example, excerpted from Sydney J. Harris's essay, "We Want a Messiah, Not a Leader," in which Harris defines *true leadership*. After constructing the problem for his readers in the first paragraph—that is, after explaining what warrants the definition—he defines the term through oppositions:

> People keep saying, "We need a leader" or "We need leadership," but that is not what they really mean. What most of them are looking for is not a leader, but a Messiah.

---

*The practice of defining by contrast goes back to ancient Greece, where the philosophers Aristotle and Plato both argued that we know things through their opposites: joy through sadness, sickness through health, goodness through evil, and so on.

They want someone who will give them the Word. And the word would be one that is agreeable to them, that appeals to their preferences and prejudices, so that they can follow it wholeheartedly.

But this is not what a true leader does—a leader tells people hard truths, gives them a difficult path to follow, calls upon their highest qualities, not their basest instincts. A true leader does not tell us what we *want* to hear, but what we *ought* to hear.

Backing Through Examples

Definitions are abstract, so most writers cite and interpret examples of their claims, as does Martin Luther King, Jr. in exploring his contrasts:

> Let us consider a more concrete example of just and unjust laws. An unjust law is a code that a numerical or power majority group compels a minority group to obey but does not make binding on itself. This is *difference* made legal. By the same token, a just law is a code that a majority compels a minority to follow and that it is willing to follow itself. This is *sameness* made legal.

And Sydney J. Harris mentions two people as examples while examining the traits of false or true Messiahs:

> A false Messiah—such as a Hitler, in our time—caters to and inflames the fears, hates, angers and resentments of his people, and drives them to destruction rather than to salvation or self-realization.

> A true Messiah—such as Jesus, even taken on the worldly plane—rebukes his people, shows them their errors, makes them want to be better, not stronger or richer, and asks them to make sacrifices for the common good and for the good of their own souls. He is never followed by very many, usually killed by the majority, and venerated only when he is safely dead and need not be taken seriously.

Writers don't limit themselves to sharp contrasts, but often cite borderline cases to illustrate subtle distinctions. For example, King presents and interprets his own experience with a borderline example of an unjust law. His readers can then understand why even some seemingly just laws must be disobeyed:

> Sometimes a law is just on its face and unjust in its application. For instance, I have been arrested on a charge of parading without a permit. Now, there is nothing wrong in having an ordinance which requires a permit for a parade. But such an ordinance becomes unjust when it is used to maintain segregation and to deny citizens the First-Amendment privilege of peaceful assembly and protest.

Try brainstorming a list of contrasts during invention, and add contrasting examples as they come to your mind during composing and revision.

Providing Warrants and Responses to Counterarguments

A simple list of the criteria—even with examples of each—that define a term is often not enough to create a coherent argument. Your final draft may need to show what warrants the definition; that is, why a definition is needed, why your examples back your claims, and why the objections you anticipate from readers are unfounded. Here are warrants from Parker and King:

> You say in your clean clothes coming from your clean house, "Anybody can be clean." Let me explain about housekeeping with no money. . . .

> Paul Tillich has said that sin is separation. Is not segregation an existential expression of man's tragic separation, his awful estrangement, his terrible sinfulness? Thus it is that I can urge men to obey the 1954 decision of the Supreme Court, for it is morally right; and I can urge them to disobey segregation ordinances, for they are morally wrong.

Collaborative Activity: Deriving a Definition from Specific Instances (25 minutes of class time)

Suppose a civic organization has appointed you and several classmates to a committee that will honor people who have performed courageous acts. Your first task is to determine the criteria for identifying acts of courage. Discuss each of the following examples, and take notes on the committee's conclusions. (Or consider the issues by yourself.) Does any single example demonstrate true courageous action? If not, what elements from each example might contribute to a definition?

1. The evidence suggests that President Richard Nixon knew about the Watergate burglary—at least soon after it occurred in 1972. He certainly was aware of and probably involved himself in the cover-up, a politically dangerous act that ultimately led to his resignation. Should Nixon's probable involvement in the cover-up be considered courageous? Why or why not?

2. Captain Smith newly arrives at a battle zone in which enemy troops have occupied a village important to supply routes. Soldiers warn the captain that the area surrounding the village is heavily mined and that gun emplacements and machine gun nests are probably hidden throughout the village. Smith, however, says that the village must be captured immediately and heads three squads of soldiers in a frontal attack. Is the captain courageous? Why or why not?

3. Corporal Jewkes is lost in the woods near an enemy-occupied village surrounded by mine fields and under heavy guard. Unaware of these dangers, he miraculously makes his way into the village, and not knowing what he will

find, enters the first house he comes to. Jewkes immediately discovers several guards sleeping beside a gun emplacement, so he quickly kills the guards and takes the guns. Should we consider Jewkes' actions courageous? Why or why not?

4.   The members of two rival gangs, the Archangels and the Devil's Helpers, meet on the street. Zip, a young man undergoing initiation into the Devil's Helpers, is told to confront Big Mike, the leader of the Archangels. He knows that if he refuses, the members of his own gang will ridicule him, probably beat him, and certainly throw him out of the gang. Therefore, Zip approaches Big Mike and begins to taunt him. Are Zip's actions courageous? Why or why not?

5.   One day Big Mike arrives at school in a brand new pair of basketball shoes and promptly dares anyone to step on them. Being something of a poet, he says, "Put your soles on my shoes; I'll put my knife in your life." Are his actions courageous? Why or why not? Would someone be courageous if he or she tried to step on Big Mike's shoes? Why or why not?

6.   A woman has been beaten repeatedly by her husband over the last several years. Finally, during a severe beating that threatens her life, she runs to the kitchen and grabs a paring knife. When the husband catches her arm, she turns and begins flaying him with the knife. Are the woman's actions courageous? Why or why not?

7.   After incurring heavy losses on the front lines for several days, Corporal Kallikak's squad is pinned down by machine gun fire. When his best friend is killed at his side, Kallikak flies into a rage. Swearing at the enemy, he grabs a grenade launcher, charges across open ground, and fires at the gun emplacement, destroying it. Are the corporal's actions courageous? Why or why not? Would your opinion change if he had been killed before he could fire back? Why or why not?*

Follow-Up Activity: Composing a Definition

Based on your notes from the previous activity, compose a definition of courageous action. Specify what criteria that action must meet, and illustrate your definition with an incident—real or imagined—that satisfies all of these criteria. You may also back your definition with contrasting or borderline-case examples from the list above or from your own experience, knowledge, or imagination.

---

*Adapted from Larry R. Johannessen and others, *Designing and Sequencing Prewriting Activities* (Urbana, IL: NCTE, 1982) 34–35.

Collaborative Activity: Evaluating Your Definition (25 minutes of class time)

Take turns with your group reading the first drafts of the definitions. Stop at the end of the first paragraph and periodically throughout the paper so listeners can predict what will follow and then test their predictions against what you actually say. The Postdraft Analysis questions may also guide your discussion.

Postdraft Analysis
(To be completed by the writer or peer reader)

1. Locate the definition of the term. Does the term need to be defined formally? Is the definition clearly and gracefully written? If not, how might the definition be improved?

2. Locate the criteria that explain and clarify the definition. Are the criteria sufficient? Are they adequately developed? If not, what might be added or changed?

3. Look at the examples for each claim. Are they sufficient? Do the examples illustrate and test the criteria? How could (or should) they be changed? Is the stated or unstated connection (the warrant) between claim and example clear? If not, what should be added or changed?

4. Does the argument include contrasting examples? If not, what examples might be added and where?

5. Does the argument include examples of borderline situations? If not, what examples should be added and where? If examples of borderline cases are included, does the argument explain why they don't satisfy the criteria? If not, what explanations might be added?

6. Is the flow of the argument clear and graceful? If not, what transitions and explanations of warrants would improve the flow, or how might the information be rearranged?

Concluding Activity: Revising and Editing Your Argument

Consider the responses to the Postdraft Analysis questions, and then do a final revision of the argument—adding and rearranging material, rewording ideas, clarifying connections between ideas and events, and editing the paper carefully for matters of mechanics, grammar, and spelling.

WRITING IN A SOCIAL CONTEXT: THE QUEEN V. DUDLEY AND STEPHENS (AN ACTUAL CASE)

The law is not concerned with trifles.

—Legal Maxim

The following activity simulates a real situation in which you and your classmates can gain first-hand experience, devise reports, discuss and question them, and then communicate your ideas in writing. You'll read the material provided before coming to class, choose one of three roles to play, and then make your argument in an open meeting. The entire activity should require no more than forty-five to eighty minutes, divided as follows:

- five minutes for choosing roles
- ten to fifteen minutes for determining strategy
- twenty to forty minutes to present arguments
- ten to twenty minutes for rebuttal

After choosing or being assigned to a group representing one of the roles, you and the other group members will meet to discuss the arguments you'll make, based on the definitions and information provided. Then your instructor will convene the whole class in a mock trial, first allowing the prosecution to present its case, followed by the defense attorneys, and then followed by rebuttal of the arguments. Finally, again within your role, you will compose a written argument addressed to a specified audience.

Alternatively, you may simply read through the materials and discuss them in class before composing a report within your role.

The Context

Two Englishmen, Thomas Dudley and Edwin Stephens, were indicted for the murder of Richard Parker on the high seas on July 25, 1884, and will be tried under English law, which is similar to the legal system in the United States.

The Circumstances

1. July 5, 1884, English yacht sinks in a storm about 1,600 miles off the Cape of Good Hope, Africa, and its crew—Dudley, Stephens, a third man named Brooks, and an eighteen-year-old boy named Richard Parker (now deceased)—enter small boat.

2. Boat drifts probably more than 1,000 miles from land.

3. No fresh water available except for rain that the men are able to catch in their oilskin capes. Only food available: two one-pound cans of turnips and a small turtle men catch on the fourth day at sea.

4. After twelve days, men finish all food and do not eat again until the twentieth day, when act is committed.

5. On eighteenth day—having gone seven days without food and five without water—the prisoners speak to Brooks about sacrificing one man so remaining three can survive. They suggest Parker, with whom they do not discuss the matter.

6. On July 24, Dudley proposes to Stephens and Brooks—but not Parker— that they draw lots to determine who should be sacrificed. Brooks refuses to participate. During discussion, Dudley and Stephens say their families

depend on them, so Parker is the most logical person to sacrifice if no ship rescues them the next day.

7. After no ship appears on July 25, Dudley signals to Brooks and Stephens that Parker should be killed. Stephens agrees, but Brooks objects.

8. Parker, greatly weakened by famine and by drinking sea water and lying helpless at the bottom of the boat, does not resist but does not consent to being killed.

9. With Stephen's approval, Dudley prays that God forgive them all for committing this rash act and asks that their souls be saved. Dudley then tells Parker to prepare to meet his maker and slits the boy's throat with a knife.

10. By feeding on the boy's body and blood, the three men barely survive until a passing ship picks them up four days later.

11. The men are taken to Portsmouth and then to Exeter, where they confess to their actions and are indicted for murder.

The Confessions of Dudley and Stephens:

1. Neither Dudley nor Stephens denies his actions, and both maintain that the sustenance they obtained from killing the boy afforded their only chance of survival.

2. They also claim that Parker was extremely weak and would have died soon.

3. They say that at the time of their actions, they saw no reasonable possibility of being saved soon.

4. They admit, however, that any of the four could have been sacrificed—not just the boy.

Definitions of Key Terms (Quoted verbatim from *Black's Law Dictionary*):

1. Murder: (English Common Law) The willful killing of a human being by another with malice aforethought, either express or implied.

2. Malice: In murder, that condition of mind which prompts one to take the life of another without just cause or provocation.

3. Temporary Insanity: M'Naghten Rule (1843): At the time of the committing of the act, the party of the accused was laboring under such a defect of reason, from disease of the mind, as not to know the nature and quality of the act he was doing, or if he did know it, he did not know he was doing what was wrong.

4. An Accomplice: If one willingly consents to or conspires in the commission of the crime by another, this person is also guilty of the crime.

5. Guilt: Under both English and American law, an accused is presumed innocent until proven guilty beyond a reasonable doubt.

6. Reasonable Doubt: To justify an acquittal (a not-guilty verdict), reasonable doubt must be based on reason and must arise from evidence; it is doubt that a reasonable man or woman might entertain. It is not fanciful doubt, not imagined doubt, not doubt that a juror might conjure up to avoid performing an unpleasant task or duty.

7. Self-Defense: This is the protection of one's person or property against some injury attempted by another. It is an excuse for the use of force in resisting an attack on the person, especially for killing an assailant.

8. Necessity: A person is excused from criminal liability if he acts under duress of circumstances to protect life or limb or health in a reasonable manner and with no other acceptable choice.

The Participants

The Prosecuting Team.   You believe that the actions of Dudley and Stephens constitute premeditated murder. While you acknowledge that the men were placed under extremely difficult, even impossible, conditions, you cannot condone the unlawful taking of a human life. Since the law presumes that the defendants are innocent until proven guilty, your task is to prove that guilt.

The Defense Attorneys.   You believe that the actions of Dudley and Stephens are justifiable (and certainly excusable) on a number of grounds and you will defend them using whatever strategy you can devise. However, you need not prove the innocence of the defendants—that is presumed under law. You need only establish reasonable doubt.

The Judge.   You can accept the verdict of the jury, or overrule the verdict if you believe it is not based on the evidence (if, for example, you believe the doubts of the jurors are unreasonable). You may also dismiss a case summarily—in effect, throw it out of court—if you believe the prosecution has not proven guilt.

Invention Activity: Arguing Guilt or Innocence

As the prosecuting or defense attorney, consider what to include in a legal brief to present to the judge in which you argue the guilt or innocence of the defendants. You must demonstrate whether their actions fit the legal definitions that will determine the conviction or acquittal of the men, show how your claims are warranted, and rebut the counterarguments of your opponents.

As the judge, consider what to say in a legal opinion of the defendants' guilt or innocence, and their sentencing if they are guilty. Back up your claims and explain why they are warranted.

Composing Activity: Writing a First Draft

After considering your materials, persuasive strategy, and organization during invention, compose a draft of your argument. Construct the problem at the beginning, map out your arguments, introduce relevant definitions of terms, and show how your claims satisfy or don't satisfy those definitions. Be sure to back up your claims, explain how they are warranted, and refute the counterarguments.

Collaborative Activity: Evaluating Your Argument (25 minutes of class time)

Take turns with several classmates reading your early drafts of the arguments. Stop at the end of the first paragraph and periodically throughout the paper so listeners can predict what will follow. Then test their predictions against what you actually say. The following questions may guide you further in revising.

Postdraft Analysis
(To be completed by the writer or peer reader)
1. Locate the phrases or sentences in your opening paragraph that construct the problem and roadmap the steps your argument will take. Are the construction and steps clearly articulated? If not, how might the material be revised?
2. Look at the definitions of terms. Does the argument include all those appropriate to prosecuting or defending the accused? If not, what definitions should be cited? Are the definitions introduced gracefully? If not, what language should be added or changed?
3. Does the argument provide sufficient information about the actions or circumstances relevant to its claims? Should any information be summarized or shortened? Does the argument link these matters to the appropriate legal definitions? What, if any, changes should be made to the argument?
4. Examine the warrants between claims and evidence. Are the warrants clear and sufficient? If not, indicate changes in brackets. What counterarguments does the writer anticipate and rebut? Are these rebuttals clear, logical, and strategically placed? Should more counterarguments be acknowledged and rebutted? Note these changes in brackets.
5. Are the connections between ideas unclear in any places—that is, are the ideas related in ways you haven't shown? If so, add in brackets words that explain the relationships. Look at the ends and beginnings of consecutive paragraphs. Are additional signposts needed to clarify the organizational structure? If so, indicate where with bracketed labels.
6. Does the argument conclude effectively? If not, how might the conclusion be improved?

Concluding Activity: Revising and Editing Your Argument

Consider the responses to the Postdraft Analysis questions, and then do a final revision of the argument—adding and rearranging material, rewording ideas,

clarifying connections between ideas and events, and editing the paper carefully for matters of mechanics, grammar, and spelling.

Additional Writing Assignment.   In the role of juror, weigh the evidence and
arguments of the prosecution and defense before deciding on the guilt or innocence of the defendants. Then write an argument for a news magazine or even a
tabloid in which you explain your reasons for convicting or acquitting the men.
Back up your claims and explain why they are warranted.

Additional Writing Assignment.   This case has attracted a great deal of public attention, so in the role of newspaper reporter, summarize the arguments of
the prosecution and defense in your story of the outcome of the trial. Support
your claims by quoting testimony and comments by the attorneys, jurors, and
judge.

WRITING IN A SOCIAL CONTEXT: "MOM, I WANT A DIVORCE"

The Context:

A twelve-year-old girl named Elizabeth Sampson would like to be adopted by
William and Trudy Brent, her foster parents for the last eighteen months.
Having lived in eight different foster homes and dealt with the state Child
Welfare Agency many times, Elizabeth has become somewhat of an "expert" on
the legal system. Thus, she has hired a lawyer to represent her in a suit to
"divorce" herself from her biological parents, John and Christie Sampson. John
has already consented to surrendering custody of the child, but Christie refuses. The Brents have expressed a strong desire to adopt Elizabeth but will not
testify or in any way participate in the legal proceedings.

Courts throughout the country have traditionally ruled that children are
the property (and the responsibility) of their parents, and that children have
few rights of their own. Furthermore, the states have generally tried to keep
families together through "family preservation programs," based on two
premises:

1. family affairs should be private and government has little right to interfere
   in them; and
2. with appropriate counseling and support services, a family may remain in-
   tact and handle its own problems.

Nevertheless, when child abuse or neglect is persistent and severe, the state
may deny custody to the parents and permit others to adopt the child.

A judge has scheduled a hearing to determine whether Christie Sampson
must surrender custody of Elizabeth to the Brent family, who will initiate
adoption procedures. All interested parties and their attorneys will be present.

The Participants

Elizabeth's Lawyer. You contend that Christie has deserted the child several times and is unfit to retain custody. You also believe that the Brents have given Elizabeth a loving and stable foster home and should be allowed to adopt the child.

Christie Sampson's Lawyer. You contend that Christie Sampson has done her best to raise Elizabeth under extremely difficult financial and physical circumstances. Her supposed neglect of the child can be attributed to two causes: (1) Christie's inability to support Elizabeth at various times; and (2) the state's failure to provide appropriate support services or to inform Christie of her responsibilities. You will further argue that Elizabeth wishes to leave her mother so she may benefit from the Brents' high income and luxurious suburban lifestyle. Denying custody to Christie would therefore set a dangerous precedent, encouraging children to shop around for families that provide the best living arrangements.

State Social Workers. You will argue that Christie has been an unfit mother. She has repeatedly abandoned Elizabeth and ignored state laws and the procedures of the Child Welfare Agency.

Christie Sampson. You love Elizabeth and want to keep her. Although you've made mistakes in the past, you believe they resulted from your inability to work and support her, as well as from the state's poor administration of its Family Preservation Program. You have never physically abused the child.

The Facts

1. John and Christie Sampson: high school dropouts who marry at age sixteen when Christie becomes pregnant with Elizabeth. Their son William arrives sixteen months after Elizabeth's birth. However, John often becomes drunk and beats Christie before deserting the family when Elizabeth is three. Christie lives on welfare and works in menial jobs to support the children.

2. Over a nine-year period, Elizabeth lives in four foster homes while spending six years in total with mother.

3. The Brents could sue for custody of child, but choose not to in hopes of creating a test case to further the cause of children's rights.

4. A year after deserting family, John Sampson asks for and receives permission for the children to live with him in another state. Christie reclaims William seven months later, but neither sees nor talks to Elizabeth again for a year—because, she later contends, John refuses to surrender custody. John returns Elizabeth to Christie when child is four.

5. Christie subsequently takes job in another city and leaves her two children with a friend. She does not communicate with children for six months.

6. John and Christie reconcile and reclaim their children from the state, but the reconciliation lasts only a few months. Christie retains custody of Elizabeth and William after John leaves.

7. Unable to support children, Christie asks that they be placed in foster homes. She visits children regularly, regains custody after finding a better job, and then surrenders children to the state when she is laid off—despite promising the children she'll never leave them again.

8. Christie then lives with another man and regains custody of Elizabeth. When the man leaves her a year later, Christie can no longer support the child, and again surrenders Elizabeth to the state.

9. William Brent is a college professor; Trudy Brent is lawyer. They own a large house and have two other children, who, along with Elizabeth, attend a private school.

10. Almost 500,000 children are in foster homes, an increase of more than 50 percent since 1982. Many foster children are continually shifted from one home to another.

11. Foster families provide temporary homes until children can return to their parents or be adopted, typically after twelve to eighteen months. Although state caseworkers are assigned to these families, no one ever visits Elizabeth.

12. Children's rights have broadened since 1967, when a juvenile suspect in a crime was granted the right to an attorney. Children have subsequently been granted rights to free speech in school, to abortions, and to emergency medical treatment without parental consent. Federal laws now protect children against parental neglect or mistreatment, and state laws now require court-appointed attorneys to insure children's rights in custody or abuse cases.

13. A child doesn't always recognize or acknowledge her best interests, so court-appointed lawyers must act in the best interests of child. For example, a thirteen-year-old sexually abused girl wanted to return to her mother and stepfather who had completed a four-year jail term for aggravated criminal assault against her. She was granted the right to an attorney, who did not argue that her mother regain custody.

Composing Activity: Defending the Mother's Rights or the Child's Rights

As the attorney for either Christie or Elizabeth, write a legal brief to present to the judge in which you argue for or against surrendering custody of Elizabeth to the Brents so they may adopt her. You must support your claims, explain why they are warranted, and refute the arguments of your opponent. Your argument must also define any relevant terms and show how the actions of your client satisfy the criteria of those definitions.

As a state social worker, write a document supporting Elizabeth's contention that she should be allowed to live with the Brents. You must also back up and explain why your claims are warranted, define terms, and show how your arguments satisfy the criteria of the definitions.

As Christie Sampson, write a document supporting your lawyer's contention that you be allowed to retain custody of Elizabeth. Define any relevant terms and show how your actions have satisfied the criteria of those definitions.

At various stages in the composing and revising process, discuss your paper with members of your group following the procedures (including the Postdraft Analysis questions) introduced in this chapter.

Additional Composing Activity: Reporting the Results of the Trial

Assume you are a reporter from a news magazine. Compose a story on the trial, explaining the issues, the arguments of the parties involved, and the outcome of the proceedings.

LITERARY ACKNOWLEDGMENTS

"A talent-thin sport gets thinner" by Bernie Lincicome from *The Chicago Tribune,* November 18, 1992, Section 4, page 1. Copyright © 1992 Chicago Tribune Company. All rights reserved. Used with permission. **(Pages xxiv–xxv)**

From "The Juice Craze" from *Consumer Reports,* December 1992, Volume 57, No. 12, page 747. Copyright © 1992 by Consumers Union of U.S., Inc., Yonkers, N.Y. 10703-1057. Reprinted by permission from *Consumer Reports.* **(Page xxv)**

From "Old Before Her Time" by Katherine Barrett from *Ladies' Home Journal,* August 1983, page 46. Copyright © 1983 by the Meredith Corporation. Used with permission of Ladies' Home Journal Magazine. **(Pages 23–24)**

From "Ladies' and Gentlemen's Guide to Modern English Usage" from *The Owl in the Attic,* published by Harper & Row. Copyright 1931, © 1959 by James Thurber. Reprinted by permission of Rosemary A. Thurber. **(Page 46)**

"Matinee Idler" by Robert Hughes from *Parents Magazine,* May 1994, page 138. **(Pages 54–55)**

From "Ultimate Discourse" by E. L. Doctorow from *Esquire Magazine,* August 1986, page 41. Reprinted by permission of Esquire Magazine. **(Page 65)**

"Teen gangbangers an ignored issue" by Mike Royko from *The Chicago Tribune,* January 31, 1992, page 3. Reprinted by permission of Tribune Media Services **(Pages 66–67)**

"From a grandpa, above and beyond" by Bob Greene from *The Chicago Tribune,* March 11, 1990, Section 5, page 1. Reprinted by permission of Tribune Media Services. **(Pages 72–73)**

"Love Finds A Way" by Bob Greene (appeared in *Reader's Digest,* November 1990, page 154). Reprinted by permission of Tribune Media Services. **(Pages 73–74)**

From *The Best of Sydney J. Harris* by Sydney J. Harris, pages 16 and 216. Copyright © 1975 by Sydney J. Harris. Reprinted by permission of Houghton Mifflin Company. All rights reserved. **(Pages 81, 206, 207)**

"Divining the strange eating habits of kids" by Ellen Goodman. Copyright © 1994 by The Boston Globe Company. Reprinted with permission of The Washington Post Writers Group. **(Pages 82–83)**

"Women Are Just Better" from *Living Out Loud* by Anna Quindlen, pages 31–34. Copyright ©1987 by Anna Quindlen. Reprinted by permission of Random House, Inc. **(Pages 100–101**)

From "The Layout of Arguments" by Stephen E. Toulmin, from *The Uses of Argument,* 1958. Reprinted by permission of Cambridge University Press. **(Pages 94–98, 102–104)**

From "The Claim" by Annette T. Rottenberg, from *Elements of Argument,* 3rd ed. Reprinted by permission from St. Martin's Press, 1991. **(Pages 94–95**)

From "The Decline of Gentrification" by William Stern, from *Forbes,* November 11, 1991. **(Page 109)**

From "Tenants to Buy Uptown Tower" by William Mullen, from *The Chicago Tribune,* April 28, 1993, Section 2, page 3. **(Pages 109–110)**

"A Delicate Operation" by Roy C. Selby, Jr., from *Harper's Magazine,* December 1975, Vol. 251, No. 1507, pages 118–119. Copyright © 1975 by Harper's Magazine. All rights reserved. Reprinted from the December issue by special permission. **(Pages 112–114)**

"The Median Isn't the Message" from *Bully for Brontosaurus: Reflections in Natural History* by Stephen Jay Gould, pages 473–478. Copyright © 1991 by Stephen Jay Gould. Reprinted with the permission of W. W. Norton & Company, Inc. **(Pages 114–118)**

Figure by Ben Gamit from "The Median Isn't the Message" from *Bully for Brontosaurus: Reflections in Natural History* by Stephen Jay Gould, page 474. Copyright © 1991 by Stephen Jay Gould. Reprinted with the permission of W. W. Norton & Company, Inc. **(Page 115)**

From "Speakers Voice Support for Group Homes" and letters by Steve Ostrowski, from *Wilmette Life,* January 11, 1990, page 6. **(Page 127)**

From letter by Julia Joehl to *Wilmette Life*, October 12, 1989, page 16B. **(Page 128)**

From *Ordinance No. 90-0-78,* "An Ordinance Amending Chapter 20, Article 2, 'Definition' and Article 5, 'Zoning Districts' of The Wilmette Village Code 'Zoning Ordinance'." Reprinted by permission of The Village of Wilmette. **(Page 129)**

From *Ordinance No. 90-0-5,* "An Ordinance Providing for the Licensing and Regulation of Group Homes in Wilmette, Cook County, Illinois," page 1. Reprinted by permission of The Village of Wilmette. **(Pages 128–129)**

From "Chocolate-chip cookies" from *Consumer Reports,* October 1993, Volume 58, No. 10, pages 643–644. Copyright © 1993 by Consumers Union of U.S., Inc., Yonkers, N.Y. 10703-1057. Reprinted by permission from *Consumer Reports.* **(Pages 132–134)**

From "Tougher on teen-age drinking" from *The Communicator,* #5, 1992, pages 1–2. Reprinted by permission of The Village of Wilmette. **(Pages 134–135)**

From L. Sue Baugh, from *Handbook for Memo Writing,* 1990, pages 33, 44–46. Reprinted by permission of NTC Business Books. **(Page 136)**

From "Dumber Than We Thought" by David A. Kaplan with Pat Wingert and Farai Chideye from *Newsweek,* September 20, 1993, pages 44–45. Copyright © 1993 by Newsweek, Inc. All rights reserved. Reprinted by permission. **(Pages 139–142)**

From "Saturn Rising" from *Popular Mechanics,* January 1990, pp. 44, 46–47. **(Page 147)**

From "Here Comes GM's Saturn" from *Business Week,* April 9, 1990, pages 56–57, 60–62. **(Pages 147–148)**

"Old meets new: Steamy 'Hot Spot' blends B movie, film noir" by Roger Ebert from *The Chicago Sun-Times,* October 26, 1990. Reprinted by permission of The Chicago Sun-Times. **(Pages 152–153)**

"In Our Own Image" by De'Lois Jacobs from *Essence,* June 1986, page 122. Reprinted by permission of the author. **(Pages 165–166)**

"The Invisible Mainstream" by Ken Baker from *Newsweek,* January 10, 1994, pages 10–11. Copyright © 1994 by Newsweek, Inc. All rights reserved. Reprinted by permission. **(Pages 166–168)**

From "Letter From Birmingham Jail" from *Why We Can't Wait* by Martin Luther King, Jr., pages 76–78 and 79–84. Copyright © 1963 by Martin Luther King, Jr., copyright renewed 1991 by Coretta Scott King. Reprinted by arrangement with The Heirs to the

Estate of Martin Luther King, Jr., c/o Joan Daves Agency as agent for the proprietor. **(Pages 170–172, 203–204)**

From The Antioch College Sexual Offense Policy. Reprinted by permission of Antioch University. **(Page 180)**

"The Two Ismo's" by Russell Baker from *The New York Times,* June 5, 1982. Copyright © 1982 by The New York Times Company. Reprinted by permission. **(Pages 183–184)**

"The Iks" from *The Lives of a Cell* by Lewis Thomas, pages 107–110. Copyright © 1973 by The Massachusetts Medical Society. Used by permission of Viking Penguin, a division of Penguin Books USA Inc. **(Pages 184–186)**

From *America's Other Children: Public Schools Outside Surburbia* edited by George Henderson, pages 30–34. Copyright © 1971 by the University of Oklahoma Press. Reprinted by permission. **(Pages 200–203)**

From *Theory & Research into Practice: Designing and Sequencing Prewriting Activities* by Larry R. Johannessen, Elizabeth A. Kahn and Carolyn Calhoun Walter, pages 34–35. Copyright © 1982 by the ERIC Clearinghouse on Reading and Communication Skills and the National Council of Teachers of English. Reprinted by permission. **(Pages 208–209)**

From "Irreconcilable Differences" by Pat Wingert and Eloise Salholtz, from *Newsweek,* September 21, 1992, pages 85, 86, 88. **(Pages 215–217)**

Student essays by Nancy Joanne Farrell, Otto Castillo, Diana Jeter, Terrance Mhoon, Linda Novak, Aldo Ronchetti, Carlos Orellana, Allan Schulze, Christine M. Mueller, Gerald Anderson, Robin Prosser, Emese Schweder, Kate Friedlob, Leola Culpepper, Gloria Udaundo, Mark J. Schlitt, Sidney Porter, Hua Yan, Phu V. Ngo, and Virginia Ray reprinted by permission except for an untitled essay by Mary C. Fahey and an untitled essay by Alice El Yamin, both of whom the author was unable to locate.

Index

Abstract terms, eliminating, 45
Academic journal, 10, 11–12
Adelman, Clifford, xxv–xxvi
Analogy, in comparisons and contrasts, 182
Anderson, Gerald, 33–35, 37, 38
Antithesis, oppositions and, 51, 58
Argument, 65, 93–110
   claim in, 94–95, 98, 102, 103, 104–105
   creating own, 102–104
   examples of, 98–102
   Postdraft Analysis of, 106
   qualifiers in, 95–96, 98, 104
   support in, 96, 98, 102, 103
   Toulmin's model for, 94–98
   on urban renewal, 107–110
   warrant in, 96–97, 98, 103, 104, 106
   See also Comparisons and contrasts; Definitions; Narratives, interviews as basis for; Point, statement of; Rebuttals
Aristotle, xxii–xxiii, 37, 38, 51, 164, 206n
Attitude, statement of point expressing, 84–85
Audience, 14, 21
   for free writing, 5
   in problem-solving narrative report, 122
   purpose for writing and, 21
   readability depending on, 42
   for report of results, 140
   shifting perceptions of, 14
   statement of point analyzing, 86–87

Background information, in problem-solving narrative report, 121–122
Backing, in criticism, 160–161
   See also Support
Baker, Ken, 166–168
Baker, Russell, 183–184, 199
Barrett, Katherine, 23–24
Baugh, L. Sue, 136
Beginnings
   coherence established in, 80
   of criticism, 161

flash-forward technique for, 37, 38
in medias res technique for, 37, 38
of narratives, 36–39
point stated at, 84–88
Believability, for effective writing, xxii–xxiii
Biases, reviewer acknowledging, 157–159
Brainstorming, discovering and shaping ideas by, 15–18
"Butterfly is Free, The" (Mueller), 28–29

Case, making your. *See* Definitions
Castillo, Otto, 5
Categories, eliminating empty, 45–46
"Chocolate-chip Cookies" (*Consumer Reports*), 132–134
Cicero, 14, 21, 22
Claim
   in argument, 94–95, 98, 102, 103, 104–105
   in criticism, 161
Clichés, beginnings avoiding, 38
Clustering, discovering and shaping ideas by, 18–20
Coherence, opening paragraphs and, 80
Communication service, argument selling, 193–198
Communicator, The, 134–135
Company modernization, report of results of, 144–148
Comparisons and contrasts, 182–198
   argument on ending of high school athletics using, 188–193
   argument selling communication service using, 193–198
   examples of, 182–187
   generating, 187–188
   grid developed for, 187–188
   point-to-point organization for, 187, 188
   whole-to-whole organization for, 187, 188
Conclusions. *See* Endings
Confidence, for effective writing, xxiv–xxv
Consumer Reports, xxv, 132–134, 199

223